VIRGINIA COLONIAL ABSTRACTS

Vol. X

Charles City County
Court Orders 1655 - 1658

Abstracted by
Beverley Fleet

Southern Historical Press, Inc.
Greenville, South Carolina

This volume was reproduced from
A 1941 edition located in the
Publisher's private Library

All rights reserved. No part of this publication may be reproduced, stored in a retrieval system, transmitted in any form, posted on to the web in any form or by any means without the prior written permission of the publisher.

Please direct all correspondence and orders to:

www.southernhistoricalpress.com
or
SOUTHERN HISTORICAL PRESS, Inc.
PO Box 1267
375 West Broad Street
Greenville, SC   29601
southernhistoricalpress@gmail.com

Originally published: Richmond, VA. 1941
ISBN #0-89308-368-2
All rights Reserved.
Printed in the United States of America

Preface.

Please observe carefully. It would be folly indeed to attempt a history or genealogy concerning colonial Virginia without considering the data in this old order book. Still, even if superciliously, we must forgive the many follies committed.

At the period Prince George County on the south side of James River was included in Charles City County.

As for the story of this book, sad fragment of greater records, were it not for those human frailities, thievery and disregard, we would not have it at all. Let's pass that by. The original had 653 pages. Many were torn out and lost or destroyed. Here are abstracts from 136 pages. If I can continue the series of Virginia Colonial Abstracts all that is left will be shown. The original is now in the Archives Division of the Virginia State Library in Richmond. It was obtained in recent years by Mr. Morgan Poitiaux Robinson, who is State Archivist for Virginia and also Recording Secretary for the Virginia Historical Society.

If you can read this 17th century item, please do so. Frankly I cannot. Any word, any name, is subject to correction. Let us hope some perfectly certain prig can accomplish what I cannot. I have had generous offers of assistance from such. But I stubbornly return to my own interpretation or that of Mrs. James Claiborne Pollard or that of Miss Estelle Bass who make college degrees look very, very silly. My blood be upon my own head, and yours if you accept my offering.

Beverley Fleet.

January 29th 1941.

CHARLES CITY COUNTY
Court Order Book

page 1

Att a Co'rt holden att Westov'r
Junij: 4 1655

present

Coll'n Ed'd Hill)
Capt Henry Pery) esqrs

Maior Abra. Wood   Ca: John Bishopp
mr Thomas Drewe   Capt John Epes
mr Antho: Wyatt   mr John Gibbs
mr Rice Hoe   Capt David Peibils

page 1. Whereas Henry Hawkins is indebted by bill to John Burton 600 tobbo and cask payable att Powells Creeke: Itt is therefore ordered that the sd Hawkins shall make pay'mt thereof w'th costs else exec

page 1. Whereas John Burton stands indebted to Capt David Peibils by bill and Interest 982 lb tobbo and cask: Itt is therefore ordered that the sd Burton shall make paymt thereof w'th costs els exec

page 1. Wm Lambson bindeth out in Co'rt one cow called Nansie unto Joseph Parsons for security of 475 lb of tobo and cask payable the 10th of 9'br next, and Confesseth Judgmt agst himself and - (illegible) for the sd debt, whereupon in case of Nonpayment order - - (illegible)
Test   Wm x Lambson
Hoel Pryse Cl   his mk

(Howell Price, Clerk of Charles City County)

page 1. Present mr Sparrow

page 1. The difference betweene Capt John Woodleife plt and Coll Edd Hill of the Deft concerning a title of Lands is humbly presented and refferred to the Hono'ble Gov'nor and Councill to be tryed - (illegible) (by both their Consent and agreem't) the 3d day of November Co'rt next.

page 1.   mr Antho: Wyatt ex'aed and sworn saith
     That mr Gabriell Holland lett to mr Jenkin Osborne (abo- - - - or 23 years agoe) a parcell of Land next adjoyning to the said Osborne for a Certaine time (w'ch and the quantity of Land - cannot remember) for the pastureing of his cattell, - - further saith not
                                             Anthony Wyatt
Jur: in Cur Jun: 4 1655
Test Hoel Pryse Cl

page 2.   James Parham aged 29 years or thereabouts ex'aed and sworne saith That being at the house of Ed'd (Edward) Ardingtons he and his wife told the depon't that Capt Woodleife was planting from - - - - - imployed he went in and tooke his gun and going to a heape of woods neer there shott it off and presently after they heard a hog cry and going to see whose hog it was found it to belong to Phillip Lewis; shortly after the depon't too being after a cow in the sd Capt Woodliefes ground the sd Ca: Woodlief ask'd him if he saw a black sow dead, the dep't told him no. the sd Capt Woodliefe replyed that he had shot a sow of Phillip Lewis and thought to have broke halfe a dozen of her legs but supposed he had shot her too high into the guts and further s'd not
Jur in Cur Test   James x Parham mk
Hoel Pryse   Cl

page 2. Ellias Holmes aged 28 years or thereabouts exa'ed and sworne saith That being at Edd Ardingtons house the sd Ardington and his wife told the depon't the Circumstance in the first branch of James Parhams oath, so far that they found a sow belonging to Phillip Lewis that was shott and further said not
Jur in Cur Test   Elias Holmes
Hoel Pryse   Cl

page 2. The m'rk of the cattle and hogs of Nicholas Poole
     A slitt in the right eare and the piece next the head taken off and in the Left eare two halfe moons

page 2. The difference betweene Phill Lewis plt and Ca. Jo. Woodleif deft is referred to the exa'ceon of a Jury

page 2. Ordered that the Late Sherr give accot of his collec'on at the next Co'rt, and the present Sherr then to give security according to act for the performance of his place and saveing the Co'rt harmlesse

page 2. Ordered that the publick stock of powder and shott belonging to his regim't be delivered and intrusted to Lt Coll Walter Aston and Maior Abra Wood Vidzt halfo to each of them by those in whose hands it now rests

page 2. According to act of the late assembly Itt is ordered and appointed that the m'kett of this County be held and at Westov'r and ffloriday hundred which are Conceived to be the most convenient places relateing to the act in most business

page 3. According to refference of the petition of Weynoke parish from the late Grand Assembly this cor't for full and finall determina'- con and Confirmacon of the bounds of the sd parish Itt is ordered by consent and choice and for his better convenionce and neerer adiacencia (adjacencia - adjacency) of Ca. Tho. Stegge and his family and tenants, that the sd Ca: Stegs family and all other Inhabiting below Old man's Creeke (w'ch is the Lower most bounds of Bucklands Dividends) shall be Continued and belong wholly to Weynoke and the aforesd, and shall pay all tythes and duties for the future to the sd parish

According to reference from the late graund Assembly to this Co'rt to examine and fully determine the difference betweene the Inhabitants of Woynoke and the Inhabitants of Martins Brandon, Itt is ordered according to a former ord'r of Assembly that Martin Brandon neck vidzt, ffrom Wards Creek to Chepakes brooke and all the Inhabitants therein shall from henceforth be an absolute distinct parish of themselves w'th all Im'unities and priviledges of a parish without rela'con to Weynoke parish or any other

page 3. Itt is ordered that the sherr Deteine the person of Ca: Harris till he enter into bond w'th security to appe and answer at the next Quarter Co'rt the complt of Coll Ed'd Hill esqr.

page 3. Whereas Rich'd Pace the orphan and heire of Geo Pace dec'ed hath at this Co'rt made choice of and humbly Desired Confirma'con of mr Wm Baugh to be Guardian of him and his estate dureing his minority. The Co'rt doth therefore hereby grant and Confirme his sd request requireing the sd Guardian to mannage duly and justly all estate belonging to the sd orphan giveing yearly acco't to the Co'rt of the same and the Improvement delivering the whole to the sd orphane at his full age

page 3. Whereas Henry Brigs is indebted to Curtis Laud by bill 250 lb tobbo and hath neglected to make paymt: Itt is therefore ordered the sd Brigs shall forthwith pay the sd sume to the sd Laud or his assgs also Interest and all costs or als exec.

page 4. (abstract) Deed. Dated 3 Aug. 1653. Recorded 19 June 1655. Capt. John Epps of Charles City Co., sells to Thomas Rands of Weynoke, for 2000 lb. tobo. payable 10th Nov. next, 60 acres at Weynoke formerly belonging to Mr. Humphrey Kent deceased, and by him lived on his lifetime.

"Signed and Sealed in   Signed   John Epes
Cor't the 4th Day of   Mary x Epes
June 1655
Test
Charles Sparrowe and)
Hoel Pryse   )

page 5. I Ellias Holmes do give graunt and bestowe and makov'r the sonne of James Parham and to his heires exors admrs and assgs for ov'r one cow called Browne, and one heyfer of two years old named Blossom they m'ked w'th a crop in the left eare w'th a slitt in the crop and a slitt under the same eare and two half moons in the other eare, w'th all increase thereof Dureing the life of his sd father, the female to his own use and the male towards schooling and educateing the sd child and after decease of his sd father the sd male increase to be refferred to the discretion of the County Co'rt Wittnes my hand Jan: 4. 1655
                                               Elias holmes

Signed sealed and desired to be recorded in Co'rt the day and yeare abovesayde
Test Hoel Pryse   Cl

page 5. Hatcher as Tho: ffones told me before Jo: Gilham and Sam: Woodward did say at Mr Wm Johnsons the night before he went downe (there being then present Will Baugh Tho Jones Tho ffones and his wife and John Pryse) that he would hang Mr Landsdale in England at Tyburne and that he wish'd he could meet w'th Ned Hill in England, and that he was going for England to be released of his good behavior, and that he wondered why such Could bind him to his behavior that never had none themselves, and that he would have a bout w'th Gov'nor Bennett when he came thare
                                     rec July 11. 1655

page 6.   v'Memorand' that I mr Wm Ditty do deliver in the hands of David Peibils the pattent of my Land lying at high peake in pledge of a debt of 1417 lb of tobbo w'th cask, and in case that I do not well and truly pay unto the sd Peibils his heirs the above men'coned debt before Christide next then the land w'th all houseing and fenceing to be David Poibils his heirs or ass's freely for ev'r, and do bind me to acknowledge the same in Co'rt this next Co'rt att Westov'r Wittnes my hands this 15th ffebr 1654. Moreov'r in case mr Ditty can give me other security that I shall like of then this condi'con to be voyd
Wittness
   The mk of   William Dittie
George I Breward
William Prise

Recognit in our Juni 4: 1655
by present Guilm Dittie
                    Test Hoel Pryse Cl
rec. July 11. seq

page 6. A cow to be recorded for Jo Minters sonne named Gentle and her increase by my owne free consent and desire
Test Charles Sparrowe   The mk of
rec July. 11. '55   Eliz EM Minter

page 6.
    Present   Ca: Henry Pory Esqr)   mr Rice Hoe
                 mr Antho Wyatt   )   ca: David Peibils

Memorand that Capt Wm Harris apped this day in open Co'rt without call or Sumond and w'th violent Language argued and depended that Coll Edd Hill esqr had not Just power to call witnesses by Comand of his writt from Henrico Com to Charles Citty com Co'rt further taxeing one of the Co'rt w'th untruth in the face of the open Co'rt, and boldly undertaking to answer this first assertion att the next Quart'ly Co'rt
               Certified by the Gent abovewritten
               Test Hoel Pryse Cl Cur pre'et

page 7.

Att a Vestry att Westov'r for that parish
Jun: 4th. 1655.

present

                  Coll Edd Hill)
                  Ca: Hen: Pery) esqrs

mr Tho: Drewe   mr Ja: Waradine
mr Rice Hoe   Lt Jo. Banister
Ca. Jo. Bishopp   mr Joseph Parsons
Ca. David Peibils   mr Edd Mosby

It is ordered by this vestry that 25 lb tobbo and one bushell of Corne per poll per anno be allowed and payd to mr John Dibdall minister for every tytheable person in Westov'r parish for his yeares exercise in his ministry in that parish the sd tobbo and corne to be collected secured and payd to him, vidzt By Capt Henry Pery Esqr for Buckland Westov'r and Barkley dividends, by Capt Daniell Llewellin from Barkley to the upper end of the parish on that side, by Ca. Rich'd Tye for merchants hope to Powells Creeke and the backe planta'cons, and by Capt David peibils from Powells Creeke downwards, All wch persons have power in their sd severall precincts to Com'and the same to be brought to convenient places, and in default thereof to distreine on the delinquents.

By consent and choice of mr John Dibdall minister Wm Bayly is Confirmed Clearke of this parish and to have 4 lb of tobb and one peck of Corne a head per anno collected secured and payd to him by the severall persons for their severall precints as are ingaged for the ministers tythes

(The figure shown above as 4 lb. tobo. may be 1 lb tobo. It is not clear on the original record)

page 8.

Att a Co'rt holden att Westover
Aug: 3. 1655

Present

            Coll Edd Hill Esq'r
Ma'r Abr Wood   mr Rice Hoe
mr Tho Drewe   Ca: Richd Tye
mr Antho Wyatt

Memorand that as Rice Hoe do acknowledge to have sold unto Wm Cradock 100 acres of land next adioyning to Ca: Edloes land and 152 acres or thereabouts unto Tho: Drinker bounding upon that and extending towards the land of Willm Hanett w'ch Land being acknowledged by them to be sold unto Wm ffry and desired upon their disclayming thereof to be surrendred by me to the sd ffry according to the grand and originall

pattent and accordingly to their resign'mt do render resign and fully
convey and make out to the sayd ffry and his heirs for ever the sd two
parcells of land conteining 252 acres by Survey and bind my selfe my
heirs exors and adm'rs to make such further assurance thereof as shall
be reasonably desired and devised by the sd ffry or any for him Aug:
3. 1655
Test Hoel Pryse Cl   Rice Hooe

page 8.   This present Co'rt is adjourned and removed to the 17th Day
of September next (As also the Co'rt for orphanes w'ch was appointed
for the 10th day of this month) on w'ch the 17th of September all
cawses refferences and dependences to either this or the sd orphans
Co'rt are appointed to have hearing

page 9.
                        Att a Co'rt holden att Westover
                             Sept 17th 1655
Present
                        Coll Edd Hill Esqr
            Ma'r Abra Wood   mr Rice Hoe
            mr Tho: Drewe   mr War: Horsmonden
            mr Anth: Wyatt   Ca: David Peibils

page 9. Whereas mr Jo: Gibbs complained against Ca: Jo ffrome for an
Iron chaine carried away from his ground by some of the sd Ca: ffromes
people: Itt is therefore ordered the sd Ca: ffreme shall deliver and
render the sd Chaine to the sd mr Gibbs and pay costs of suite als Exec

page 9. Henry Wentworth confessed Judgmt to Capt Thomas Stegge for 4
barrells of good Indian corne to be forthwith paid to him or his assgs,
als exec.

page 9.   To prevent the many scurrulous reproachfull and unneighborly
differences and Languages betweene mr John Gibbs and Capt John ffreme
the Court doth order that either of them first raysing or causeing any

future quarrell rayling or difference being thereof complained and justly combined shall forfeit and pay to the other partie suffering 1500 lb tobo and cask w'th costs

page 9.   mr Henry Randolph confessed Judgm't to Jo Drayton - - - for 1200 lb tobbo and cask to be pd him or his assgs, als exec and costs

page 9.   The 17th Day of September yearely is appointed for orphanes Co'rt at w'ch time all persons therein interested are to app'r and give their acco'ts: And Howel Pryse is hereby qualified and authorized to receive what acco'ts of orphanes estates shal be brought unto him; and administer oathes to the parties for Confirmacon of their severall accots

page 9.   Itt is ordered that 90 lb tobbo be paid and allowed mr Tho: Drewe at the next Levy upon Westov'r Parish

page 9.   Henry Barker confessed Judgmt in Co'rt to Michaell Master for 477 lb tobbo to be payd him or his ass'g on the 20th day of October next, als exec w'th costs

page 10.   Abstract. Indenture. 17 Sept. 1655. Rice Hoo of Charles City Co., in Va., Gent., sells to Wm. Fry of James City Co., 252 acres in James City Co., "bounding vidzt Southwest on the main riv'r South East on the Land of Capt Mathew and - North East into the woods and North West on the Land of Wm. Hanett", this land "part of a dividend formerly graunted to the sd Rice Hoe by pattent cont' 1969 acres Dated the 18th of October 1643 and since graunted and assigned vidzt the sd 252 acres by the sd Rice Hoe w'ch Thomas Drinker and Wm Cradock, vidzt to the sd Drinker 152 acres and to the sd Cradock 100 acres and by them lately reassigned and surrendered to the sd Rice Hoe to be by him in all full and ample forme conveyed and Confirmed to the sd ffry"
                              Signed   Rice Hoe the seale

"Signed sealed del'ved acknowledged and confirmed in Co'rt of Cha Citty Com the day and yeare aforesd
Test
War: Horsmonden
David Peibils and Hoel Pryse   Cl "
"rec 7br 22. sequ: "

page 12. "This Bill bindeth me Curtis Laud my heirs, exor's admr's to pay or cause to be pd unto John Howell his heirs exors admrs or assgs the full and just sume of one thousand pounds of good sound m'ckable tobacco and cask to be pd at or upon the 10th day of October next insuing the Date hereof as witnes my hand this 17th 7'br 1655

         The m'k of x Curtis Laud
       (The mark is actually an L upsidedown)

(Abstracts)
Curtis Laud binds his crop of tobo. to secure above debt. Same date, same signature. Witness William Baylie. Recorded 22 Sept. 1655.

Bill binding Curtis Laud to pay Jno. Howell 2000 lb. tobo. on 10th Oct. 1656. Security being 3 cows names Squerrell, ffortune and honny. Signature, Witness and date of record as above.

page 13. Mr Tho Drewe testifieth in Co'rt that Lt Coll Tho Swan upon an agreemt w'th Mr Robt Letherland in the business of one Parsons of London, whereon rested due 3000 lb tobbo per bill, did promise to deliver to the sd Letherland one cop'r still, or a copp kettle of 30 gallons dat 7'br. 17th Ad 1655
Test   Thomas Drewe
Hoel Pryse Cl
      rec 22 Sept 1655

page 13. Itt is ordered that the tythable parishoners of Weynoke shall pay to mr John Dibdall Clerk 5 lb tobbo per poll for the time he officiated there after expira'con of the Coven't w'th them

page 13. Itt is ordered in Conclusion of the difference betweene mr John Dibdall and Tho: Coale that the sd Coale forthw'th enter into bond of 5000 lb tobbo w'th security for his good abearing

page 13. Jo: Burton Confesseth Judgm't to Peter Mackerell m'rcht for 660 lb tobbo and cask to be pd him or his assgs, als exec'n and costs.

page 13. Itt is ordered that mr Antho Wyatt shall be accomptable to Ca: Daniell Lewellin for a bill of 700 lb tobo of mr Shipleyes left in his hands by John Bull

page 14.   Itt is ordered that Richard Wells shall prepare and bring
in place sufficient timber for eight tunne of Cask ready malled barked
and rined, whereof Ellias Webb is ordered and appointed to make four
tunne of cask and deliv'r the same first to the sd Wells by the last
day of October next als exec. And this to be Conclusive betweene them

page 14.   The Co'rt doth hereby tolerate permitt and allow Capt Wm
Rothwell to enterteine keepe and imploy an Indian, according to act of
Assembly to destroy wolfes and do other service, And Ord'r that he
enter into bond of 10000 lb tobbo that no damage detrim't wrong tres-
passe be Done or occasioned to any English people or their estates by
any Indian so by him entertained or imployed

page 14.   In full determination of the difference betweene Phill:
Lewis plt and Capt John Woodliefe defend't Itt is ordered that the sd
Capt Woodleife shall on the 10th day of November next pay to the sd
Lewis 150 lb of good tobbo and costs of suite als exec.

page 14.   Sixe hundred acres of Land appe'th to be due to Cha:Gregory
per Indentures produced and proved for importation of Rich: Gummie
Wm Morley   Herbert Margerom   John Huson   George Marler   Jo: Eells
Wm Holliman   Robt Brier   David Robts   Katherine Hockwell   Mary Hull
and Mrs ffuller

page 14.   ffive hundred acres of land app'th to be due to Peter Moyle
per Indentures produced and proved for importa'con of Walther Sansom
John Smeed   Tho: Hayward   James James   Jo: Hide   Mary Morris   John Allin
Roger Norton   Thomas Penton and Wm Keble

page 14.   Whereas severall acco'ns have beene comenced by Howell Pryse
against Mr Richard Jones Cler for 1052 lb tobbo and Non Inventus severall times returned by the sherr' Itt is therefore ordered according
to act that attach'mt issue at the sd Pryse his suite against the
estate of the sd Mr Jones for the sd sum and Costs incident

page 14.   John Harrison is hereby exempt by reason of his lamenesse
and age from all levies and taxes except parish dues.

page 14.   Due to Sam: Eallo for killing a wolfe certified by Capt Ferry

page 15.   Whereas ffrances Maylan left severall bills and accots in trust w'th Howell Pryse The Co'rt doth therefore hereby fully authorize and impower the sd Pryse or any his substitutes or assgs to receive recover and require by all lawfull wayes and meanes all the Debts so intrusted, and he to give acco't of his proceedings therein when it shal be Legally required of him

page 15.   The Co'rt doth order and allow that Morgan Jones shall have and enjoy to his owne proper use all the male Cattell proceeding and accrewing of the stock belonging to the children of James Monfort dec'd in Considera'con of educating the sd children and endeavoring to preserve their sd stock

page 15.   Itt is ordered that Mr Thomas Drewe shall out of the estate of Robt Lewellin mer'cht pay to Mr Anthony Wyatt for the use of Jerdons parish five pounds sterl money for the buriall of Peter Midleton late agent of the sd Lewellin in the sd parish Church

page 15.   Upon acc'ot of Elizabeth Minter of the estate of her late husband John Minter decd proveing that she has paid as far as assetts The Co'rt doth Certifie the same whereby the Quiet est may be graunted unto her

page 15.   Itt is ordered that 350 lb tobbo and cask be paid and satisfied to Mr James Warradine out of the next Levy of Westov'r parish

page 15.   Itt is ordered that 600 lb tobbo be raysed at the next Levy upon Westov'r parish and paid to Howell Pryse for sev'rall attendances and businesses done for the sd parish

page 15.   These are to Certifie that 1250 acres of land appe'th by testimony proQuced to be due to Howell Pryse for importation of

Jo: Walker	Barnaby Slitt	Hen: Shore	Robt Hostler	Hen Seares
Ja. Huckes	Mich: Waterford	Ja Webber	Hugh Joffers	Peter Jackson
ffranc Salter	Edd Spires	Tho: Edes	Nich Titbury	Tho: Hay
Jno Thorne	Ellinor Heads		Jane Wms	Jane Sands
Ja ffryer	Robt Haines	Jo: ffowler	John ffryer	
Gervase Byham	Jeffrey Speed			

page 15.   Itt is ordered that Capt Jo. Woodleife shall forthw'th pay to Howell Pryse or his assigs 676 lb tobo found Due for fees als exec and costs thereof

page 16.   The Co'rt of October next is removed and adjourned to the 5th day of November next by reason of the occasion of attendance of some of the Com'rs and officers at the Quarter Co'rt at that time

page 16.   Whereas Tho: ffones appe'th to be indebted to Howell Pryse for fees and other disbursements for him 400 lb tobbo and cask Itt is therefore ordered that the sd ffones shall make good paym't thereof als exec and costs thereof

page 16.   Whereas Capt John ffreme undertooke paym't of 552 lb tobbo for fees Due to Howell Pryse from Mr Ingelton and Richard Ash as per testimony of the late Collect'r appeareth
   Itt is therefore ordered that the sd Capt ffreme shall make good paym't of the sd sume w'th costs

page 16.
                    Att a meeting at Westov'r Sept: 27. 1655
Present
                        Coll Edd. Hill Esqr
        mr Tho: Drewe   Ca: Richd Tye
        Ca: Jo: Bishopp   Ca. David Peibils

Itt is ordered that untill the next County Co'rt in 9'ber the present sherr Do take the acco'ts and Invoices of all goods landed and to be landed in the sev'rall m'ketts of this Countie wch acco'ts Invoices and entries are to be made and given upon oath of the owners or m'chts of such goods to be adm'rd by Capt John Bishopp for Westov'r m'kett or in his absence by any other of the neerest Com'r

Itt is ordered that all the Com'rs of this Com Do app. and attend the next Co'rt the 5th day of November for the settlement of some speciall business and that the sherr' Do give each of them particular notice thereof

page 17.
                    Att a Co'rt holden att Westov'r
                         9br. 5th. 1655
Present   Coll Edward Hill)
                     Ca: Henry Perry   ) osqr
        Major Abr: Wood   Ca Jo Epes
        Mr Tho: Drewe   Ca: Richd: Tye
        Mr Antho Wyatt   Mr War: Horsmonden
        Mr Rice Hoe   Capt David Peibils

Note: These abstracts were taken in pencil according to the severe and exact rules of Mr. Morgan Poitiaux Robinson, based upon those of the Public Record Office in London. Mr Robinson is so exacting that it makes work in the Archives Division of the Virginia State Library a delight to and for the student who actually comes to work. Then having taken the notes I had the temerity to lend them to that most remarkable lady, Mrs. Martha Woodroof Hiden, who not only makes a success of the largest export warehouse business in Newport News, but also has time to be the most accomplished genealogist in the Virginia field, an active member of the Virginia Library Board, supervise the education of her children, be a director in various enterprises, and still has further time to go with Mrs. James Claiborne Pollard to obscure County Court Houses, obtain and have restored the most important original records of Virginia. She is an authoritive Latin student, particularly in regard to early colonial records. As if all this were not enough this lady manages somehow to always be courteous and kindly to those hundreds of us who would be her friends. See below:

"Thank you so much for your kindness, Mr. Fleet, I have greatly enjoyed this   M.W.H. "
Which might truthfully have been 'Go on, you pest, I hav'ent time to bother'.
Then another note for me:
"Have you noticed how keen the writers were for abbreviations, using 7br for September, etc. ? This 'br' is for 'bris' an adjectival ending, 'on the 5th day of the 9th month', Novembris. "

Now then, on with the Court proceedings of 9br. 5th. 1655.

page 17.   Whereas James Hugnet privately killed and carried away a hogg belonging to Richd Baker whereof he hath made compl't and proofe
     Itt is therefore ordered that the sd Hugnett shall remaine in the Sherr's custodie untill he give caution to pay the sd Baker 2000 lb tobbo or two yeares service according to act w'th costs &c. And that Symond Symonds who is suspected to have induced the premises shall also rest in custodie untill he enter into bond w'th good Caution for his good abearoing

page 17.   Itt is ordered that Lt Coll Walter Aston shall pay to Capt Daniell Llewellin one terce of good Sack according to bill of Mrs Susanna Major, or produce the person or lawfull attorney of Capt Batt who married the sd Mrs Major (Maior) to answer the same at the next Co'rt w'th costs &c.

page 17.   Upon the choice and request of Tho: Boyce orphane of Mr Cheney Boyce dec'd that Ca: Richd Tye be Guardian of him and his estate dureing his minority; The Co'rt doth order and appoint that the sd Capt Tye do keepe educate and maintain the sayd Boyce, being allowed therefore out of his estate and endeavor the preserva'con of the sd orphanes estate and give yearely acco't thereof

page 17. The difference betweene Lt Coll Tho: Swan and Lt Coll Walter Aston is reffered and respited till the next Com Co'rt, at w'ch time if Lt Coll: Aston cannot prove paym't of the claime against him, a Judgm't is to be granted and entered for the same and costs.

Further notation by Mrs. Hiden: "Comitatus, a gathering or following. Evidently the county was considered an enlarged borough whose citizens would form a gathoring. "

page 17. Attachm't is graunted to Tho: Huxe agt   Tho. Peters upon non Inventus retourned agt him according to act

page 17. Attachm't is graunted to Humfrey Shipley agst Henry Wentworth upon Non Inventus for 700 lb tobbo and cask w'th all costs incident

page 17. Attachm't is graunted to Hioromo Ham agst Phill: Mintorne upon Non Inventus for 633 lb tobb and cask w'th costs ec

Note: Non Inventus, not found.   B.F.

page 17. Jo: fflower confesseth Judgm't to Walter Salter for 500 lb tobo and cask to be pd him or his assgs w'th Costs, als exec.

page 18. Abstract. Indenture. 5th Nov. 1652. "Lt Coll Walter Chiles of James Citty in Virginia esqr" solls to "Robt Coalman of the Com of Cha: Citty in Virginia aforesd planter", for a "valuable sume of tobacco", 813 acres, "lying in Appamattuck riv'r in the Com of Cha Citty in Virginia", according to a patent granted sd Chiles by Sir Wm. Berkeley, dated 5th Nov. 1649, and since patented by sd Chiles under patent under the hands f Richard Bennett, Esqr., Govr. and Coll Wm. Claiborne, Secretary of Virginia, dated 25 Oct. 1652.
Wit: Signed
Anthony Wyatt   Walter Chiles
Rob: Hubord   the seal
                 Rec. 5 Nov. 1655.

page 19. Marmaduke Brookes hath confessed Judgm't to Jo: Drayton mercht for 1400 lb tobb and cask to be paid him or his assigs als ex: costs

page 19. Jo: fflower confessed Judgm't to Howell Pryse for 240 lb tobb Due for fees, to be paid him or his assg's w'th costs, als exec.

page 19. Itt is ordered and appointed that the marketts of this Com shal be held and kept att Westov'r and Martins Brandon vidzt: from the great marsh upwards two miles in extent and all goods and serv'ts henceforth imported for sale, and to be landed according to act in the sd sev'rall marketts to be entered w'th the severall Clearkes vidzt Mr Nicholas Perry for Martins Brandon Markett and Howell Pryse for Westov'r markett, who are to keepe acco't of the sd entries being made by oath of the owners or mer'chts of any such goods or servants before the next in authority qualified to the admr'acon of an oath; as also to Certifie the removall of any goods or ser'vts from one markett to another

page 19. Itt is ordered that Mr War: Horsmonden shall pay to Jo Shale (or Shap) 23/8 resting due of wages for time past in tobb at 20 lb per Cents: and to Jo Turner 2 lb 6/8 at the same rate and they to give acquittance for the time past upon receipt thereof

page 19. Itt is ordered that Mr Anthony Wyatt have power to survey and lay out four hundred and fiftie acres of land according to a pattent assigned and surrendered to him by Coll Edd Hill Esqr

page 19. All Cawses depending and untryed at this Co'rt are generally referred and adjourned to the next Com Co'rt the third day of December next

page 20. By Consent of John Arrow serv't to Tho: Gregory Itt is ordered that the sd Arrow shall serve halfe a yeare after expira'con of his time by Indenture in considera'con and recompense of Damages and lost time wherein he absented himselfe w'thout licence and pay costs hereof

page 20. Itt is ordered that 3 lb tobbe per poll be raised w'th the generall levie on Jordons parish and paid to Wm Heyward for charges and according to ord'r of Vestrey

page 20. A probat is graunted unto Thomas Greene of the last will and testamt of Thomas Pierson dec'd this day pro'ved in Co'rt

page 20. Memorand that I Rice Hoe gent do for me my heirs exr's adm'rs and asigs firmly and by these presents bargaine and sell and turne ov'r unto Wm Hanett his heirs ex'rs and assgs all my right and title of a parcell of Land bounding from Tho: Drinker Wm Hanetts old bounds all the Land lying from Henry Okams hundred acres to Joining to Wm Hills - - - bounds both into the woods and to the riv'r up all priviledges belonging to the pattent w'thin certified for ev'r x x x witnes my hand and seale this 20th of March 1654.
Test   Signed
William Cowley   Rice Hooe   the seale
Thomas T.S. Speeding
                Recorded 20 Aug. 1655

page 20.

                By the Com'rs of the Militia Sept: 17: 1655
                        Coll Edd Hill esqr
        Lt Coll. Walter Aston   Ca: David Peibils
        Ma: Abra: Wood   Capt Wm. Harris
        Ca: Rich'd Tye   Ca: Daniell Lewellin

Ordered that the Comand'rs of the sev'all companies in this regim't be as foll: vidzt

Capt Wm ffarrer from the falls to four mile Creek includeing neck of land
Capt Wm Harris for the rest of Henrico Com, except Bristoll parish
page 21.
Major Abra Wood for Bristoll parish to the Cittie Creeke on S side
Capt John Epes from the Cittie Creeke to the Lower end of Jordons Except the back planta'cons
Capt Richd Tye from the howse of Richd Colsey includeing that to Powells Creeke
Capt David Peibils from Powells Creeke to Wards Creeke
Coll: Edd Hill esqr from Wards Creeke to Wm Radawayes including that family
Lt Coll: Walter Aston from Turkie Island Creeke (except Essex) to Joseph Parsons house and att Westov'r side and so from Jordans
Capt Daniell Lewellin for Essex the rest of Buckland, Windsor Weynoke to Tho: Moodyes and includeing that
Capt Jo: ffreme for the rest of Weynoke the family of Lt Aston, the families and ten'ts of mr Webs and mr Hamelin and thence to the lower end of the Com on that side and twenty three persons at Chepokes to the howse of Tho: Reynolds.

And that the sd severall Comand'rs in their severall lymitts exercise and traine their sd severall companies in the use of their armes postures of war and twice in the yeare, or oftener upon Comand, or emergent causes

page 21.   Att a Co'rt holden att Westov'r Dec: 3d 1655
    Present   Coll: Edd Hill esqr
                mr Tho: Drewe   Ca: Jo. Bishopp
                            mr Jo Gibbs

page 21. A Comic'con of adm'ra'son is graunted to Mrs Sara Hoe widd of the estate of her late husband Mr Rice Hoe decd she giveing Caution as is accustomed

Note: Mrs. Hiden, in her notations remarks here "Widd is just anglecizing vidua, the Latin, don't you think ? "

page 21.   Tho: Greene confesses Judgt. to Howell Pryse for 360 lb. tobo for fees, to be pd 3 days after the next season.

page 22. Itt is ordered that 26 lb tobbo per poll be forthw'th levied by distresse if needful by the sherriffe on the tytheable persons of this Com and p'd as followeth

		lb (tobbo)
Coll: Hill burgesse charge and attendance		1400
Ca: Pory por acc't		1400
Wm Burford per list		0300
Jos: Parsons for 4 dayes worke		0040
Mich: Master for transport burgesses		0200
Mr Hamelin for Tho. Pierson		2000
Howell Pryse for cop acts		0600
Lt Banister for 3 wolves		0600
Tho Hamond " 1 -		0200
Ja: Ward " 1 -		0200
Sam Calle " 1 -		0200
Wm Short " 4 -		0800
To Ca Wall " 1 -		0200
Coll Hill " 1 -		0200
Lt Coll Aston " 1 -		0200
David Ramsay " 1 -		0200
Richd Nicholas for arreares assigned		1500
to make good defective and exempted persons		1000
Wm Thomas of Jordons for 1 wolfe		0200
Mr Holford for 4 wolves		0800

		12240
	Sallory	1224

		13464

Itt is ordered that 7 lb tobbo per poll be levied on the parish of Westov'r and paid as foll vidzt

To Coll Hill for H Pryse	600
To Mr Waradines exerc	350
To Mr Drewe	090
To Joseph Parsons	150
To Sallery	119

	1309

Itt is ordered that 14 lb tobo per poll be forthw'th levied on the tytheable Inhabitants of Weynoke and Martins Brandon parishes and payd as foll vidzt

To Mr Hamelin for 2 burgesses charge	2400
to him for fees of their businesse	0150

	2550
To sallory	0255

	2805

page 23.   By reason of the concurrance and meeting of the Inhabitants of Weynoke and Martins Brandon in the elec'oon of Mr Stephen Hamelin for burgesse for those precints for the last Assembly and that the sd places were not then absolute distinct parishes. It is ordered that the Inhabitants of both the sd parishes be equally and jointly charged and shall contribute in the defraying of the charge by Joint Levie proporc'onably amongst them

page 23.   This present Co'rt is adjourned by reason of the bad weather until the 17th Day of this present December

page 23.

                  Att a Co'rt holden att Westover
                      Decemb'r: 17: 1655.

present
                  Capt Henry Perry esqr
          Mr Tho: Drewe   Ca: Richd Tye
          Mr Antho: Wyatt   Ca: David Peibils
          Mr John Gibbs

page 23.   Charles Gregory confesses judgm't to Sam: Smith for 726 lb tobbo and cask to be pd him or his assgs w'thin 6 dayes w'th costs als exec

page 23.   Itt is ordered that ffrancis Grey pay within 6 Dayes to Lt Coll Walter Chiles or his assgs 241 lb tobbo and cask w'th costs, als exec

page 23.   A probat is graunted to Mrs Mary ffreme of the last will and testam't of her late husband Ca. Jo. ffreme dec'd prouv'd in Co'rt
    The Co'rt doth hereby graunt and allow unto Mrs Mary ffreme one third of the Land of her late husband dureing her life

page 23.   Itt is ordered that the ex'or of Ja: Waradine dec'd shall pay to Mr Tho: Drewe 2248 lb tobbo and cask Due on ball of acco't, w'th costs, als exec

page 23.   The Co'rt doth hereby graunt and allow unto Elizabeth Warradine widd the third of all Lands and app'tenances of her late husband James Warradine dec'ed Dureing her life, and of all his chattells and moveables for ev'r

page 23.   Itt is ordered that the heires or exors of Ca. John ffreme dec'd shall give assurance to m'r John Dibdall of certaine Land sold unto him by the sd Capt ffreme, and pay costs thereof, als exec

page 23. Jacob Covell (?) confesseth Judgm't to Lt Jo: Howell for 1215 lb tobo and cask to be forthw'th pd him or assgs, als exec w'th costs

page 24. Abstract. Deed. 17 Dec. 1655. William Clay of Westover Par., sells John Dibdall, minister, for 2500 lb. tobo. and cask, 550 acres. This land part of 1000 acres "bought by my father John Clay dec'd of Capt Edd Hooke of Virginia aforesd com'only called and Knowne by the name of Clayes Clossett". Of the balance of 450 acres, 400 acres was sold to Willm Bayly, and "fiftie given by me to Cornelius Clemence". Land lying on the South West side or South and by West of the Crosse Creeke.
Wit: Signed " Wm Clay
S. hamelin   the scale
R Pryse   his x mk "
                  Rec. 22 Dec. 1655

page 25. Itt is ordered that Mr John Dibdall minister shall w'thin 6 dayes pay to Mrs Mary ffreme ex'rx of Capt John ffreme dec'd two thousand four hundred thirty three pounds of tobo and cask Due for severall specialties w'th costs als exec

page 25. The whole difference betweene Capt David Peibils and Ja: Crewes is referred to the award and finall determinacon of Coll Edward Hill esqr Capt Henry Perry esqr Mr Thomas Drewe and Mr Anthony Wyatt, or an Umpier by them or the major part of them elected, And to be done the 20th day of January next

page 25. The difference betwoone John Cogan plt and George Atkins is referred to the next County Co'rt

page 25. Itt is ordered that Edd Richards pay to Tho Morgan one thousand pounds of tobbo and cask due by bill w'th costs, als exec

page 25. Itt is ordered that Edd Richards pay to Richd Carter 1092 lb tobbo and cask, w'th costs, als exec.

page 25. Richard Bayley Confesseth Judgmt to Edd Richards for 1500 lb tobbo and cask, to be forthw'th pd, w'th costs, als exec

page 25. A nonsuit is graunted to Capt Daniell Lewellin agt Henry Isham w'th 40 lb tobo costs for his attendance

page 25. Itt is ordered that Wm Wheeler pay to Mr John Dibdall 100 lb tobbo for damages and costs, als exec.

page 25. Itt is ordered that James Salmon shall in full of all claimes pay to Robert Letherland 484 lb tobbo and cask, w'th costs, als exec

page 25. On petic' of Joseph Parsons Itt is ordered that the suite of Andrew Meldrom agst him be exai'ed and tryed by a Jurie

page 25. Itt is ordered that the Juries charge be pd by Joseph Parsons according to act.

Note: Meldrum - a good old Perthshire Presbyterian name, to become well known in Virginia later on. The beloved Thomas Meldrum Rutherfoord who was named for his grand-mothers Scottish family, etc. etc. B.F.

page 25. The Co'rt hath ordered that ffrancis Grey shall produce to the next Co'rt a true Inventory upon oath of the estate of Bartholomew Whitehead dec'd. And referred the Doubt whether the sd Grey as greatest Cred'r or John fflower as neerest of kin shall have the adm'r'acon of the sd estate, the pretended will being found null and invalid in Co'rt

page 26. Abstract. 20 Nov. 1655. "Wm Dittie of high peake w'thin the parish of Jordans and Charles Cittie Countie" sells Joseph Parsons, for a "valuable sume of good m'chantable Virginia tobo and caske to him in hand already paid", 403 acres, "all that his planta'con com'only called or knowne by the name of High Peak". 200 acres thereof being his part of 350 acres purchased from James Waradine with Robert Langman, as by patent dated 3rd Dec. 1637, which said 350 acres abutting westerly upon Baylyes Creeke,"next upon the land of Mr John George, vidzt Beginning upon the third Island and so running along the Creeke Easterly into the woods."

The other 203 acres being at the head of the abovesaid 200 acres and on the South side of Baylies Creeke "and running into the woods South by East by the sd Mr Jo: George his Land", this 203 acres granted him by patent dated 7 Oct. 1653.
Wit: Signed   William Dittie
Patrick Jackson
Evan Derwas

. . . .

The following items, out of order, are of the Court proceedings of Dec. 3rd 1655.
page 21. Curtis Laud being convict for hog stealeing, and an idle person voyd of Industry and endeavored to mainteine his chargo is ordered to give Caution for his good behavior, and to save the parish harmlesse from charge, or remone where he formerly Dwelt

page 21. Judgmt is graunted to Howell Pryse agt Mr Richd Jones Cler for 1052 lb tobbo and all costs incident

. . . .

(Court proceedings of Dec. 17th 1655 continued)

page 27.   Curtis Laud acknowledged Judgm't to Capt Abra: Read and comp for 600 lb tobbo and cask to be payd him or them or their assgs, als ex'o w'th costs

page 27.   In conclusion of the difference betweene Andrew Moldrom plt and Joseph Parsons Deft Itt is ordered that the sd Moldrom pay all costs occasioned therein on both parts, als exec

page 27.   Abstract. Mrs Sara Hoe, admx of Mr. Rice Hoe decd., ordered to pay Mr. Tho: Drewe 2893 lb. tobo. due on bill. Also to pay Thomas Hamond 520 lb. tobo. due to him.

page 27.   The Co'rt hath reversed the order graunted to Mrs Mary ffreme widd for a third of her late husbands Land, she clayming and cleaveing to the benefit of the will

page 28.   The Co'rt hath graunted and allowed to Rice Hoe the son of Mr Rice Hoe dec'd, out of the estate, one gun and a share of the last Crop in Considera'con of his care and paines in the sd Crop

page 28.   Present Mr Horsmonden

page 28.   Itt is ordered that John Lucas shall surrender unto Joseph Harrison all the rights of a parcell of Land sold to him and pay to the sd Harrison for damage 1000 lb tobo and costs als exec

page 28.   Itt is ordered that Mrs Sara Hoe shall out of her late husbands estate pay to Mr Anthony Wyatt for Capt Tho: Darnell what shall appear due upon examina'con of accts of a bill of 5693 lb tobo and cask, w'th costs als exec

page 28.   A Com'ison of admra'con is graunted to Capt John Bishop of the estate of Wm Hienders decd he finding Caution as is accustomed

page 28.   Attachm't is graunted to Stephen Hamelin agst Geo: Brownes estate for 580 lb tobbo and Costs

page 28.   Absen: Ca: Perry

page 28.   Itt is ordered that ffrancis Grey shall forthwith pay to Mrs Ann Downes or her assgs 560 lb tobbo and cask Due per bill w'th costs als exec

page 28.   Hugh fforshaw confesseth Judgm't to Robt Nicholson for 2050 lb tobo and cask to be pd him or his assgs wThin 10 dayes als exec and costs

page 28.   A probat is graunted to Kidby ffrere and Tho: Cleark of the last will and test'mt of John Bromwell dec'd

Note: Kidby ffrere is refered to March 4th 1661/2 "By reason of his great age". Cleark is indexed as Clarke.   B. F.

page 28.   Abstract. Morgan Jones ordered to pay Capt. David Peibils 264 lb. tobo due por bill.

page 28.   Itt is ordered if John White do not make good 90 lb tobbo the rest of a hhd unto Morgan Jones that Capt David Peibils shall according to his promise make good and satisfie the same

page 28.   Quietus is graunted to Mr Warham Horsmonden from Ca: Coce his estate, w'ch he hath rendered according to ord'r

Note: This name is illegible. It may be Core, Cone, Cope or Coxe. B.F.

page 28.   Itt is ordered that Phill Ellyott pay to Mr John Dibdall 524 tobbo and w'th costs als exec
page 28.   And that the said Mr Dibdall shall Deliver to the sd Ellyott a note past to Mr Edwards for the sd Debt or otherwise save him harmelesse from itt, and Deduce of the abovesd 524 what that thereof shall app'e' to be p'd to Mr Edwards according to that note

page 28.   Itt is ordered that Nich Perry forthw'th pay to Howell Pryse 645 lb tobbo Due for fees w'th costs als exec
            Nich: Perry appealeth to the third day of the next Quarter Co'rt from the Judg'mt aboves'd

page 29.   Abstract. N. Perry ordered to give bond re above appeal.

page 29.   Itt is ordered that 1976 lb tobbo returned by the late sherr Mr Anth: Wyatt in bills of severall men for arreares of the last yeares Levie be Collected and rec'd by the present Sherr and p'd to the Cred' of the last yeares publick Levie together w'th 1500 lb tobbo Due by ord'r to Rich Nicholas and 2000 lb tobbo raysed to make good Deficient absent insolvent and exempted persons in all 4476 lb tobbo so that the sd Mr Wyat may be acquitted of so much

page 29.   The Co'rt hath referred the Comp'lt of Nich Perry agt Phillip Mintorne till the next Co'rt and ordered that if the sd Mintorne shall not then appe' and show cause to the contrary Judgm't shal be graunted ag'st him for the just claime and costs

page 29. Itt is ordered that James Parham forthw'th pay to Ca: David Peibils 525 lb of tobbo and cask Due by bill w'th costs, als exec

page 29. Itt is ordered that Nich: Poole shall deliver on demand to Capt David Peibils all the tooles lately belonging to John Allison Dec'd upon oath

page 29. Daniell Scott confesseth Judgmt in Co'rt to Howell Pryse for 3000 lb Good tobbo and cask to be pd to him or his ex'ors adm'r or assgs, als exec and costs
Dec 17. 1655   Daniell Scott

page 29. Daniell Scott confesseth Judgmt in Co'rt to Capt Abra. Read and company for 680 lb of tobbo and cask to be pd to them or any of them or their assgs als exec w'th costs, dec. 17. 1655 being in full of all debts to the sd Read and company
Test Howell Pryse Cl   Daniell Scott

page 29. I Daniell Scott confesse Judg'mt unto Howell Pryse to deliver and record by the 10th of Aprill next one good cow w'th calfe for the use of my children Elizabeth and Daniell Scott w'th all increase thereof to be and come to them or the surviv'r of them or unto the sd Pryse in case they shall both Dep't this life w'thout issue in case of fayling wherein I confesse Judgmt as aforesd to the sd Pryse or his exors admrs or ass'gs for 1500 lb of good tobbo and cask to be pd him or them als exec, for the same and costs Dec. 17 1655
                                           Daniell Scott

page 30. Whereas Phillip Mintourne being bound in an obliga'con of 10000 lb tobo: to appe and answer what should be objected ag'st him by Mr Cha: Sparrow, hath attended two Co'rts, and nothing moved ag'tt him and is sued to Surry Com Co'rt upon the same cause: It is therefore ordered that the sd bond be deliv'ed up unto him

page 30. Itt is ordered that Capt David Peibils forthw'th pay to Howell Pryse or his assgs 532 lb of good tobbo due for fees w'th costs als exec

page 30. A Comi'con of admera'con is graunted to Howell Pryse of the estate of Wm Midloton dec'd he giveing Caution as is accustomed

page 30.   Howell Pryse hath proved right by testimony produced to 1600 acres of land for importation of

Wm Helman	Susan Bury	James Coxe
Tho: Holder	Jane Blanes	Edd Burley
James MacDonnell	Rebecca Jackson	Richd Atkins
Hugh Cartie (sic)	Wm Huntley	Richard Allcock
Robt Barnes	Roger Harlston	Mich: Waller
Robert Hewett	Judith Page	Walter Bird
Edmond Taylor	Elizab: Moaner	Wm Lacie
Richd Johnson	Elizabeth Major	Willm Lee
Peter Edwards	Mary Smith	Jeremy Lawes
Robt Jones	Hannah Dixon	James Lewis
Jane Bentlet	Mary Jones	

page 31.

Att a Co'rt holden att Westov'r
ffebr 4th 1655

Present
Coll Edd Hill esqr

Ma'r: Abra Wood   Capt John Epes
Mr Tho Drewe   Mr Warham Horsmonden
Mr Antho: Wyatt   Capt David Peibils

page 31.   The Co'rt on request of ffrancis Grey hath referred the claimes concerning the estate of Barthol: Whitehead dec'd untill the next Com Co'rt, And ordered that the sd Grey shall preserve and keepe intire the sd estate and seeuro it to his power what is perishable and give a true Inventory thereof to the sd next Co'rt

page 31.   Whereas there is due to Wm ffisher from mr John Dibdall 5500 lb tobbo and cask to be paid forthw'th: It is therefore ordered that the sd mr Dibdall shall (according to his offer in Co'rt) pay and deliver to the sd ffisher one good breeding mare and one filly of a yeare old w'thin six monthes from the date hereof, and pay unto him the next winter one thousand pounds of tobbo and cask remayning of the sd Debt and 870 lb tobbo and cask w'ch he Confesseth in Co'rt to be due and remayning in full for the house and Land formerly of his father mr ffisher Dec'd

page 31.   Lt Coll Walter Aston appealeth from the comp'lt of Lt Coll Thomas Swan to the next Quarter Co'rt
Itt is ordered that the appealant enter into bond according to act in Case of appeale

page 31.   Itt is ordered that John Drayton mer'cht possesse himselfe of the estate of Marmaduke Brooke Dec'd for paym't of the debt Due to him and give acc'ot to the Co'rt of the overplus

C 10

page 31. A Comi'con of admer'acon of the estate of James Waradine dec'd is graunted to Elizabeth Waradine Widd she giveing Caution as is acaustomed

page 31. The difference betweene Robt Letherland plt and mrs Mary ffreme deft is refferred untill the next Co'rt

page 31. Joseph Parsons surrendreth in Co'rt all his right and title of a parcell of Land at High Peake by him lately purchased of Wm Ditty unto James Parham and his heires ex'rs adm'rs and assgs for ever

page 32. To All &c I S'r Jo: Harvey knt Gov'nr &c give and graunt unto James Waradine three hundred and fiftie acres of Land scituate lying and being in the Com of Charles Citty butting westerly upon Baylyes Creeke next above the land of mr Jo. George vidzt beginning at the third Island and so running along by the Creeke easterly into the woods &c et in als dat 3 9br 1637
John Harvey

page 32. Abstract. 3 Oct. 1651. James Waradine transfers above to Wm. Ditty and Robt. Langman.

page 32. Abstract. Wm Ditty transfers his title to 200 acres of above to Joseph Parsons.

page 32. Abstract. Joseph Parsons transfers his title to above to James Parham. This name appears in this entry as 'James Paddam'. Signed by Jos. x Parsons. Witnessed by Robt. Marshall and Richd. Martyn. Dated 4th February 1655. (1655/6).

page 32. Abstract. Patent issued by Governor Richd. Bennett dated 7 Oct. 1653, for 203 acres, to Wm Ditty. Land adjs. above. Also assignment of this by Wm Ditty to Jos. Parsons dated 17 Dec. 1655. Also assignment by Parsons to James Parham. This name again spelled 'Paddam' in the entry.

page 33. Abstract. Deed. 4 Feb. 1655/6. Joseph Parsons to James Parham, the foregoing land.
Wit: Signed   Joseph x Parsons
Robert Marshall
Richard Martin   Recorded 26 Feb. 1655/6

page 35. Abstract. Deed. 23 Jan'ry 1655/6. Anthony Wyatt "of Chaplins choise in Virga" sells Robt. Burgiss of Apomattocks, 400 acres in Apomattock "com'only called and knowne by the name of Henry Millers, and part of it now in the posession of Wm Willms, the sd Land beginning

next to the Land of Samuell Woodward, his being two hundred acres and extending towards the land of mr Tonstall Dec'd as per pattent appeareth".
Wit: Signed Anthony Wyatt the seale
Ab: Wood
John Epes   Rec. 27 Feb. 1655/6

page 36. Abstract. Mrs. Sara Hoe ordered to pay to Capt; Richd. Tye, 703 lb. tobo. out of her late husbands estate. Also to pay Tho: Nothway merchant, 400 lb. tobo.

page 36. Abstract. Bill binding John Gaby to pay Walter Salter 400 lb. tobo. by 10th Nov. next, his plantation as security. Dated 1 Feb.1655/6.
Wit: Signed   John x Gaby
Mary x Owen
Peter Plumer   Rec. 27 Feb. 1655/6

page 36. Abstract. Mrs. Sara Hoe ordered to pay Morgan Jones 860 lb. tobo., out of her late husband's estate.

page 36. Itt is ordered that execu'n shall forthwith issue ag't certoine estate of mr Richd Jones attached for 300 lb tobbo and costs due to the Hono'ble Edd Diggs esq'r Governor &c

page 36. Abstract. fferdinando Aston confesses Judgm't. to Coll Edd Hill, esqr., for 440 lb. tobo.

page 36. Abstract. Curtis Laud confesses Judg't. to Mrs. Mary fframe for 700 lb. tobo.

page 36. Itt is ordered in full conclusion and Determinason of the difference betweene Tho: Huxe plt and Tho: Peters Deft depending these three Co'rts that the sd Peters shall forthw'th pay to the sd Huxe 700 lb of tobbo and cask w'th all costs of this present suite als exec

page 36. Itt is ordered that Corne and cleathing according to custom be forthw'th paid to Thomas Chappell late serv't to Jo Richards dec'd out of the sd Decedts estate by the exo'r or adm'er thereof als exec w'th costs

page 37. I George Worsuham Do hereby testifie and Depose in Co'rt that Wm the sonne of Wm Worsuham of Jordans in this County in his childhood had the accident of a fall whereby happened a small cutt in his eare w'ch (least future times should Convert to a Calumny) was Desired to be testified to vindicate him from any thought of the sd Cutt being infamous
Jurat' in Cur per'dt   George   GW   Worsuham
Test Hoel Pryse Cl

page 37. Itt is ordered that Certificat graunted upon this and the testimony ⌐   of m'r Antho: Wyatt be fully Drawne up in authentick ample forme

Mr Antho: Wyatt affirmeth testifieth and doposeth in Co'rt that Wm the son of Willm Worsuham of Jordans in this Com of Ch: Citty by the accident of a fall he recd in his childhood had a cutt in the upp' part of his eare, w'ch is Desired to be manifested to prevent what future infamy the mistakes or malice of ensuing times or persons may endeavor to cast upon him concerning that
Jur in Cur   Anthony Wyatt
Test Hoel Pryse Cl

page 37. To All to whom these presents shall come or may concerne Greeting
   I Coll: Edd Hill esqr, and the Com'rs of Cha: Citty Com in Virg'a haveing rec'd suffic't testimony by oath of Mr Antho: Wyatt mr George Worsuham that Willm the son of Wm Worsuham of Jordans in our sd Com receiving a fall in his childhood had the accident of a cutt in one of his eares and being desired by his father the sd Wm Worsuham Sen'r to manifest by our publick Certificat how the sd cutt hapened, do hereby upon the sd testimonies rec'd Certifie assure and make knowne that the sd cutt or slitt came by accident as afores'd, this being to prevent and take off all ill thoughts that may futurely be Conceived or imagined that the sd cutt or slitt might be any mark of Infamy and have publickly manifested the same and given this our Certificat (inserting the same in our records) to prevent the mistakes or malice of future times concerning that cut, the 4th Day of ffebr. 1655

page 38. Abstract. Walter Salter confesses Judgt. to Capt Jo. Wall for 450 lb tobo.

page 38. Itt is ordered that Mrs Sara Hoe admrx of m'r Rice Hoe dec'd pay to Capt David Peibils 924 lb tobbo and cask for the estate of Mrs Elizabeth Maxwell dec'd w'th costs als exec

C 10

page 38. Attachm't is graunted to Capt Wm ffarrar agst Michaell Mastres estate for 893 lb tobbo w'th costs incident

page 38. A probat of the last will and testam't of Wm Pryse dec'd is graunted unto Ann Prise the relict and extrx of the sd Decedt

page 38. Execu'con is graunted to Stephen Hamelin ag'st certaine estate of Geo: Browne attached for 500 lb tobbo w'th costs &c

page 38. Whereas m'r Richd Jones was arrested by the sherr at the suite of Stephen Hamelin for 514 lb tobbo and no bayle taken nor appean'ce made to answer: Itt is therefore ordered that Lt Coll Walter Aston the present sherr shall produce the person or suffic't estate of the sd m'r Jones at the next Co'rt or satisfie and pay the sd debt w'th Interest and Costs als exec
    Attachm't is graunted to Lt Coll Walter Aston ag't the estate of m'r Richd Jones for 514 lb tobbo w'th Interest and costs &c

page 38. The Co'rt doth hereby graunt and allow to mrs Mary ffreme widd the third part of all Lands and appertenances of her late husband Capt John ffreme decd, dureing her life, w'th the use of the best house thereon; The sd Lands to be divided and shared by some indifferent neighbors betweene the sd widd and the decd'ts heires

Note: Well ! I've had indifferent neighbors myself at one time and another, but would hardly have selected them to divide my property. This is a perfect example of the change in value of the English word.
                                                                       B.F.

page 38. Abstract. Attachment granted Howell Pryse agst est. of George Browne for 1200 lb. tobo. and costs.

page 38. Itt is ordered that Mrs Sara Hoe shall pay to Ca: David Poibils for Peter Salmon 1000 lb tobbo. 4 barrells of Corne: 1 shirt and 2 pare shoes Due per cov'ent w'th costs als execu'con.
    Bedusoing and Discounpting therefrom what shall app'e by the next Co'rt to be formerly pd thereof

page 38. A probat is graunted unto Robt Killingworth of the Last will and testam't of Willm North Dec'd this day prouved in Co'rt

page 39. Itt is ordered that Phillip Minterne pay unto Nichol' Perry 653 lb tobbo and cask Due per bill w'th costs, als exec

C 10

page 39. Itt is ordered that a full Co'rt be there had and held tho third day of March next to such Co'rt all suites and Differences now depending and unheard are also referred

page 39. Howell Pryse hath proved right by testimonyes produced to 4450 acres of Land for the right and charge of the transportation of these persons assigned unto him vidzt

Herbert Greene	Wm Cooper	George Mothley
Elizabeth Tanner	Joseph West	Richd ffarnham
Margaret Hally	John Nelson	Wm Stafford
Robert Bouy	Tho: Barker	Cha: Morley
David Humfreyes	Tho: Coalman	Phillip Bayley
Jo Ellyot	Richd Grey	Elizabeth Morris
Ellinor ffowler	Henry Hart	Edd Hall
Alice Tawney	Wm ffreaton	Richd Lawrence
Bryon Watts	Steven White	Jane Hughes
Wm Whittingham	Mathew Harrison	Jone Bennet
Tho Beale	Alice Mercer	Roger Play
Robt Korby	Phill: Langham	Martha Robinson
Antho Royes	Mary Ayres	Phill Chester
James Preston	Peter Sherwood	Andw: Berry
Humphrey Paine	Androw Stevenson	James Joyner
Henry Speed	Katherine Burdet	Edd Allen
Edd Charington	Walter Ray	Peter Browne
Robt Smith	Rebecca Major	Jane Griffith
ffrancis Hull	Symon Johnson	ffrancis Gregory
Wm Wells	James Heyward	Ellis Benson
Arthur Arnold	Tho: Jenkins	Robt Walker
Archebald MacCraw	Henry Mason	Tho: Senior
Jo: Comings	Mary Rosser	James Kirbie
Hugh Moris	Roger Hide	Wm Seale
Sara Lacie	Richard North	Alic: ffarrell
Jane Mabbett	Tho: Jett	Tho Pond
Henry Wrench	Wm Poynton	Michaell Longe
Tho: Wood	Tho: Man (or Maw)	Joseph Kent
Bernard Hallywell	Marmeduke Keybler	James Williams
Edmond Price	Richd Moore	

page 40. Att a Co'rt holden att Westov'r
Martij 3d 1655.

Present

Coll Edd Hill esqr
m'r Thomas Drewe   m'r Charles Sparrow
m'r Antho: Wyatt   Capt David Peibils

page 40. A Comi'oon of admr'acon is graunted to ffrancis Grey of the estate of Barthol: Whitehead dec'd he giveing Caution as is accustomed

page 40.   Ralph Poole aged 28 yeares or thereabouts
            ex'aed and sworn saith
That
   Major John Westhrope about a weeke before he dyed Desired the Depon't to go and request mr Sparrow to come and make the sd Major Westhropes will whereupon mr Sparrow came to him, and the sd Ma'r Westhrope told him he had brought the copie of a will out of England in his chest, wherein, he sayd, he had made no ad'mr, or had no adm'r, in Virginia, and being demanded whom he would putt in trust w'th his estate, he answered, Capt Tye and m'r Sparrow, further saying to mr Sparrow being then present, you know my estate as well as myselfe, therefore pray do by mine, as you would have yo'rs Done by (or to that effect) and you know my estate is cleere
Jur in Cur
Test Hoel Pryse Cl   Ralph Poole

page 40. Elizabeth Poole aged 25 yeares or thereabouts ex'aed and sworne saith and Deposeth the very same as is abovemenconed in every particular; and that Major Westhorpe being Demanded whether he would have his father Sadler or whether he would have his brother Thomas, intrusted w'th his estate, (or to that purpose) Answered No.
Jur in Cur
Test Hoel Pryse Cl   Elizabeth Poole

page 41.   Willm Short aged 42 yeares or thereabouts
            ex'aed and sworne saith
That being at the house of Ma'r Westhorpe shortly before his Death (mr Sparrow and mr Grey being w'th him) he heard them demand whether he had a will made or no, whereto he answered that he had a copie of a will that he brought out but told them it was lost, whereupon he desired a new will should be made, whereof mr Grey demanded who should be overseer, to w'ch Major Westhorpe answered, Capt Tye mr Sparrow and your selfe, w'ch he iterated
Jur in Cur   Wm WS Short
Test Hoel Pryse Cl

page 41. Abstract. Mrs. Sara Hoe ordered to pay George Potter 462 lb. tobo. out of her late husband's estate.

page 41. Itt is ordered that Ann the extrx of Wm Pryse dec'd shall pay unto Tho: Holford gent, attorn' of tho No'thway mer'cht 1000 lb tobbo and cask, with costs, als exec

page 41.   Attachm't is graunted to Capt David Peibils ag'st the estate of Tho: Nothway m'cht for 2000 lb tobbo and cask w'th costs incident

page 41. The Difference betweene Gilbert Platt plt and Capt Willm Rothwell Deft is referred to the next Co'rt

page 41. Capt Wm Rothwell confesseth Judgm't to Coll Edd Hill esqr for 1400 lb tobbo and cask payable the 20th Day of November next, als exec. w'th Costs

page 41. Itt is ordered that the DelinqTs in paym't of tythes in the precints undertaken for by Capt Henry Perry esqr shall upon notice given bring and deliver the severall quantities of tobbo and corne due from them to the house of m'r John Dibdall att Westover otherwise to be Distrained upon for their neglect

page 41. Wm Greene confesseth Judgm't to Walter Brookes for 740 lb tobbo and cask to be pd him or his assgs w'th costs als exec

page 41. Itt is ordered that Walter Salter shall forthw'th pay to Coll Guy Molsworth esqr or his assgs 300 lb tobo and cask, w'th costs als exec

page 41. Attachm't is granted to Capt David Peibils agst the estate of m'r Richd Jones for 700 lb tobbo and cask w'th costs incident

page 42. Whereas Capt John ffrome dec'd stood indebted per remainder of two bills to Wm Barker dec'ed 5 lb: 22 s: 6 d Sterl money, and twenty pare of mens shoes: Itt is therefore ordered that Mrs Mary ffrome shall forthw'th pay unto Robert Lotherland who married the Admrx of the sd Barker the sd 20 pare of shoes, and the sd money in tobbo, at 20/s per Cent
(Deduceing thereof 300 lb tobbo Due per Contra w'th Costs als exec

page 42. Whereas Capt Wm ffarrar sued out an attachm't agst Mich: Master for his nonappearance in the suite of Gilbert Platt and the sd Master now offereth to Joine issue: Itt is ordered that the sd attachm't be suspended, and that the sd Master give security to answer the sd Platt at the next Co'rt in Henrico County, to w'ch the businesse is recomended and refferred

page 42. A Comi'con of adm'erac is graunted to Richd Prise and Antho: Allen of the estate of John Richards dec'd, they giveing Caution as is accoustomed, and to Defray all just claimes ag't the sd estate and give acc't thereof to the next Court

page 42. Abstract. The Admrs. of John Richards, dec'd., ordered to pay Mr. Thos. Drewe 842 lb. tobo.

page 42. The Co'rt doth grant and allow unto Temperance Smith widd out of her husbands estate one bed w'thout acct to assets for the same

page 42. Quiet. is graunted to mrs Sara Hoe from the estate of her late husband m'r Rice Hoe, she paying all Levies and fees Due from her sd husband, or the estate

page 42. A Comi'oon of admeracon is graunted to Mary Longman widd of the estate of her Late husband Robt Longman Dec'd she giveing Caution as is accustomed

page 42. Attachm't is graunted to m'r Richard Dibdall agst the estate of Joseph Dunne for 1500 lb tobbo and cask w'th all costs incident

page 42. A Comico' of admera'con is granted to Ann Lewis widd: of the estate of her late husband Phillip Lewis Dec'd, she giveing Caution as is accustomed

page 42. A Comicon of admer'aenm cum testamento annexo, is granted to Jane Gregory widd of the estate of her late husband Tho. Gregory Dec'ed, she giveing Caution as is accustomed

page 42. A probat is granted to James Parham of the nuncupative will of Richd Colbrooke Dec'd this Day proved in Co'rt

page 43. Know all men by these presents that I Mary ffreme Do give unto my five children 2000 wayt of neate tobbo to be pd to them when they come of age or at my decease to Arther Willm James Sara and Jonne, and the sd tobbo to be Equally Divided amongst them, and the whole stock of sheepe excepting the Ram - Lambes and the wooll, and my daughter Ann to have her stock when she pleaseth out of them; I give also to my Daughter Sara a cow called old Browning and a hoope ring and a bodkin and a dutch Iron pot w'th a bayle to it, and to surrender the house and land w'ch I live in to my Sonn Will' lands to have as soone as I please after my day of marriage, also I give him a testam't w'th a gilded Cover, and a small testam't w'th a cloth cov'r to my daughter Sara also I give to my sonne James a practice of piety. Wittnes my hand this second Day of March 1655
Test
William Burford
Robert Rowse

the mk of
Mary MF ffreme

Rec. 6 March 1655/6

C 10   33

page 43.   ffeb'ry the 20th 1655
          Rec'd of Lt Coll Walter Aston two thousand pounds of tobbo
Due to me per order being in full of all accts and reckens or any guift
Due formerly by will or any bill or bonds. I say rec'd by me the 2000
lb of tobbo given me by will by Thomas Mathews witnes my hand the Day
and yeare above written
Test William Burford   John West
                              Rec. 6 March 1655/6

page 43.   These are to certifie that Howell Pryse hath proved right by
testimony produced to 1950 acres of Land for importacon of

Roger Bell   Randoll Jackson   Ales Tiller
James Arden   Tho. Beale   George Ray
Cornel' May   Peter Hughes   ffrancis Covey
Robert Rodes   Mary James   Antho: Barwick
Timothy Lawrence   Martha Hiller   Walter Pratt
Bernard Nash   Judith Croshaw   Jasper Gray
Jo Darnell   Wm Batty   Arthur Newcome
Edd Cooper   Wm Gill   Tho. ffarrington
Lawrence Seines   Rich. Heath   Prudence Greene
Daniell Armstrong   Elizabeth Arnold   Wm Corey
Hugh Davids   Rebecca Stone   James Slaner
Tho. Madrin   Jane Hunt   Isabell Moldrom
Nicholas Peake   Amie Browne   Jane Montfort

Note: If names mean anything, then I'd have liked to have seen Prudence
Greene come ashore in this strange Virginia.   B.F.

page 44.   Lt John Banister hath proved right by testimony produced to
500 acres of Land for importacon of
Humfrey Paydon. Hulda Speed. Susan Charington. (blank space left on
page for rest of names which were never recorded)

page 44. Abstract. Claims agt. estate of Maj. Jo. Westhorpe refered to
Gov. and Council at next Quarter Court.
Captain Wm. Thomas ordered to keep entire the est. of Maj. John Westhorp
and give a/c to Mr. Cha. Sparrow. The est. ordered to pay Howell Pryse
585 lb. tobo. due.

page 44.   Att a Co'rt holden at Westov'r
                       the 3d of April 1656
Present   Coll Edd Hill   )
                       Capt Hen: Perry) esqrs
            mr Tho: Drewe   mr Cha: Sparrow
            mr Antho Wyatt   Capt Rich. Tye
            Capt Jo: Epes   Capt David Peibils

page 44. Whereas by an act of Assembly held at Ja: Citty the 20th of Mc'h last and a comi'oon graunted unto Coll Edd Hill by the Gov'ner for the raysing of a Considerable party of men out of Charles Citty and Henrico Counties, w'ch men being raised, Itt is ordered by this Co'rt that their work be made good by those that stay at home of their sayd Companies proporconably

page 44. Robert Scott aged about 40 yeares and Tho: Douglas aged 26 yeares sworne say that Jo: Armstrong late dec'd and Andrew Armstrong were brothers children and further say not
Sworne in Co'rt

page 45. Itt is ordered by the Co'rt that exec be issued out agt the state (sic) of Michaell ffletcher for the value of 1818 lb of tobbo and cask and all charges at the suite of Capt Henry Perry esqr And whereas it appe'th to the Co'rt that the sd ffletcher hath Deceitfully and fraudulently taken tobacco out of severall caskes rec'd and in the roome thereof putt in bad tobbo, tobbo stalkes and dirt, Itt is ordered that the sd ffletcher shall forthw'th be Comitted to the sherr' custody and there remaine till such time that he stand at the Co'rt doore for one hour w'th a paper in his hatt written in Capital L'res w'th these words BEHOLD & BEWARE BY MY EXAMPLE HOW YEE CHEATE AND ABUSE TOBB'O ALREADY REC'D. and that he stand one whole yeare bound to his good behavior, and give in security for the performance

Note by Mrs. M.W.Hiden "I've several times seen the 's' of estate omitted if the preceding word ends in 'e', as in this instance".

Note by B.F. The penalty here is light, even if exceedingly undignified, considering that this was right close kin to chipping, which in turn is not too distantly related to counterfeiting. Certainly every effort seems to have been made to keep the Virginia tobacco of a high grade.

page 45. Itt is ordered that Capt Henry Perry esqr and Capt David Peibils pay unto Wm Burford under sherr 683 lb of tobbo out of the estate of Capt John Bishopp dec'd

page 45. Capt Daniell Lewellin was this Day sworne high shorr' for this Com for this ensuing yeare

Daniell Scott sworn as under sherr

page 45. Capt Tho: Stegge and Capt Robt Wynne sworne Com'rs for this Com, according to elec'oon

page 45. This present Co'rt is adjourned and removed to the 21th Day of this instant Aprill 1656

page 45. I acknowledge to have rec'd of Richard Bradford full paymto of all debts Dues and Demands from the beginning of the world to this Day ffebr 12. 1655 being neere 500 lb tobbo
                                Abra Wood
Test Hoel Pryse Cl
                      Rec June 29th 1656

page 46.   Att a Co'rt holden att Westov'r Apr 21. 1656
present
                Capt Henry Pery esqr
     Major Abr. Wood   mr Cha: Sparrow
     mr Tho: Drewe   Capt David Peibils
     mr Antho: Wyatt   Capt Tho: Stegge
     Capt Jo: Epes   Capt Robt Wynne

page 46. Abstract. Tho: Beadles confesses Judgt to James Crewes, merchant, for 224 lb tobbo. A cow bound for security. Dated 22 Apl. 1656

page 46. Abstract. Michaell Master confesses Judgt. to Capt. Thomas Darnell for 1255 lb tobo. to be pd 10 Dec. next.

page 46. Be it knowne unto all men by these presents that I Tho: Rands of Weynoke in Cha: Citty Com have bargained and sold unto Joseph Harwood his heires exors and assgs the one halfe of my plantacon being by estimacon thirty acres or thereabouts being that part of my plantacon next adjoining unto David Jones his plantacon, w'th leave to outt and carry away what timber he shall find upon any other share of my plantacon for his present occasion of building upon his share of the plantacon and not otherwise, excepting and refereing this to my selfe what houses are now built upon the same part of the land, And I do hereby warrent to Defend him from any others laying claime unto it so far forth as in me lyeth, as witnesse my hand and seale this 20th of December 1655
Wit: Thomas
Thomas Broome   Rands the seale
   the mk of
Wm x Viccars
                    Rec. 26 April 1656

page 47. Know all men by these presents that I Susanna Major the relict of Lt Coll Edd Major do ratifie and Confirme the guift of my

dec'd husband, that is to say, one mare fole that fell last August of a bay Collo'r unto my brother Walter Aston, And Do disclaime all my claime of the sd fole. As wittnes my hand this 24th Day of Aprill 1655.
Test.
Mathew Edloe
Edmond Smith
                                                Susanna Major

                         Rec. 21 Apl. 1656

page 47. Know all men by these presonts that I Thomas Malory for and in consideracon of marriage w'th Mary the relict of Robt. Langman dec'd and for and in Considera'con of my love and good affec'con to Mary Langman Jun'r the daughter of the sd Dec'edt, and for her better subsistance hereafter do give graunt bestow and Confirme unto the sd Mary Langman Junr two Cowes and foure yearling female calves, all marked vidzt w'th a Crop and a hole in the right eare, and swallow tayle in the leaft eare, being all in my present possession and custodie, wch sattell w'th all female increase thereof accrewing, I bind my selfe to keepe and preserve w'th all care and endeavor for the use of the sd child, giveing a yearely acc'ot thereof according to law, and deliver the whole to her at her full age or day of marriage whether shall first happen, As also to give and deliver to her at the time or day aforesd one man servant for the tearme of four yeares at least, or, in defect thereof, two thousand pounds of good merchantable tobbo and cask Witnesse my hand this 21th Day of Aprill 1656.
Test
Hool Pryse Cl   Thomas Malory

                       Rec. 26 Apl. 1656.

page 47. Abstract. Michaell Master confesses Judgt. to Richd. Hobs, mariner, for 600 lb tobo. payable 10 Dec. next (1656). Also (page 48) to James Crewes, merchant, for 606 lb tobo., payable" by the 10th day of December next w'th one yeares Interest at 8 per c ".

page 48. Abstract. Wm. Lambson confesses Judgt to Capt. Tho: Stegge, for 2800 lb tobo., payable 10 Nov. next (1656) "at my now dwelling". Also to Jo: Richards, merchant, for 248 lb. tobo., payable same date. Also to Jo: Drayton, merchant, 236 lb. tobo., payable the same date.

page 48. Abstract. Curtis Laud confesses Judgt. to Capt. Tho. Stegge, for 938 lb. tobo., payable 10 Nov. next (1656).

page 48. Whereas Joseph Dunn rec'd of Rich'd Dibdall for the use of Wm ffisher certain bills amounting to 2500 lb. tobbo and cask, whereof 500 lb tobbo is allowed to the sd Dunn for charges expended, Itt is therefore ordered that the sd Dunn shall deliver and restore to the sd Dibdall now Guardian of the sd ffisher the sd bills rec'd or 2000 lb tobbo and cask in kind and pay costs, als exec

page 48. A probat is graunted to Mrs Mary Shipley of the noncupative will of her late husband m'r Humfrey Shipley dec'd and this day proved in Co'rt

page 48. A Comicon of admineracon of the estate of Edd Ham'ond dec'd is graunted to Cornelius Clemence, for the use of the orphane, he giveing Caution as is accoustomed

page 48. ffrancis Redford sworne constable for Weynoke parish
Joseph Harwood sworne Deptie constable

page 48. Refference granted Inter Ca: Peibils and Sam: Smith to the next Co'rt

page 49. Abstract. The admr. of Jo: Richards, dec'd., ordered to pay Capt. Tho. Stegge 550 lb. tobo. by 10 Nov. next. Also to pay Wm. Bird 290 lb. tobo. by the same date.

page 49. Abstract. In full of differences Capt. David Peibils is ordered to pay James Crewes 2640 lb. tobo. "and that the sd Crewes give acct to the sd Ca: Peibils of three hogsheads of tobbo Consigned and intrusted into London to be sold for him".

page 49. David Jones and Howell Edmonds are hereby exempted from all publick services and taxes, except parish dues

page 49. Wm ffisher by consent of his present Guardian Doth freely and voluntaryly bind and ingage himselfe apprentice to Richard Parker chirurgeon for the tearme of two yeares and ten months from the date hereof, to be taught and instructed in the art and profession of the sd Parker, to be accomodated w'th dyett lodging and habit as his sd master, and to have two suites of apparell at the end of his sd time, w'ch the Co'rt hath Confirmed and ordered that Indentures be Drawne to that purpose

page 49. Abstract. Attachment is granted Capt. David Peibils agt. the est. of Henry Banks for 650 lb. tobo.

page 49. Itt is ordered that the admrs of Major John Westhorpe dec'd forthw'th pay to Capt Abra: Read or his assgs 4 l: 7 s. 6 d sterl money proved Due in Co'rt, als exec

page 49. A probat is graunted to Elizabeth Moyles of the last will and testa'mt of her late husband Peter Moyles dec'd this day proved in Co'rt

page 50.   Itt is ordered that Capt David Peibils pay to Theodorick Bland mer'cht 360 lb of merchantable tobbo Due per a note under his hand, w'th costs, als exec.

page 50.   Wm Justice hath proved right by testimony of Capt Thomas Stegge and Mrs Mary ffitzgarrett, to 1200 acres of land for the charge of Importa'con of

Mary Sherwood	ffrancis Nelson	Ann Lawrence
Wm Phillips	Jo Barber	Arthur Lawrence
Alex Michell	Joseph Erreene	Sara Lawrence
Mathew Bayle	Wm Prise	Wm Ballance
Tho: Whittior(Whitter)	Edmond Joyner	Jo: Halley
Rebecca fframe	Tho: Hayslwood	Eliz: Heath
Rich: Lee	Wm Lawrence	Peter Plum'er
Wm Coleman	Mary Lawrence twice	

page 50.   A probat of the last will and testam't of John Harrison Dec'd this day proved in Co'rt is granted unto Jo. Tate who married the relict and exerex of the sd Harrison

page 50.   Itt is ordered that the adm'r of Major Jo. Westhorpe dec'd forthw'th pay to John Hally chirurgeon 350 lb tobbo and cask for physicall meanes and attendance in the sickness of the sd Maj'r Westhorpe

page 50.   A Comi'con of admi'acon of the estate of George Armstrong dec'd is graunted unto Andrew Armstrong, he giveing Caution as is accustomed

page 50.   Itt is ordered that Richard Parker performe and perfect the Cure of the legge of John Mathews for wch he hath already served two yeares

page 50. Abstract. David Ludeons (?) confesses Judgt. to Tho: Drewe for 2981 lb. tobe. and 2 lb. sterl. money to be pd forthwith.

page 50.   All the Cred'rs of John Gaby here present haveing released and remitted their debts, The Co'rt hath thought fitt and ordered that the widdow enjoy all that small estate is left for her and her childrens reliefe, and that the Cow w'th her increase be and remain to the use and property of the sd children onely

page 50.   Exec is granted to issue for H Pryse agt Geo Brownes estate formerly attached at his suite for 2200 lb tobbo and all costs incident

page 51. Abstract. Admrs of Capt John Bishop dec'd ordered to pay 646 lb tobo to Tho: Northway or Erasmus Miller or either of them

page 51. The Co'rt upon the voluntary choice of James Warradine, Doth confirme mr Tho: Holford to be Guardian of the sd Warradine and his estate untill his full age

page 51. Itt is ordered that the adm'rs of Ma'r Jo. Westhorpe dec'd shall pay to Ralph Poole 800 lb tobbo for severall imploymts and attendances by him and his wife in the sicknesse of the sd Major Westhorpe, als exec.

page 51. Abstract. Admrs. of Capt. Jo: Bishopp ordered to pay Gilbert Platt for the estate of Reignald Evans dec'd 420 lb tobo., less discount for contra a/c

page 51. Whereas there is a runaway apprehended and accused to have consumed certeine gunpowder from mr Theo'd: Bland, Itt is therefore ordered that the sherr' officer do forthw'th inflict on the sd offender twenty lashes w'th a whip on his bare sholders

page 51. Itt is ordered that 200 lb tobbo be pd out of the estate of Edward Hamon dec'd to John Hodges for two Coffins by the admr of the sd estate, als exec.

page 51. Howell Pryse hath proved right by testimony produced to nineteene hundred acres of land for the charge of Importa'con of

Hen Thornton	Eliz Norton	Tho Dallison
Ja: May	Pru: Neale	Jo: Hall
Ja: Jolly	Diana Johnson	Daniell Rosse
Robt Brooke	Margt Bell	Marmaduke Clanton
Jo: Battin	Jane Denny	Grace Harrison
Jo: Covell	Paul Hinson	George Burton
Edd Mason	Roger Andrews	James Dawes
Syl: Baker	Isaac Hart	Nich Coleman
Edd (name blotted out)	Wm Hatley	Hen Rowse
Math Short	Mary Meredith	Margery Linton
Lancel: Haines	Katherine Hermy	Joice Coventon
Peter Greene	Ales ffoy	Andrew Mosse
Patrick Davison	Jeffrey Munson	

page 51. Abstract. Admr of est. of Edd Ham'ond ordered to pay 155 lb. tobo. to Howell Pryse.

page 52. Abstract. Wm. Greene having been arrested by Wm. Burford at suit of Tho. Drewe for 1314 lb. tobo., no bail taken and no appearance made, Burford ordered to pay.
    Attachment granted Burford agt Greene for 1314 lb tobo. with costs.

page 52. Abstract. Wm Burford having arrested Geo: Haraham at suit of Tho. Drewe for 1307 lb. tobo., no bail taken and no app. made, Burford ordered to pay. Attachment granted him agt Haraham for 1307 lb tobo and costs
    Burford having arrested Tho: Huxe for Thos. Dixon for 480 lb tobo., no bail taken and no appearance made, Burford ordered to pay. Attachment granted Burford agt Huxe for 480 lb. tobo. and costs.

page 52. Whereas m'r Wm Lawrence dec'd by his last will gave and bequeathed to each of his children two ewe lambes to be Del'rd as soone as his stock of sheepe should produce them, for accomplish'mt whereof, and in addition whereunto Mary his wife, late the relict of Capt John ffreme dec'd, in her widdowhood, gave and Confirmed by her deed on record to the sd children all the sd stock of sheepe extent, w'ch the Co'rt, on her explana'con of her intent therein conceiving confirming and declareing to be, not onely a compleate performance, but also an inlargem't and advancem't of the sd bequest by the sd will, Doth therefore cleere and acquitt her and her present husband Edward ffitzgarrott their heires and exrs and admrs off and from any future claimes to be made of the sd legacie, it being Comprehended and included in her sd guift

page 53. Itt is ordered that the estate of Edd Hamond dec'd be sold att an Outcry on the 20th Day of May next reserving what portion thereof the adm'r shall think needfull and Convenient for the use of the orphane, and the reste, after Debts paid, to be layd out to some proffitable use for the sd orphane, the adm'rs charge and paines and the keepeing of the sd orphane being allowed for

page 53. Whereas Robt Abernathie hath produced and proved an acc't of disbursemts and also charges for Geo: Armstrong dec'd amount' to 2186 lb tobbo wch he hath paid and ingaged for; Itt is therefore ordered that Andrew Armstrong adm'r of the sayd George shall pay or secure the sd sume to the sd Abernathie before removeall of the sd Dece'dts estate, als exec

page 53. Whereas Ann Parke serv't to Elizabeth Hacker widd is Complained of and proved to have Comitted ffornica'con and borne a Child in the time of her service: It is therefore ordered that the sd Ann shall double the time of service due to be performed by her sd mistresse or her assgs, from the time of her sd pro-ure, according to act in that Case made and provided

page 53.   Att Westov'r Junij 3. 1656
    present
        mr Tho: Drewe and Capt David Peibils

page 53.   Tho: Madder is sworne Constable for fflow'r de hundred precinct

page 53.   The Co'rt intended to have beene held this Day is adjourned and removed (by reason of apperoance and attendance of most of the Com'rs at this present Quarter Co'rt) to the 25th Day of this instant month of June

page 54.   Att a Co'rt holden att Westov'r
                Junij 25: 1656
present
                Coll Edward Hill)
                Capt Henry Perry) esqrs
    mr Tho: Drewe   mr Cha: Sparrow
    mr Antho Wyatt   Capt David Peibils
    Capt Richd Tye   Capt Tho: Stegge

page 54.   Whereas James Reyner being wounded in the late service agst the Indians and being offered a perfect cure of his sd hurt by Tho: Culmer for 700 lb tobbo and cask Desireth to addresse and offer himselfe to the sd Culmer for his sd Cure. It is therefore ordered that the sd Culmer for the cure of the sd Reyner shall receive 700 lb tobbo and cask in case he performe and perfect the same

page 54.
(Entered in margin)   Wm Short confesseth Judg'mt to James Crewes
Satisfac'con   mer'cht for 704 lb of good merchantable
acknowledged   tobacco and cask, and thirtie one good large
by mr Crewes   Beaver skins in season to be payd him or his
in Co'rt   assgs the 10th day of November next als exec
8br. 3. 1659   and costs
Test H Pryse Cl

page 54.   Itt is ordered that the Guardian of Wm ffisher shall att the next Co'rt pay and satisfie to Joseph Parsons 810 lbs good merchantable tobbo and cask, provided it shall not appere at the next Co'rt that the sd ffisher by his performances in the crop of Tho. Gregory dec'd hath Deserved a share of the sd Crop

page 54. Itt is ordered that Richard Nicholas shall by the third day of August next restore and deliver to Joseph Parsons one horse rec'd att Westov'r belonging to the sd Parsons w'th his sadle bridle and other furniture and appurtenances att Westov'r aforesd unimpaired and undamnified, als exec and costs

page 54. Abstract. David Luderas confesses Judt. to Capt. Henry Perry, esqr., for the est of Capt. Jno. Bishopp, dec'd., for 2500 lb tobo. Also to Tho. Drewe for 5186 lb tobo.

page 54. Abstract. The dif. betw. Wm Clay and Edd ffitzgarald ref. to next Court.

page 52. To all Christian people to whom it may Concerne: whereas there is a marriage intended and concluded betweene me John Powell of the parish of Westov'r and Hester Cradock of Westov'r aforesd widd, and she desired to dispose of part of her estate before marriage to the benefitt of her children for their future benefitt and maintenance, These are to acknowledge that I the sd Hester Cradock Do w'th the free and voluntary consent of the sd John Powell before marriage aforesd had and obteined give and bequeath to my children whose names are here under expressed these severall cattell there under written for their proper use benefitt and behoofe Vidzt I give to my sonn Robert Cradock of the age of ffifteene yeares or thereabouts one steere called by the name of Darling m'ked w'th a Crop on each eare and in each cropp a slitt of the age of three yeares or thereabouts, provided that if the sd steere aforesd may be exchanged for a Cow under the age of six yeares and recorded for the use of the sd Robt my son w'thin three monthes after the date hereof, that then the sd Cow shall be in lieu of the sd steere. It. I give my daughter Hester one heyfer of a yeare old and better called by the name of whiteface marked as aforesd w'th all her increase both male and female to be recorded for her sd use w'thin three months after the day of my marriage. Id I give to Jone Cradock my youngest Daughter one heyfer of the age of one yeare or thereabouts called by the name of starr x x x x Do set our hands and bind ourselves Jointly and severally in the sume of 10000 lb of tobbo for the true performance as witnesse our hands this 6th Day of may 1655
Wit:
John Dibdall   The m'k of X Hester Cradock
Michaell Master   The m'k of X Jo. Powell

M'd It is Concluded that this present deed of guift shall be left in the hands of John Dibdall minister till the sd Deed of guift be recorded at the charge of the sd Jo. Powell
Witnesse Michaell Master Margarett X Master

Recorded 27 June 1656.

page 56. Abstract. David Peibils ack. receipt from Mr. Jo. Holmwood of a bill due by Capt Roger Marshall for 1200 lb tobo. Dated 18 Feb.1652/3 Signed David Peibils. Recorded 27 June 1656.

page 56. Abstract. Deed of Gift. 25 June 1656. Nicholas Poole "in consideration of my good will and affection to the three Children of Peter Moyle dec'od and in consideration of marriage w'th Elizabeth the relict of the sd Moyle" gives 3 cows to the children. Recorded 27 June 1656.

page 56.

Loveing Brother

These are to give y'u to understand that I rec'd your let'r Dated the 11th of Aprill 1655 wherein y'u Do expresse your Desire to heare from me, and that in regard y'u grow auncient that y'u are willing to satisfie that tobacco that is due unto me. I give y'u thanks for the same, and do not doubt but y'u will porforme what y'u so freely offer, but I shall not send out for the same, it so falling out that my sonn in law Thomas Hallam is now entering upon a voyage for Virginia and I hope shall deliv'r this he himselfe into your hands if the Lord be pleased to send him a safe passage, w'ch if it please God so to Do I beseech y'u and my sister to give him kind entertein'mt as the sonn of my predecessor mr Tho: Hallam; truth it is he hath had crosses both by sea and land and by that meanes is put besides any calling there, and upon severall debates betweene his uncle Wm Hallam my selfe and my wife and himselfe all did agree the best way was that he should goe for Virginia, himselfe being fully resolved, haveing some good incouragem't that he should come to a loveing uncle and aunt who would well advise him and assist him that so he might be setled in some way for his future good as I have said before so beseech y'u againe to Do him all the good y'u can, and my selfe and my wife shall ever rest obliged but y'u and my sister, who I presume will not forgett the Cartesies of my predecessor, as for the tobbo that is Due unto me I Do freely give this same to my sonn Tho: Hallam be it more or lesse, for my part I have so little minded the same of late that I do not know how the acc'ot Doth stand at present, but I shall reffer the same to your owne conscience, and upon that acc'ot shall wholly Discharge y'u Delivering on the sd tobbo to my sonn Thomas Hallam unto whom I Do wholly consigne the same, but let him have that which is good and well cured, and upon the receipt of a lre' from y'u and my sonn that y'u have concluded the same, by the next I will if God permitt send y'u a full and suffic't Discharge; my sonn doth come out in the ship called the adventure m'r Young being Capt and hath pd for his passage six pounds, and he hath laded on board on (sic) Long deale chest w'th some soverall things in the same to passe off in Virginia, w'ch I pray good Brother let him have your best advice in, and that he may have good goods for the same, he hath also one boxe w'th some other necessaries, and one bed and 2 blanketts w'ch I hope w'th himselfe will all have a safe arrivall at his intended haven: And further these are to give y'u to understand that if att any time if y'u think good to send me ov'er any hhds of good tobbo. I shall be very willing and industrious to putt them off for y'u and to retorne y'u goods according to yo'r order and shall as faithfully performe every thing for yo'r good, and upon as easie tearmes as any y'u shall imploy, so Comitting the Contents hereof unto yo'r considera'con intreating yo'r favor and love towards my sonn Thomas Hallam in every particular that y'u are able to Do him good in, I take leave w'th mine and my wives kind love and best respects to y'u and my sister remembred, and should be glad to see y'u both here in England in the meane time rest

October the 5th 1655

Yo'r Loveing brother
William Mason

Subscribed

To his most respected brother
Mr Daniell Llewellin esqr   (sic)
present

Recorded Jun: 28. 1656

page 58. Be it knowne unto all men by these presents that I Thomas Hallam Salter of London by order from m'r Willm Mason and his wife my mother both of London aforesd as also by vertue of a lre of Attorney from Wm Hallam have remised released and quitt claimed x x x x unto Daniell Lewellin of Essex in Virginia of and from all x x x accompts x x x Dues or demands as also of and from one bill of Eight thowsand seaven hundred and fivetie pounds of tobbo and cask due to the estate of my late father Mr Thomas Hallam dec'd x x x In witnesse whereof I have hereunto sett my hand and seale this 14th Day of Aprill 1656
Test
James Crewes
John Aste

Tho: Hallam the seale

Recorded Jun: 28. 1656

page 58. Abstract. The dif. betw David Ludeons and Wm Burford to next Court. Burford ordered to give security.

page 58.

The Deposition of Jo. Stith exa'ed and sworne
Saith
That when he passed by the planta'con of Tho. Gregory dec'd he often saw Wm ffisher at work in the field w'th the sd Gregory's people and that the Dep't tooke him to be a sharer in the Crop

page 58. Whereas Elizabeth Heath ser'vt to Edd ffitzgerald comitted the act of ffornica'con and bore a child in the howse and service of her sd master: Itt is therefore ordered that the sd Elizabeth shall double the remayning time of service Due from the time of her Delivery and suffer such other corporall punish'mt as the Co'rt shall Consure to be inflicted for her sd offence according to Law to that purpose

page 59. Abstract. Capt David Peibils ordered to pay Jas. Crewes 356 lb tobo for 8 bushels of salt now due.

page 59. Abstract. Order that all differences be settled betw. Mr Jas. Crewes and Capt. David Peibils by Dec. 10th. Capt Henry Perry security for Peibils.

page 59. Abstract. Rice Hoe confesses Judgt. to Col. Edw. Hill for 350 lb. tobo.

page 59. A probat of the last will and testamt of Lt Coll Walter Aston dec'd this day proved in Co'rt is graunted to Mrs Hanna Aston the relict and ex'erix of the sd Dece'dt

page 59. Itt is ordered that the estate of James Warradine the sonn of James Warradine dec'd be fogaethred and delivered into the hands of his Guardian mr Tho: Holford

page 59. The Co'rt doth graunt and allow unto Elizabeth fforshaw widd two barrells of Corne one bed and one pott out of her late husbands estate towards her subsistance

page 59. Itt is ordered that the estates of Hugh fforshaw and John Gibson Dec'd be sold by Outcry the second Day of July next, and acct thereof given to the next co'rt

page 59. Itt is ordered that the generall list of tytheables of this Com be forthw'th taken by the sherr or his officer and presented to the Co'rt

page 59. Abstract. Wm Reines ordered to pay 600 lb. tobo. due to Richd. Price, admr. of the est. of Jo. Richards, dec'd.

page 59. Abstract. Discharge granted Richd. Price and Anth: Allen, exors. of est. of John Richards dec'd, they having already pd. beyond the assets

page 60. The Co'rt Doth hereby bind and ingage Henry the orphan of Hugh fforshaw dec'd apprentice unto Phillip Ellyott untill the sd Henry shall attaine to the age of eighteene yeares, And Itt is also ordered and enjoyned that the sd Ellyott shall educate his sd apprentice in the rudim'ts of Christian Religion teach and instruct him in the full knowledge of his trade or profession find and provide him sufficient of all necessaries dureing the sd tearme and at the end thereof give and deliver him such cloathing provi'con and tooles as are usuall and necessary in that case

page 60. Capt David Peibils is hereby tolerated and permitted to retoine and keep an Indian according to the rules and proscriptions of the Law in that Case provided

page 60. Abstract. Tho: Huxe ordered to pay Wm Lea 300 lb tobo on 10th of November.

page 60. Abstract. Bond. No date. 20000 lb tobo., to abide by settlement of dif. betw. Peibils and Crewes, by Capt. Henry Perry and Mr. Antho: Wyatt.
Wit: Signed   David Peibils
John White   James Crewes
Patrick Jackson
                         Recorded 12 July 1656

page 60. Abstract. Receipt. No date. 1656 lb. tobo from Richard Bradford in full of debts, excepting a bill due to Mr. Johnson of 373 lb of tobo.
                                  Signed   Thomas Stegge
                         Recorded 21 July 1656.

page 60. Howell Pryse hath proved right by testimony extant to 1450 acres of Land assigned unto him for importation of

Thos Slaney (or Tho'h)   Robt Wilson   Susan Browne
Jo. Russell   Robt Turner   Axander Dutton (sic)
Jo. Carey   Henry Shell   Geo Wyat
Ralph Barnes   Wm Chatterton   Edd Smith
Wm Talbot   John Crawley   Edd Simpson
James Goodheart   Ja: Radford   Simon Hatley
Richd Coxe   Roger Oxenden   James Nash
Tho. Galer   John Pike   Thomas Braine
Jo. Read   ffran: Bull   Tho: Jugle
Luke Monnace   fran: Marble

page 61.   Att a meeting of the Militia of Chas Citty
            Com at Buckland this 25th July 1656
  present
                    Coll Edd Hill   )
                    Capt Henry Perry   ) Esqrs
     mr Thos Drewe   Capt Richd Tye
     mr Antho Wyatt   Capt David Peibils

   Whereas there are certeine Intelligences brought to us by the King of Weynoke of severall strange Indians w'ch are come from the Northwards to the head of James river w'ch he calls Mastehooks, who (as he Conceives) come to fight the Rickohookans by some Certeine Intelligence he hath from some of his owne Indians, As also Peter Lee haveing given notice to Major Wood of certeine Indians who have killed severall hogs in the upper parts, upon w'ch notice Major Wood sending out to discover what Indians they were he found by Confident Intelligence that there had beene severall strange Indians upon the head of Swift Creeke, w'ch he Conceived to be Rickohookans; And whereas there are severall other reports of a suddaine Invasion intended by strange Indians w'ch Conduce much to the Disturbance and feares of these frontier Counties; ffor preven'con whereof therefore, and secureing themselves and others in case any such unexpected warr should breake forth, We the Militia above men'coned Do order that there be forthw'th prest out of Coll Hills comp' at Martins Brandon 15 men, out of Capt Peibils his comp' 20 , out of Capt Tyes comp. 10 out of Capt Epes his comp 10. and out of Maj Woods comp' 6 men all to be in readinesse at an howers warning w'th their armes and 12 shott of powder and ball a man for the security of the South side of James river. And for the north side 50 men be raised and in readinesse at an howers warning w'th armes powder and shott as aforesd. And that any one of the Militia shall have power to Comand the sd fiftie where any enemy shall appeare to assault

page 62.
            Att a Co'rt holden att Westov'r Sept primo 1656
  present
                    Coll Edd Hill   )
                    Capt Henry Perry   ) Esqrs
     mr Thomas Drewe   Capt Tho: Stegge
     mr Charles Sparrow   Capt Robt Wynne

page 62.   Itt is ordered that mr Rice Hoe shall Deliver to m'r Theodorick Bland two Cowes according to his fathers obligacon to the sd mr Bland and the increase thereof, if any be, als exec.

page 62. Abstract. Thos. Coale ordered to deliver to Wm. Wheeler a heifer and a bill in his hands for 800 lb tobo.

page 62. Abstract. Ordered that 300 lb. tobo. be pd. Richd Rawlins from the est. of Capt. Jno. Bishopp dec'd.

page 62. Ordered that maintenance be allowed and assessed for Magdalen Luck a poor impotent woman out of the parish of Weynoke

page 62. Abstract. All suits agt. Wm Burford to next Court "by reason of his present sicknesse".

page 62. This present writing witnesseth that I Richard Parker Do freely give consent to and w'th Mary Perkins that she shall make over unto her selfe all the estate w'ch her late Dec'd husband left her by his will Doth appe', both here and in England and further I do injoyne my selfe to bring her children up to Learning to the true intent and meaneing hereof I the sd Richd Parker hereunto sett my hand   Dated this last Day of July 1656
Test   Rich Parker
Richard Delabere
                         Recorded "7br. 5. seq."
                              (5th Sept. 1656)

page 62. Abstract. Mich: ffletcher confesses Judgt. for 5000 lb tobo payable 3rd Apl. next. Record does not show who to.

page 62. Abstract. Nicholas Perry confesses Judgt. to Mr. Theoderick Bland for 1800 lb tobe to be pd 10th Nov. next in Charles City Co.

page 62. Mr Thomas Drew Capt Richd Tye Capt Tho: Stegge and mr Theod: Bland are appointed and requested to Divide the estate of Capt John Bishopp dec'd according to the will amongs the Children   (sic) Capt Jo: Bishops estate is Cred'   per Inventory   15075 and cask

page 63. Being by Gods grace bound for England know all men by these presents that I Do hereby no'iate and appoint my welbeloved wife my true and lawfull Attorney to aske and receive all debts to me belonging, and to that purpose to arrest sue and imprison any Debt'r and at her pleasure againe to release and Discharge, and to do all and every such act and acts -ing and giving as I my selfe could were I personally here present, and in case of her mortality I do constitute Charles Tyler (my overseer) my Lawfull attorney Witnes my hand this 3d Day of Aprill 1656

Test   Warham Horsmonden
Robt x Nicholson
Hoel Pryse
                       rec 8'br 4   (4th Oct. 1656)

page 63. Abstract. Power of Atty. Dated "this last of August 1656". Mrs. Hannah Aston to Howell Pryse, to transfer land "bequeathed to me by the last will and testament of my late Dec'd husband Walter Aston", to Col. Edward Hill.
Wit: Signed   Hannah Aston
James Crewes
                       rec. 8ber. 4. sequ:
                       (Recorded 4 Oct. 1656)

page 63. Abstract. Anthony Nicholas, planter, discharges Mr. Anthony Wyatt of Chapling in Virga, of all debts due. Dated 18 Sept. 1656.
Wit:
Richard Nicholas   Signed   Anthony Nicholas

                       Recorded 4 Oct. 1656.

page 63.   Mr Theoderick Bland mr Stephen Hamelin and mr Robt Letherland are hereby humbly reccomended and presented to the Hono'ble Governor and Councell to be added to the Como'con of this Countie

page 64. Abstract. Deed. Dated 20 August 1656. Daniell Llewellin of Essex in Charles City Co., sells to Col. Edw. Hill of Shirley Hundred in the same county, 60 acres, "lately purchased of Dorothie Baker on wch I lately lived". x x. "Provided alwayes and it is agreed upon betweene me and the sd Coll Hill that the sd Coll Hill shall keepe the howseing free for the enterteinm't of one Mr Thomas Noathway for and dureing the tearme and time of seaven yeares"
                       Signed Daniell LLewellin   (sic)
                       Recorded 4 Oct. 1656.

page 65. Abstract. Mr. John Dibdall allowed to keep an Indian according to law.

page 65. Mr James Powell, Richd Hamelett Tho: Blankes, and an old negro man belonging to Mrs Hanna Aston are hereby exempted by reason of their long Continuance great age and inability from all future taxes except parish dues

Note: One cannot but wonder what God in his mercy thought of that. B.F.

page 65. The order of Joseph Parsons ag'st Wm ffisher is respited till the next Co'rt

page 65. Abstract. Admr of est. of Edd Hamond dec'd. ordered to pay 130 lb. tobo. to Daniell Scott.

page 65. Abstract. Com. of admr. of est. of Edd Sparchett dec'd. granted to James Salmon. Will annexed.

page 65. Abstract. Jas. Salmon, admr. Edd Sparchett ordered to pay Mr. Tho. Drewe 324 lb. tobo., also to pay Capt. Tho. Stegge 700 lb. tobo., also to pay David Ludccas 465 lb. tobo. "for physick" for Edd Sparchett dec'd.

page 65. Abstract. Probate granted Capt. Henry Perry esqr and Capt. David Peibils of the will of Mrs. Elizabeth Bishopp dec'd., this day prov'd in Court.

page 65. Itt is ordered and requested that mr Antho: Wyatt Ca. Rich. Tye Ca Robt Wynn and Lt Jo: Banister do at their next leisure equally divide and sequester the land late of mr James Waradine in three parts, and allot as they shall so just Convenient two thirds thereof to the heire and one third to mr James Barker in right of his wife to be enjoyed Dureing her life time, also the remayning estate being about 13400 lb tobbo in three parts, whereof one third to the sd Barker and two thirds amongst the three children, w'ch two thirds is also to be shared and proportioned into three parts, and one third of the sd second division to be and remaine in the hands and trust of the sd Barker for use of Sara Waradine and the remayning two thirds of the sd second Division to be Deliv'ed to mr Tho: Holford halfe in right of his wife and halfe for the use of James Waradine Junr the sd Holford giveing caution to bear proporconable part of w't debts or other charges shall justly appe' ag'st the estate of mr Ja: Waradine hereafter: Hereby is meant and intended the estate to the value of the sd tobbo in kind

page 66. Abstract. Jo: Gibson owing 300 lb. tobo. to Jo: Marshall, who appointed him to pay like amt to Mr. Williams, Marshall now given power to collect

page 66. Abstract. Admr of est of Capt. Jno. Bishop, dec'd.; ordered to pay Nich: Perry 200 lb tobo. due.

page 66. Abstract. The dif. betw. Nichol: Perry and Michael Master to next Court.

page 66. Abstract. The dif. betw. Howell Pryse and Richd. Wells to next Court.

page 66. Whereas Richard Bradford being indebted to mr Henry Randolph per acc'ot 800 lb tobbo. and cask hath Done certein worke att the mill late of Capt Richd Bond Dec'd, for whom the sd mr Randolph was agent, to the value of 500 lb tobbo and cask, for wch Wm Midleton dee'ed gave receipt and undertooke paymt, but never performed the same, as appeareth by testimony of the sd Bradford upon oath at this Co'rt
    Itt is therefore ordered that the sd Bradford be acquitted paying onely the sd remayning 300 lb tobbo. and cask (in wares according to agreem't) And the sd mr Randolph is left to his remedy for the sd 500 lb tobbo and cask agst the estate of the sd Midleton

page 66. Whereas Capt Tho: Stegge as greatest Cred'r was appointed to be first payd out of the estate of Wm Thomas late of Jordens dec'd, and the Inventory thereof being produced by Jone Thomas the relict of the sd Deced't amounting by apprisement but to 1018 lb tobbo, far short of the Debt,
    Itt is therefore ordered that the sd Jone Thomas shall enjoy that small estate paying or secureing the sd sum to Capt Stegg, and have her Quiet est from all further claimes

page 66. Whereas mr Stephen Hamolin made Informa'con to the Co'rt agst Coll Guy Molesworth esqr mr Cha: Sparrow for Majr Westhorpes family Mrs Susanna Horsmonden, Robt Nicholson, Edd ffitzgarald and Richd Rixe of a defect in their severall lists by Concealing some of their tytheable people Contrary to acts of Assembly Itt is therefore ordered that the severall parties be Cited by writt to appe' at the next Com Co'rt to answer the sd Informa'con agst them

page 67. A probat of the last will and testam't of Nichol: Perkins Dec'd this Day proved in Co'rt is granted to Richd Parker who married the relict and exerx of the sd Dec'edt

page 67. Abstract. Respite granted Richard Nicholas to 10th of Oct. for the recovery of Jos. Parker's horse.

page 67. Ordered that the orphane of Edward Hamond decd be educated provided for and instructed in all tearmes to her capacity and quality by and at the charge of Cornelius Clemence untill her full age or marriage for 3000 lb tobbo to be allowed the sd Clemence out of the sd estate and the use of three heyfers of about 1 1/2 yeare old a piece w'th their male increase duroing the sd tearme;

And Coll Edd Hill and Capt Henry Perry esqrs Do ingage two mares - - security to Deliv'r to the sd child 40 lb sterl money for 5000 lbs of the tobbo and cask of the sd estate, the sd money to be Deliv'ed at her full age or marriage

page 67. Itt is ordered that the Vestry of Westov'r parish or the major part of them meet at Westov'r aforesd the 9th day of this month for decision and settlem't of some Church differences and that any Delinq't in appearance shall forfeit 100 lb tobbo for his sd Default

page 67. Coll: Edd Hill my most humble service presented These are to intreate so much favor of the Com'ers that I may have refferences graunted to all those Ac'ons that are ag'st me this Co'rt for at present I am not able to come up in regard of an extreame fluxe of blood and a Continuall vomiting ever since the last tuesday w'ch makes (me) not able to go or stand but in a very weake measure, therefore I do most humbly intreat the favor of the Co'rt once againe that no Ord'r may passe ag'st me now in my absence, but that all the Acc'ons Concerning me be referred to the next Co'rt, and I shall in the meane time rest

           Your sick and humble servt
August the 29th 1656   William Burford

Subscribed
To the right worp'll Coll Edd Hill and the rest of the Com'rs of Cha: Citty Com
       these present

page 67. Howell Pryse hath produced and proved right by testimony to 1200 acres of Land assigned to him for importa'con of

Marg: Gates	Roger Slee	Jo Trevett
Dorothie Michell	Edmond Lucas	Charles Davison
Ann Reymond	Mathew Batt	Wm West
Tabitha White	James Mahne (or Malmo)	Nath: Crosby
George Covell	Theoph: Clemenee	James Holicresse
Jane Dawson	Hugh Thomas	James Male
Mary James	Joseph ffairepoint	Symon Hall
Wm Newcome	Wm Nicholls	John Markeham

page 68.

              Att a Cort holden att Westov'r
                  Octobr 3d 1656

present

        Coll Edd Hill   )
        Capt Henry Perry) Esqrs
  mr Tho: Drewe   Capt Tho: Stegge
  Capt John Epes   Capt Robt Wynne
  Capt Rich Tye

page 68. Whereas Informacon hath beene given to the Co'rt agst Coll Guy Molesworth esqr for concealing severall persons from the list, vidzt, Negr' women wch upon ex'aiacon of the matter do not appe by the Law to be tytheable, wch the Co'rt hath resolved and declared, and do therefore Dismisse and acquitt the sd Coll Molesworth from the sd Informacon and Compl't

page 68. Inter mr Crewes and Ca: Peibils refference to the next Co'rt

page 68. One old negr' man of Coll Guy Molesworth esqr is exempt from taxes being past the age and ability to be taxed

page 68. Abstract. Order formerly granted Howell Pryse for 676 lb. tobo. agt. Capt John Woodleife renewed.
Also Pryse agt Thomas Whethall for 420 lb. tobo.

page 68. Robert Letherland hath proved right by Indentures produced to 650 acres of Land for the charge of importa'con of

Richd Hughes	Arthur Downes	Martin Holdsworth
Ann Tinker	James Salmon	Jo: Price
Mich: Talbott	Edd Ameson (?)	James Bingley
Edd Wilson	Robt Wyes	
Ja: Bayley	Robt Gyles	

page 68. Abstract. Exor. of Jno. Bishop, decd., ord. to pay Jas. Crewes 800 lb. tobo.

page 68. Abstract. Cornelius Clemence ord. to pay John White, mercht., 638 lb. tobo. from the est. of Edd Hamond, decd.

page 68. Itt is ordered that the Levies and fees tobbo be first pd out of the estate of Wm Burford dec'd, next parish dues and tobbo rec'd to that use and lastly Debts according to rule of priority

page 69. Memorand Itt is testified and manifested in Co'rt that Joseph Parsons did in his life time give and appoint to and for the use of Thomas Gregory the sonne of Tho: Gregory dec'd and his heires for ever one roane mare of 2 1/2 yeares old or thereabouts now going and pastureing in Weynoke, wch he had of mr Stephen Hamelin

page 69. Ann Prise widd Doth give graunt and Confirme to her daughter Elizab: Williams one young heyfer named Browning m'ked w'th a Crop in each eare, and a piece taken out underneath each eare wch she desired to be acknowledged and authenticated by me her Attorney
                                        William Dittie

page 69. The ord'r for 700 lb tobbo and caske for James Reyners cure is transferred and --ined to Tho: Reynolds who hath performed the sd Cure

page 69. Abstract. Mr. Richd. Dibdall guardian of Wm Fisher ordered to pay the adm'r. of the est. of Tho: Gregory dec'd. 400 lb tobo.

page 69. Abstract. Capt John Wall chosen guardian of Robt. Herdman and his estate, which he is to receive from Austin Willyard.

page 69. Abstract. Tho: Tomkinson ord. to pay Howell Pryse 700 lb. tobo. and that his bill to Geo: Browne be void.

page 69. Capt Thomas Stegge is hereby tolerated allowed and permitted to reteine keepe and imploy an Indian according to the Lawes to that purpose

page 69. Abstract. Order that Cornelius Clemence pay from the est. of Edw. Hamond 590 lb. tobo. to Capt. Henry Perry, also "89 foot of sawne boards 10 lb of gun powder, and satisfie for a Case of Drams bought of Capt Stegge".

page 69. Ordered that Daniell the orphane of Hugh fforshaw dec'd shall remaine and continue w'th Cornel' Clemence, and by him be educated untill his full age according to request of his ffather.

page 69. Abstract. Wm. Dolling ordered to pay Mr. Theoderick Bland 205 lb tobo and settle the "bill of m'r Richd Bland dec'd form'ly due to m'r Eveling".

page 69. The Co'rt doth hereby tolerate permitt Licence and allow Robt Rowse to keepe a publick Inne Ordinary or Victualling house at Westov'r and to vend all sorts of liq'rs according to law.

page 69. A probat of the nuncupative will of Tho Moody dec'd this day proved in Co'rt graunted to ffrancis Redford who married the extrx of the sd will

page 70. Itt is ordered that John Marshall shall pay unto Daniell Scott for three hogs illegally killed and Destroyed 300 lb tobbo and the Costs of this present Co'rt als exec.

page 70. Abstract. Release granted Jane Parsons, widow, late the relict and admrx. of Tho. Gregory dec'd., she having pd. beyond the assets of the est.

page 70. Abstract. Allowance of 1000 lb. tobo. additional to Cornelius Clemence for keeping the orphan of Edw. Hamond.

page 70. Itt is ordered that the estate of Wm Burford Dec'd be sold at an outcry the 20th Day of this instant October

Note: One day, as I sat in the Archives Division of the Virginia State Library, filling the heavens with lamentations at the stupidity of my effort, Mr. Floyd W. Sydnor who sat hard by (the one cushion had been given me to help keep me quiet), remarked "If you copy 10000 names and one of them is of value, your time has not been wasted", all of which is an exact valuation of the whole Virginia Colonial Abstracts series to date, perhaps for all time. B.F.

page 70.

Mr Rice Hoe
    And Lo: ffriend Lo: &c Sr   shall desire y'u to pay to the bearer hereof John Sanders the five pounds sterl Due to m'r Sadler and comp' being a fine for the Land y'u hold att mer'chts hope therefore pray faile not send it by the Bearer hereof and in so doing this shal be yo'r suffic't Discharge and also ingage me to acknowledge it upon the back side of yo'r Lease or otherwise as shall be thought fitt:
    Wittnes my hand this 5th Day of Aprill Ao. Dom: 1655
                                     (Will: Thomas)
                                     (1655   )

Subscribed
ffor mr Rice Hoe at his howse
mer'chts hope   these
                    rec 8br 29, 56
             (Recorded 29 Oct. 1656)

"Patrick pray tell Mrs How that I sent her husband a discharge for the five lb sterl w'ch I rec'd for the use of mr Jo: Sadler and comp' I say rec'd by me
                          Will: Thomas

                  rec 8 br 29, 1656

page 70. Recd of m'r John Pratt 2d of March 1653 one hog'd of tobbo
Conteyning three hundred and thirteene ponuds of tobbo nett w'ch is
by y'r appointm't of m'r Richard Johnes minister I say rec'd
                                            James Crewes
                        rec Jan'ry 26. 56.

page 71.
         Att a Cort holden att Westov'r Octobr: 27. 1656.
present
            mr Tho: Drewe   Capt Richd Tye
            mr Antho: Wyatt   Capt David Peibils
            Capt Jo: Epes   Capt Tho: Stegge
            mr Cha: Sparrow   Capt Robt Wynne

Ordered that 26 lb tobbo per poll be forthwth Levied and Collected by
the present shrr on every tytheable person in this Com being 516 and
paid as foll vidz   lb tobbo
mr Wyatt for burgesse charge   1852
Capt Llewellin per ser'er (services)   1400
Coll Hill for   1 wolfe   200
John Evans for   2   "   400
Ca: Wynne   2   "   200
Jo: Stith   1   "   200
mr Gibbs   1   " (assigned by Phill Owen) 200
Henry Newcome   1   "   200
Wm Short   2   "   400
Capt Stegge   1   " (assd by Laud)   200
James Ward   1   "   200
Jo: Gilham   1   "   200
mr Walter Aston   1   "   200
Nath: Tatham Junr   1   "   200
Walter Brookes   1   "   200
Ca: ffran Epes   1   "   200
mr Tho: Epes   1   "   200
Isaac Hermison   7   "   1400
Lt Banister   1   "   200
Capt Wall   1   "   200
David Ramsay   1   "   200
Robt Scott   1   "   200
Tho Blankes   1   "   200
Jo: Adams   1   "   200
Howell Pryse for cop acts cr   600
Capt Lewellin to make good 21 persons overcharged   714
page 72.
Christofer for 4 dayes Com service   40
John Ast for his man and boate   60
Capt Lewellin for takeing list   400
Nathan Casby for 9 dayes work   090
John Thomas for 9 dayes work   90

                        (continued)

Charles City County Expenses 27 Oct. 1656 (continued)

Major Wood for 1 wolfe	200
Alexander Major 1 assd to mr Wyatt	200
Richd Hamlett 1 assd to Major Westhrope	200
James Sambook for 3 dayes work	30
Pond Evans for 9 dayes work	90

	11966
The publick levy is 34 per poll	
To Sallery	1196

	13162

page 72. Abstract. Com'rs ordered to verify tytheables for 1655.

page 72. Abstract. Lieut. John Banister allowed to have an Indian in his service. Also Capt. Dan'l Lewellin the same. Also Major Abra Wood two Indians. Also Capt Robt Wynne an Indian.

page 72. Abstract. Walter Salter to have plantation sold to him by John Gaby, by deed recorded.

Note: Book mutilated here. Pages 73 - 74 - 75 - 76 torn out. The index in the original, which I've omitted in these abstracts, shows the following entries that have been destroyed.

Jan'ry Co'rt adjorned	page	74
Letherland) p. probat		74
Lucas)		
Lewis v/s King)		76
Ead & Quitus)		
Mascall de stray cow		74
Northways lre to Ca: Wynne)		75
Id note de Ellis)		
Id v/s Master		76
Ord'r per Co'rts at merch'ts hope		75
Parsons per Quietus		70
Id estate to be Inventoried)		
Pryse per attachm't)		73
Id v/s Clemence)		
Id per Laud (Land ?))		
Pratt per Land		74
Rose per 600 lb tobbo Levy		73
Ramsey her guift		74

C 10   59

Items from index (continued)

Salter per possession   page 72
Id & ord   )
Stokes v/s Sharpe   )   76
Ward Constable   73
Wright probat   )
Wishert v/s mrs Hoe   )   76

page 77. Abstract. Lt. Coll Edd Major releases Lt. Coll. Walter Aston from any debts or claims from the estate of Humfrey Lister decd. Dated 17 November 1652. Signed Edw: Major. Wit. Edw. Hill. Recorded 18th Feb. 1656/7.

page 77. Abstract. Susanna Major, widow of Lt. Coll. Edd Major,"have rec'd of my father Lt Coll Walter Aston" full satisfaction for all debts due and obligation from the estate of Mr. Lister. Dated 23 April 1655. Signed by Susanna Major. Witnessed by Mathew Edloe and Edmond Smith. Recorded 16 Feb. 1656/7.

page 77. Abstract. Wm Short ord. to pay Mr. Anthony Wyatt for the use of Geo. Potter, 5 lb. sterl. "or the full value thereof in good Beanes or other rendible Comoditie".

page 77.   Ordered that 1600 lb tobbo and cask be raised and payd to Mr Anthony Wyatt at the next Levy for his burgesse charge at the last Assembly

page 78.   Debts due to mr Lister estate
            Wm Havit per bill   0804
            Capt Marshall per bill   1818
            Rice Woolfe per bill and booke   0904
            Mr Rice Hoe per booke   0170
            John Grinehow per booke   0150
            Sʳ Wm Bartlet   0500
            Mr Salmon   0340
            Phillip Cooper   0834
            Mr Loveine 2 bills   0660

These debts I do acknowledge do romaine in my hands, witnes my hand this 24th of Aprill 1655
                                        Walter Aston
indorsed
        Recd of my mother mrs Hanna Aston the bills and accots wᵗʰin

specified witnes my hand this 24 day of September 1656
                                        Will Batt

                    rec ffebry 16. 1656

page 78.   These presents witnes that I Willm Batt have sold x x unto my mother mrs Hanna Aston one browne steere about four yeares old and one browne cowe, wch cattell belonged to the estate of mr Humphrey Lister for wch I acknowledge to have rec'd full satisfaction, witnes my hand this 24th Day of September 1656.
Test   Will Batt
Mathew Edloe
                    rec febry 16: 1656

page 78. Abstract. Will Batt gent, for 2150 lb tobo, pd by Mr. James Crewes, sells to Mrs Hanna Aston, 6 head of cattle "all wch cattell are now in the possession of the sd mrs Aston and more lately belonging to my now wife mrs Susan Batt". Dated 4 Dec. 1656.
Wit:
Daniell Llewellin   Signed   Will Batt
James Crewes
                    Recorded 16 Feb. 1656/7

page 79. Abstract. Thomas Hamond ordered to pay Tho: Gilnutt (or Gilmit) 200 lb tobo from the estate of Jo: Peach.

page 79. Abstract. Nich. Perry arrested at suit of Mich: ffletcher, for 370 lb tobo, failed to appear. Dan'l Scott his security ord to pay. Attachmt granted Scott agt Perry's estate.

page 79. Abstract. Samuel Ealle chosen constable for Westover precinct. John Marshall, now constable, to be released when Ealle is sworn.

page 79. Abstract. Michaell ffletcher ordered to pay Robt. Elam 564 lb tobo bal. on bill.

page 79. Abstract. Peter Salmon arrested on suit of Jo: Stith, for 928 lb tobo, failing to appear, the sherif ordered to bring his person, estate or security to the next Court.

C 10   61

page 79.   Attachmt is graunted to Daniell Scott undersherr agst Peter Salmon or Tho: Arner for security of 928 lb tobbo and cask wth costs

page 79.   Whereas Capt Daniell Lewellin produced a generall acquittance under the hand of Arthur Bayly marin'r Dated in 1645
    Itt is therefore declared that all Debts due from the s'd Capt Lewellin to the sd Bayly untill then be null, and that all bills of such claimes, bearing date before that discharge be rendred up to the sd Capt Lewellin

page 79.   Ordered that Edd Mosby pay to m'r Tho: Drewe 1 lb: 16 s. sterl found Due in Co'rt per bill for necessaries for the funerall of Joseph Parsons and other dues, als exec and costs

page 79.   Ordered that John Stith pay to Edd Mosby 30/8 sterl' pd by him to m'r Thomas Drewe for necessaries for the funerall of Joseph Parsons dec'd als exec and costs

page 79.   A probat of the last will and testamt of Jo Letherland dec'd this day produced in Co'rt is granted unto Thomas Tanner the ex'er of the sd will

page 80.   The ord'r for Confirmacon of Capt Lewellins discharge from mr Arthur Bayly is hereby reversed and made voyd, And it is ordered that the bill therein menconed be restored by the sd Capt Lewellin to the Co'rt and to Robt ffox marin'r the Agent of the sd Bayly

page 80.   Itt is ordered upon the accot of m'r Rich Dibdall of the estate of Wm ffisher that the sd Mr Dibdall paying the debts wherew'th he charged the sd orphaneand delivering to the sd orphane one young mare two Cowes and one heyfer be acquitted from the sd estate, wch mare, cowes, and heyfer are to be rendered into the possession of the sd ffisher, but not to be Disposed by him untill his full age of 21 yeares

Wm ffishers accot
Due to Wm ffisher   5500

	Contra Credit	lb. to.
for the mare		3000
a suite of cloathes he gave bill for to one Owen		0400
for shoes		70

(continued)

William Fisher's Account (continued)

for linnen to make him shirts	146
pd to Dr Dunne and costs of suite	500
to Jo. Stithe	500
to mr Prise for fees	307
to Capt Lewellin	45
for my fathers tythes for corne and tobbo	200
for recording the Lre sent to this Co'rt at Surry Co'rt	50
for my charges for 2 dayes and 1/2 being arrested by mr Stanton at his suite	60

	5173

So due to Wm ffisher 322 lb to

More due for fees at the Quarter Co'rt   55

    rec febr: 17. 1656
    (17 Feb. 1656/7)

page 80. Itt os ordered that Capt Tho: Stegge or mr Cha: Sparrowe admrs of Major Jo. Westhrope dec'd pay unto the Co'rt of Cha: Citty Com five pounds sterl money for their attendance on the businesse of the sd Decedts estate at a private Co'rt att Buckland, als exec. and costs

page 80. It is ordered that Capt Stegge or mr Cha: Sparrow forthwth pay to the parish or vestry of Martins Brandon 3000 lbs of good tobbo and cask out of the estate of Major Jo. Westhorpe dec'd, wch sum was given and bequeathed by the sd Decedts testam't to the sd parrish or the Church thereof.

page 81. Whereas ffrancis Toms serv't to ffrancis Grey hath illegally and negligently absented himselfe from his Duty severall times amounting to tenn monthes; Itt is therefore ordered according to act that the sd Toms shall give satisfaction by Doubling the time of service so neglected after expiracon of his Indentures or customarie service, als exec and Cost.

page 81. Abstract. Release granted Jo: Drayton, merchant, as exor. of estate of Marmad: Brookes, Decd., he having pd. beyond the assets of the estate.

page 81. Itt is ordered that John Stith who married the relict of Jos: Parsons dec'd Do give a full and true Inventory of the sd Dece'dts estate within fourteene dayes x x x at Buckland x x x for the division thereof according to the will.

page 81. Ordered that the Difference betweene Jo. Hatley plt and Edd ffitzgarrett Defte, betweene mr Stephen Hamelin plt and Cha: Tyler def'te, betweene mrs Sara Hoe plt and ffrancis Redford Defte, be tryed by a Jury

The Jury

Capt Wm Rothwell foreman	Ca: Edd Mathewes
mr James Barker	mr Wm Sanders
mr Jo. Banister	mr Morgan Jones
mr Ed Mosby	mr Walter Holdsworth
mr ffr. Grey	mr Tho: Mather
mr Cornel' Clemence	mr Jo: Hodges

Verdict Intr' Hatley plt and ffitzgarret Deft It appeeth to the Jury by circumstantiall evidence that the w'thin menconed John Hatley is free, and therefore they do set and adjudge him to be free, as for his damages because the Indenture is lost and the Day of his freedome appe'ing not to the Jury but by circumstances, The Jury in consideracon thereof do allot him three barrells of corne according to custome and double clothing from head to foot, one being a new cloth suite, And Cost of suite cr.

Judgm't is graunted according to verdict above sd to be performed by the Defte Edd ffitzgarrett, als exec.

page 82. Verdict Inter Hamelin plt and Tyler def'te
We find for the plt 400 lb tobbo and cask Damages w'th Costs.
Judgm't is graunted w'th costs, according to the verdict, to be pd by the def'te Charles Tyler, als exec.

page 82. Abstract. Elias Webb arrested at suit of Chas. Sparrow, for 420 lb. tobo., failing to appear and no bail taken, Capt. Daniell Llewellin, sherif, ordered to bring the person or estate of Webb to next Court or pay.

page 82. Isaac Hermison Wm Sheffield and Robt Jones being sumoned for witnesses for James Barker are ordered and allowed satisfac'con for their attendance according to a generall ord'r for that purpose

page 82.   Howell Pryse hath proved right by testimony produced to 4800 acres of Land by assignem't for the charge of importing of

Andrew Gorton	Wm Mason	Robt ffarrington
Steven Webb	John Sanders	Sam: Chapman
ffrancis Dixon	Barthol: Wolls	Richd Boare
Jeremy Ward	Robt Harris	Christopher Trenser
Richd Marks	Roger Harris	James Willard
David Thomas	James Bristow	Geo. Baycock
ffrederick Smith	Tho Wood	Willm Crosse
Tho: Crauford	Edmond Allison	Wm Wilks
Wm Harwood	John Bayly	Sam Ray
Austin Yates	Jo Sheffield	Tho: Andrews
Christopher Baker	Wm Hiller	Symon Browne
Margar Newsham	Mary Lane	Tho: Dod
Daniell Ashley	Dorothy Johnson	Edd Owen
Walter Knolls	Alice Bury	Tho Martin
Elizab: Lodge	Mary Grey	John Wright
Josua Baker	Phillip White	Wm Chaundler
Robt Holland	ffrances Brewer	James Preston
Mary Crewe	Alexand'r Jay	Roger Bates
Tho. Anderson	Tho Rogers	Phillip Royston
John Sacker	Robert Milles	Robt Clayton
Tho: Best	Robt Rose	Robt Banister
Wm Cooper	Bryon Oneale	Sam: Jackson
Mary Brookes	Daniell Allen	Marmaduke ffletcher
James Eley	Richard Barnett	Thomas Hay
ffrancis ffoord	Myles Hewet	Wm Moore
Thomas Wray	Richd Corbett	Mich: Nelson
Peter Crane	John Dorman	James Butler
Thomas Nelson	John Peckett	Jo Rosse
John Ball	Michaell Clarke	Jeremy Hancock
Jo Mason	Tho: Smart (or Smurt)	Henry Blackman
fferdinando ffenner	Sam: Marshall	Richd Saines
Wm Cromer	George Haines	Jo Myles

page 83   Att a Co'rt holden at Westov'r ffebr: 4 1656 present

                Capt Henry Perry esqr
mr Tho: Drewe   Capt David Peibils
mr Antho: Wyatt   Capt Robt Wynne
Capt Tho: Stegge

page 83. Abstract. Order that 3000 lb tobo due Col. Edd Hill for levies be pd by his debt to Wm Burford's estate of 1460 lb tobo, and five bills rec'd by him amounting to 1592 lb tobo belonging to the estate

page 83. Itt is ordered that the Co'rt of Cha: Citty Com Jointly or severally pay to Capt Henry Perry esqr 970 lb tobbo Due in arreare of the last yeares collection, als exec.

page 83. Mr Charles Sparrow, Capt David Peibils, Capt Robert Wynne, and Lt Howell Pryse are hereby nominated and presented to the Hono'ble Governor and Councell (according to act) whereof one to be elected sherriffe the next ensuing yeare

page 83. To the worp' Co'rt of Cha Citty Com
James Crewes humbly presenteth   That whereas Capt David Peibils recorded ord'r agst y'r pet'r at the late grand Assembly for 2000 lb tobbo and being indebted to the petn'r a greater sum as per his acct annexed appeareth
The petn'r therefore humbly tendreth paymt of the sd sum so recorded ag'st him by Discompt according to Law of the Countrey, and that the s'd tender and discount may be satisfactory to acquitt the petn'r or be recorded to signifie the petn'rs forwardnesse to Discharge that Claime
And he shall pray &c

```
Capt David Peibils Dr to mr Crewes
        To one Judgm't                    1600 and cask
        to the cask at 10 per Cent         160
        to costs of the Judgmt             171
        to one other Judgmt                356 and cask
        to the Cask                         35
        to Costs of that Judgmt             37
                                          ----
                                          2359

By tobbo Cred' by Judgmt of the Assembly  2000
by costs of suite per the same Judgmt
```

M'd. Capt David Peibils Demandeth his tobbo according to ord'r of Assembly
Rec febry 20, 1656
(20 Feb. 1656/7)

page 84. Att a Co'rt holden at Westov'r April 2, 1657
    present
            Capt Henry Perry esqr
        mr Thomas Drewe   mr Cha: Sparrowe
        mr Antho Wyatt   Capt Richd Tye
        Capt Tho. Stegge   Capt Robt Wynne

page 84. Itt is ordered that Walter Salter forthw'th pay to Capt Abraham Read or his assgs 1250 lb of good neat pork according to two specialties produced, and 5 s sterl money due by a note under his hand, all found due in Co'rt, wth Costs als exec

page 84. Itt is ordered that David Ludeens forthwth pay to Howell Pryse 100 lb tobbo and cask appe'ing for fees and other dues w'th costs, als exec

page 84. Itt is ordered that David Ludeens forthwth pay to John - - (faded out) - or agggs 775 lb tobbo and cask Due per Bill wth costs, als exec

page 84. Itt is ordered that Mrs Hanna Aston pay to Geo Atkins - - (faded out) - - lb tobbo in full satisfaccon of his claime and demand for recovering and fetching home of a horse belonging to the sd mrs Aston wth Costs

page 84. Abstract. Nicholas Poole confesses Jud't to Capt Tho: Stegge for 1140 lb tobbo. Also to Tho. Drewe for 1882 lb tobbo.

page 84. Ordered that Anth: Allen shall at the next Com Court produce and present a true and perfect Inventory of the estate of John Gallis Decd

page 84. The Ingagem't of Michaell ffletcher and recognizance for the peace and good abearing to Continue till this day is hereby released and nulled, he paying all the Costs and append't charges of the sd businesse

page 84. Inter Capt Peibils and John Green having the refference to the next Co'rt to be then finally Determined by their mutuall agreem't

page 85. Following entry faded and partly illegible.

Loveing Brother and sister
- - - my - - respects prosented to y'u and to - - - I know not I have not recd any Lre from y'u of - - - not this three yeares I am

certaine of and therefore know not - - y'u are all Liveing or how it hath pleased the Lord to dispose of yu I praise the Lord I am at those present in good health wth Robt Hallam yo'r sonne who doth remember his Duties to y'u and love to all his sisters and brothers - - - but it hath pleased the Lord to take away from me - - - - - - since as in my form'r lre I gave y'u an acc't of woh I hope y'u have or will receive, to that as yet I am a single man and unmarried till it shall please the Lord to ordr it otherwise

    Now brother and sister the bearer hereof my kinsman Tho: Hallam eldest sonne of my late brother Thomas Hallam haveing - - - to go beyond sea in regard of a troublesome land that we have - - - - - - - very very bad and haveing rec'd great losse at - - - - - - was left him by his late ffather is much Decayed - - - - it lost - - - advice of his friends to Comend him to yu - - - - - sister that as I have beene and am carefull to provide - - - - - way that if he takes good courses may an- - - - - helpe and Comfort to yu the rest of his friends, so - - - - - much as in yu lyeth so long as he shall Continue wth - - - - - - carefull over him and advise him the best way y'u can - - - - his good. I am the more bold wth y'u (not that I Doubt of yo'r - affecoons and love to me woh I and my wife found whilst we continued in the land w'th yu woh I Do thankfully acknowledge) to urge - - - on this young man in regard that he is now far from his friends - - perhaps the voyage may be - - tedious to him not being used to the - - - therefore I pray let him not want any thing that lyes in yo'r power to help - - I would Desire that the portion of tobacco woh is due to me from y'u to pay - over to him that so he may have somewhat to send over into England this - - -. I shall expect and be very glad to heare from yu by the first in the mean- - - my desires to God shal be for yo'r health and preservacon Comitting yu and yo'rs to the protecion of God I shall remaine ever
                         Yo'r affectionate Loveing Brother
                               William Hallam

Burnham in Essex 20th 7br 1655
subscribed
ffor his Loveing Brother mr Daniell Llewelling
at Sherley hundred these I pray D'ld
    in
        Virginia
                    Recorded Apr 13. 1657

page 86. Abstract. Power of Atty. 20 Sept. 1655. "Wm Hallam of Burnham in the Com of Essex Salter", England, to "my welbeloved Cozen Thomas Hallam of the same towne and Com", to receive accounts due from Daniell Llewellin of Sherley hundred or elsewhere in Virginia.
Wit:
Edmund Clover   Signed William Hallam
Hugh x Sherborn
                    Recorded 13 April 1657

                (see further entries next page)

page 86. Abstract. Receipt. 20 March 1657. Rec'd of Daniell Llewellin, 2284 lb tobo. 420 lb being on a/c of "my uncle Wm Hallam in full of all accts betweene him and the sd Llewellin", and 1384 lb "upon a debt of 8750 lb of tobbo and cask due from the sd Llewellin to my mother mrs Margarett Hallam". Signed Tho: Hallam.

page 86.   1st ffebr: 1650
     Recd of Daniell Llewellin upon the ac'ot of Wm Hallam of London Salter one hd tobbo weyghing grosse 480 lb   I say recd
          per me by ord'r of mr Arth'r Baley
                                Edward Dunninger

                    rec. Apl 13. 1657

page 87. Be it known by all men by these presents that I Capt George Bond do acknowledge to have rec'd of mr James Crewes two hogsheads of cake tobacco in rowle, as also three hogsheads of Leafe tobacco, And I do firmely bind myselfe my heires and assgs to Dispose of the sd tobacco in Holland and to give a true and just accompt of the same unto the sd James Crewes or his assgs at the returne of the next shipping the sd Crewes paying frayght for the same at the rate of Seaven pounds per Tunn: In witnesse whereof I have hereunto set my hand this 7th Day of Aprill Ano Dom 1656
Wit.   Geo: Bond
Henry Perry
Daniell Llewellin
                         Recorded 13 Apl. 1657.

page 87.   Whereas I Richard Parker chirurg' did x x freely consent and agree to the signing sealing x x estate belonging to my now wife Mary Parker now know yee that I the sd Rich Parker for divers good causes x x freely Confirm the sd Deed x x and freely make over unto my sd wife all the Crop that her two boyes or ser'vts shall make this ensueing yeare and after se long as they have to serve, or any other things or servts which shall be sent from her father at any time or times whatsoever, To have and to hold as her owne property and free the sd two servts w'th goods or servants already sent out to be sent unto my sd wife, unto her for ever wthout any let or hinderance of me the sd Rich: Parker x x In witnesse whereof I have hereunto set my hand and seale this 17th of Mch 1656
Wit.   Richard Parker
Daniell Llewellin
John Aste
                         Recorded 15 April 1657

C 10   69

page 88. Entry faded. Partly illegible.

                          7br 4th 1650
Brother Llewelling
    I recd yo'r lre' and am very sorry to heare of y'r Dangerous sick-
nesse wch I shall Desire of the Lord if it be his pleasure to strength-
en you againe I praise God I and my wife and Robt are all of us in
good health w'th the rest of o'r friends onely we live in troublesome
times still and we are like to Continue, the Lord fit us to undergoe
them but our kingdome is in a sadd Condicon the sover' still raigning
still amongst us so that tradeing is very dead - - - - a man and his
family that hath lived well heretofore are - - - - brought low and to
want: Concerning the tobacco yu intend to send me the next yeare I
have taken ord'r wth mr Arthur Bayly to take it in and do desire yu to
take - - lbs of Lading from him in my name. I am satisfied wth what
yu write you will send me being 15 C weight and Cask. I desire yu good
brother that it may be good tobacco and that I may not fail of it by
this retorne of mr Bayly according as you have written yu will doe. I
heartily thank yu for yo'r paines in it. I hope when it shall please
the Lord to send it to my hands I shall in some capacity to send yu and
my sister something, unto whom I Desire yu that both mine and my wifes
love may be remembered and to the rest of yo'r children: I have spoken
to Roger Preston - -t his tobbo, and w't he intends to Do in it I know
not, But however for my part I accept of yo'r proffer, and shall be
ready to give yu what discharge yu shall require if mr Bayly Doth not.
I hope yu have and will Do w't yu can for me in it and I desire yu to
be carefull of my sister Mason that she may be satisfied for her debt.
I could wish I could heare in w't condicon yu live in for I feare if
these times hold long amongst us we must be all faine to come to
Virginia
    This wth my desires of all y'r good health and love to all our
friends remembered for present I comitt yu to God resting
                          Yo'r Lo: Brother
                                William Hallam

Subscribed
To his very loveing Brother
   mr Daniell Llewelling
at Sherly hundred there I pray Del'r
         in Virginia

Note: Even the typewriter and mimeograph cannot destroy the flavor in
the address on this letter.   B.F.

page 88.   mc'h 24th 1656
    Recd of Daniell Lewellin the Day and yeare abovewritten three
thousand six hundred and sixtie pounds of tobbo and cask being the
remainder of his tobo Due out of Charles Com
                       I say recd
                       per me William Berkeley

page 89. Entry faded. Almost any word below subject to correction.

Loveing Brother
  Itt is fallon unto me by reason I - - - w'ch yo'r sister in law mrs Margaret Hallam to write yu an answer of a lre that yu writt unto her bearing date ffebr - -- - - - yu - - - - oxceptions as it doth appe' by yo'r lre of a O'rd that was writt unto y'u by my wifes sonn She gave no such ord'r as to write any thing that might justly give yu - -see -ent but that I shall intreat yu to passe by as proceeding from a young man, but these are to give yu to understand that w'thin this - - - 6 weekes at furth'st I have rec'd for the 3 hds of tobbo of mr Llewellin from Lond- what I could get of him wch was but a small - - and I do understand that these were the first three sent - - agreem't one yeare being neglected since yu sent out the first 3 hds and therefore yo'r sister do'th intreat yu and I shall also intreat yu likewise that y'u will send over so much as will make up the - - due by agreemt f- time past. I will assure that we have - - severall great losses that have befallen us and o'r charge is great and by reason of the differences that are in our kingdome tradeing is dead that we must of necessity labor to compasse what is ab- - into - - - if possible mr Bayly can certifie yu w't ends - - - - of mr Llewellin Concerning the 3 hds of tobbo and truly had not mr Bayly proved a very honest man in that businesse - - - - - - very hardly got any satisfaccon of mr Llewellin for that - - - - pray S'r be pleased to take the Contents hereof into yo'r brotherly Consideracon and let us heare from y'u as soone as Conveniently y'u may if possible by the first retorne, so not Doubting - - - kind love and best respects unto yu and my sister unknowne as - - my wifes I com'it y'u and all yo'rs to the protec'con of the Almighty - - and will ever rest
         Yo'r Loveing brother
           W Mason
London the 19th of 7br 1648

I thought good to acquaint yu and mu sister that my litle Cozen yo'r son in law is very well and a prettie schollar yu will have Comfort of him

Subscribed
To his loveing brother mr Daniell Llewellin
liveing in Virginia in Sherley hundred
   these present
pray mr Bayly Doliv'r this w'th yo'r owne hands

       Recorded 14 April 1657

page 90.

Loveing Brother y'r lre per mr Bayly I have recd Dated the 4th of m'ch 1649 wherein yu expound unto me that yu will pay mr Bayly - - - (80 ?) bushells of English wheate at the rate yu sell at in Virg'a to yo'r neighbors w'ch is 50 lb of tob and cask yo'r bushell and the

C 10

Mason to Llewellin (continued)

rest yu say yu will pay in tobbo and cask according to the agreem't -
- - - is I should yeeld to any reasonable motion but as far as I do
apprehend I shal be a great looser considering the great charge that
will every way arise upon the same. I would rather - - that yu/y'u would
performe the agree'mt that was made w'th mr Bayly w'ch I hope/may performe brother you write of yo'r hinderances that yu have had the truth
is both my wife and myselfe are very sorry to heare of it but you know
that we must looke for troubles in this world man is borne to sorrows
as the sparkes fly upwards our savior saith and in the world ye shall
have troubles but in me ye shall have peace. God give us a lively faith
to get into - (Jesus) - Christ in whom is peace that passeth all understanding - - - - - may meet w'th troubles heare yet to learne that - -
- - that the Apostle hath taught us in all condi'cons to be content and
willingly to beare the punishmt of our iniquitys laboring to keepe
faith and a good Consciences in all things Brother it's not my Desire
to presse y'u beyond your abilitie which is best knowne to yo'r selfe,
onely keepe and a good conscience w'ch I hope is Yo'r endeavo'r, the
businesse that is in difference betweene us cannot be Denyed but it is
a due debt from y'u to me and my wife and truly there is a many of
little children that claime also a portion in it and I must inform y'u
that our tradeing since our troubles began in England is much decayed
and since I was married to y'or sister there hath beene much of her
estate lost that both my selfe and she thought would have been very
good and therefore I would desire y'u to take this into yo'r considera-
a'con, for my part I will reffer this businesse to mr Bayly and hope
that y'u performe that first agreem't w'ch I do Confirme by this my lre,
and that of necessity I must come to a new agreem't I must and do by
this lre' refer the businesse to mr Bayly and what he and y'u shall
agree on I will stand to and do Confirme by this my lre onely I desire
that conscience I meane a good conscience may have a share in the
agreem't that what shal be agreed on may be w'th a good conscience and
also performed yo'r litle son in law Robt Hallam is in good health
and doth remember his Duty to yu and my sister his mother he is placed
set prentice to the trade of a salter to my son in law Wood that
married w'th my wifes Daughter Ann Hallam and he is in a fine way of
trade liveth well - a honest man maketh acct the boy is provided for
and shall not want - - - - - the best of my endeavors and I believe
other of his - - - for him hees a - prettie witty boy and well approved
of - - - (several words faded out here) - -

  I have beene somewhat tedious but I hope yu will excuse me onely
w'th my kind love and my wifes - - unto yu and my sister and com'iting
yu and yrs and all that y'u have unto the blessing and proteccon of the
almighty will ever rest

                  Yo'r lo. brother
Lond the 21th of Aug 1650   (Signature faded out)

Supsor'
To his loveing brother mr Daniell Llewellin
- - - in Virginia   I pray yu
mr Bayly I pray Deliv'r this lre w'th yo'r
owne hands   Yrs
         Willm Mason

Recorded 14 April 1657.

C 10

page 91.   ffrancis Redford is by Judg'mt of this Cort com'itted to the
custody of the sherr untill he shall make legall answer upon oath to
the Channcery comp'lt of mrs Sara Hoe concerning a parcell of Land and
appertenances, and certeine timber in controversie

page 91.   By consent and in presence of Wm ffisher the orphane of John
ffisher dec'd mr John Dibdall and his sonn haveing manifested in this
Co'rt their full Disbursem't of the estate of the sd ffisher dec'd are
hereby acquitted and cleered from the sd estate as either principalls
or securities, and more especially and --ially from a parcell of land
formerly apperteyning to the sd ffisher as that of the Assetts of his
estate the sd mr Dibdall or mr Richard Dibdall rendering to the sd
ffisher two Cowes and 1 heyfer according to form'r ord

page 91.   Sam Lucie haveing recd a bill Due to Jo: Gibsons estate of
277 lb tobbo Discompteth 114 lb tobbo Due to him and 100 lb tobbo for
the sd Gibsons coffin and undertakes paymt of 80 lb tob to Tho: Beadles
for the sd estate

page 91.   Sam: Ealle sworne Constable for Westov'r precinct

page 92. Entries badly faded. All shown here subject to correction.

Mr Robt Hallam in - - - (looks as though Contra and Dr) - - -

		L.	s.	d.
1636	To me Thomas Hallam for - (several ?) gasgazones of goods - (sent ?) - this yeare	217:	16:	10
1637	ffor goods unto him this yeare	119.	9.	4
1638	ffor goods sent his wife this yeare	110.	5.	2
	Ditto for a bill of - pd her for her acc't	230.	-.	-
1637	for my p- of - 16 hds tobbo - sold - - - 1637	28.	-	-
1638	for my - - of the sale of 28 hds tobo sold	28		
		633:	11:	4

Ballance - - (expressed in terms I cannot read) - -

I take no p- for the 28 hds on Contra being the last parcell nor any
allowance for his ball of 210 L. 16 s. 5 d though it hath beene
forborn - - Ano 1638

                                    per me Thomas Hallam
rec   Apr: 14: 57

Note: I have tried in vain to identify the word 'gasgazones' which may
be 'gargazones'. The nearest I can come is that it means a miscella-
neous shipment of goods. It is just possible that it may be from the
French 'qu'est que c'est', broadly translated meaning 'whatever'. B.F.

page 92. Be it knowen unto all men by these presents that I Dan:
Lewellin of Sherley Hundred in the Com of Cha: Citty in Virga Do bind
me my heirs and assgs to pay or cause to be pd unto Margarett Hallam
of Brodstreet in the Citty of London widd or her assgs the full and
intire sum of eight thousand seaven hundred and fiftie p'ds of good
tobacco and cask at seaven severall paymts vidzt 1250 lb of tobbo and
cask at or upon the 20th Day of December next after the date hereof
and 1250 lb of tobbo and cask at or upon the 20th Day of December 1647,
and so yerely till the like sum and cask untill the sd debt be satisfyed, but if the sd Daniell Lewellin or his assgs can pay the sd sum
before the sd times of paymts are expired or can pay more then the
yearly propor'con of 1250 lb of tobbo and cask then the sd Margaret
Hallam or her assgs accompt of it and give discharges for so much out
of the principall Debt of 8750 lbs of tobbo and cask. In witnes whereof
I have hereunto set my hand this 6th Day of Mo'h 1645
            Daniell Llewellin
Signed and deliv'd in the presence of
The true copie of a bill made to
my sister Hallam   Witness   (sic)
          rec Apr. 14. 57

page 92. Lt Jo. Howell and Jo: Aste are appointed to view the struc-
ture and preperacon at Sherley hundred reserved by Capt Daniell
Lewellin for mr Thomas Nothway according to bargaine and make report
of the value thereof to the next Co'rt and that to be satisfied by
Discompt out of two bills of the sd Capt Lewellin past to sd Nothway

page 93. Entries faded. Those shown here subject to correction.

Mr Robt Hallam - - - - -

		L.	s.	d
1636	By me Thomas Hallam - - of our accts	7.	00.	4
	for this tobbo Due			
	Ditto for a surplus allowed - acct Did amount to	30.	-	-
1637	ffor 22 hds tobbo sold for his acct	115.	12:	-
	Ditto for 16 hds more sold for -	116.	-	-
1638	ffor 28 hds tobo sold for - - at 3 d lb -			
	cleere of all charge - - - make 2 d per			
	lb of - - - - - - - -	122.	-	-
1639	ffor 28 hds tobo for her acco recd wch I value at 50.	-	-	
		422:	14:	11
resting ffor ball of this acco't and is due to me			
Tho: Hallam this 16th Day of September all	220.	16.	5
		633:	11:	4

Ballance - (illegible) -
        per me Thomas Hallam
rec Apr 14. 57

page 93. Be it knowen unto all men by these presents that I Arthur Baily mer'cht - - - of a lre of attorney to me Directed from Margaret Hallam of - - London beareing date the 7th Day of October 1644 in the -th yeare of the reign of our Sovereign Lord King Charles &c - - - - and quit claimes and by these presents Do remise release and quitclaime unto Danl Llewellin of Sherley hundred in Charles Com Virginia of and from - - - all manner of accons as well reall as personall Debts acc'os - - - - bonds duties or demands w'tsoever w'ch she the sd Margaret Hallam - - adm'rs or assgs or any of them x x x - - - - or assgs of the Dec'd Robt Hallam for - or Concerning any matter - - x x. Witnes my hand this 5th Day of mch 1645

Wit:
Leon Ball- (?)
Wm x Johnson

Arthur Baily

rec Apr 14. 57

page 93. Recd of mr Lewellin in Ao 1646 for the accot of mrs Marg: Hallam 976 lb of tobbo w'th cask to Conteine it and in 1647 I recd of him part of a bill of James Robesons whereof 450 and cask belonged to her acct and is payable in 1647 the totall being 1426 lb of tobbo w'th cask and is in part - - bill of 8000 and odd. Witnes my hand this 25th of Jan'r 1647

Arthur Baily
rec Apr. 14. 1657

page 94. First entry illegible. It is a receipt, apparently to Dan'l Llewellin from Arthur Baily for tobo. dated 24 Feb. 1650;

page 94. This second entry on the page badly faded. Words transcribed below subject to correction.

Mr Lewellin my love remembered to y'u and to yo'r wife and family - - - - of yo'r health as my owne. I have Desired by the unto- - - - to make and end w'th y'u if yu will be - - - let him do what he can for me I shalbe a - - - however w't he Doth Do I shall subscribe unto and Consent to as if I were there my selfe thus hoping yu will make paymts this yeare to him for my use I rest and shall remaine

Yo'r Loveing ffr'd
Roger Preston

- - - -
London this 7th of 8br 1650
supr'ter
to mr Daniell Lewellin liveing at Sherley hundred
in Virginia
these

rec Apr 14. 57

page 94. Abstract. Receipt. 1 May 1652. Signed by Tho: Swann "by x power to me Directed from Roger Preston of London in England", releases Danl. Llewellin from all claims "left by Wm Hallam". Paper witnessed by Wm Whitby. Recorded Apl. 14. 1657.

page 95. This page stained, spotted and scratched over.

Md That I Tho Nothway do bind me my heirs - - to pay unto Daniell Lewellin or his assgs - - - in Cha: Citty Com so much good and - - - goods - - Dowlas canvas shoes and stockins and other goods as shall amount unto the full sum of twenty six pds thirteen shillings - pence at the first - - onely the sd Lewellin is to allow fifteen pence charge on every pound Witnes my hand this 12th of June 1655
Test John Sloman   Tho Nothway

md these words thirteene and four pence - - interlined before the sign-
- -. John Sloman
                          rec A- - 57

page 95.   ffebr the last 1645
   Recd of Daniell Llewellin the Day and yeare above menconed one bill for one thousand fortie and six pds of tobbo and cask bearing date the 6th Day of march 1645 in full of all accots and recconings from the beginning of the world to this Day excepting one hundred and fiftie pds of - - - - for smiths work witnes my hand
                                   Arthur Baily
                          rec April 14. 1657

page 95.   Ordered that the Co'rt make good the debt and damage - - - against Capt Daniell Lewellin for the escape of Elias Webb for want of a prison according to act

page 95. Abstract. Samll Lucie ord to pay Tho Madder 247 lb tobo by 20 Nov. next.

page 95.   The Co8rt hath by Consent bound and ingaged Dorathie the daughter of Jane Osborne dec'd unto Edd Mosby for five yeares to serve him his exors admrs or assgs as an apprentice and to be by him or them educated and maintained and at the end of the sd tearme to have cloathing and other necessaries according to custome and this to be Confirmed by Indenture

page 95.   Itt is ordered that Tho Smith serv't to ma'r Jo Westhorpe dec'd shall serve according to his Indenture produced in Co'rt except one yeare given and remitted by his sd Master in his life time

page 96. Abstract. The Court binds Frances the daughter of Jane Osborne decd to John Marshall until her full age. Wording as above order re. her sister Dorothy Osborne.

page 96. Upon complt and suite of mrs Sara Hoe that ffrancis Redford hath trespassed on a parcell of Demised Land contrary to Lease Itt is ordered that the sd Redford satisfie and pay all costs and charges expended or occasioned in any suite or suites about the premisses als exec

page 96. Know all men by these presents that I Wm Batte gent doe willingly allow that my brother (sic) Thos: and Henry Batte (in consideracon of their interest in Virginia) shall have eleven cowes one heyfer of two yeares old two yearling heyfers wth their increase the sd cattell to remaine upon our plantacon in Charles Com untill they come to age I do also allow that they shall have each of them two men serv'ts wth good clothes and bedding for four yeares wch is according to the Custome of the Countrey, and each of them a featherbed wth Curtens blankets rug and two p'r of sheets to each bed, and that they shall have sufficient meat drink apparell and lodging w'th other necessaries untill they come to age as above sd reserving onely out of this the male cattell for my owne use. Lastly I do allow that the plantacon shall be sold onely for their proper use and benefit lying in the Isle of Wight Com, and that they shall equally have as much Interest in the plantacon at Charles County comonly called Spring Gardens as my selfe Witnes my hand this 3d of May 1654
Testis
Phillip Malory   Wm Batte

Recognit in Cur Apr 3. 1657 per Thoms Malory and Guilm Batt present
                    Test
                              Hoel Pryse   Cl

        rec Apl 24. 57

page 97. Abstract. Bill of Sale. 1st April 1657. Hannah Aston widow, sells to Col. Edward Hill, for 3500 lb. tobo., "one Iron gray mare of the age of three yeares or thereabouts wth a white spot on one of her thyes". Signed by Hannah Aston. Witnessed by Edward Hill Junr.

page 97. Abstract. Col. Edw. Hill sells the above mare to John Dibdall minister for 46 barrels of Indian corn. Signed Edw: Hill. Witnessed by John Jacob.

page 97. I John Dibdall Do in open Co'rt assigne and make ov'r this bill of sale to Wm ffisher wth all her increase as witnes my hand this 3d of Apr 1657
Test H. Pryse Cl   John Dibdall

            Rec. Apr 25 seqr
            (25 April 1657)

page 98.   To the worp'll Com'rs of Charles Citty Com
            at the Co'rt at Westov'r the 3d of Apr 1657
The humble peticon of Sara Hoe
Sheweth
      That whereas yo'r petn'r hath beene much wronged by ffrancis Redford by his conveying away timber off of the land yo'r petn'r desireth yo'r worp's to graunt him (sic) reliefe in chauncery that y'r petn'r being able to make it appr by sufficient evidence
      And for that the Injuries recd by the petn'r may be more plainly made appr yo'r petn'r proceeding in chauncery humbly craveth that the sd ffrancis Redford may take his oath to these Interrogatories foll' in a distinct manner to every particular

1   Whether or no that the sd ffrancis Redford Did not carry away or cause to be carried away or transported timber of of yo'r petn'rs land.
2   What sorts or quantity of timber he hath carried or caused to be carried away
      Upon the appereance of yo'r petn'rs Damage he (sic) humbly craveth yo'r worp's to graunt him (sic) reliefe according to Lawe
            And yo'r petn'r shall ever pray &c

                  rec Apr 25 seq

page 98.   Those presents witnes that I Robt Abernethy Do consent and agree that my now wife Sara Abernethy do make over to her child Sara Cubishe one cow called Goodluck and a heyfer called Browne and another heyfer called Jug to remaine for the use and good of the child, and if it please God to call this child by death then the next child to succeed heire to its sister, And this we desire to be recorded in Co'rt wittnes our hands this 3d of Aprill 1657
                        Robt x Aberneathie
                        Sara x Abernathie
                              her m'k
Ack in Court same date
                  Rec. 25 Apl. 1657.

page 99. Abstract. Mr Charles Sparrow and Capt. Robt Wynne having examined the a/cs of Capt. Danl. Llewellin and found them satisfactory, the Court grants him Quietus est for 1656.

page 99. Abstract. Capt. Danl. Llewellin having been instructed to sell the estates and settle the affairs of Hugh fforshaw, John Gibson and William Burford, all dec'd., and having done so to the satisfaction of the Court is given Quietus est.

page 99.   Howell Pryse hath produced and proved right by testimony to
3500 acres of land assigned unto him for importacon of

Phill Harwood	John Tyler	Mich: Wills
Robt Salter	Morgan Lewis	Alex: Mont
Marmad Long	Mathew Hughes	Mark Allester
Thomas Warnham	James Robts	Geo Reyman
John Spire	Roger Clayton	Sam Burton
Roger Plumer	Tho. Knightley	Cuthbert ffletcher
Edd Playce	Robt fferne	fferd: Downes
Jervis Wilkinson	Wm Strood	Wm Edmonds
Wm Lancaster	Symon Allen	Josua Gibson
Tho ffecknham	Jeremy Ward	Robt Read
Tho Panton	Rich'd Cord	Henry Harper
Edd Bourne	Rich. Smith	Tho: Dunning
Phill Ashby	Sam. Warren	Tho: Beale
James Beare	Ja. Bird	John Marston
Symon Salter	Tho. Davis (Davies)	Roger Grey
John Wray	Edd Snealls (Sneath ?)	Henry Talbott
Jo. Cotes	Wm Tanner	Mich: Orton
Thomas Preston	Robt Wheeler	James Neale
Abra Johnson	Henry Weston	Tho: Murrey
Edd Johnson	Isaac Scott	Luke Bayley
Wm Gayler	Jo. Atkins	
Tho Gyles	Jo. Sheffield	
Henry Sterne	Nich. Wilson	
Roger Symmons	Ralph Sharpe	
Jo Philpot	Wm Balesman (Batesman ?)	

page 100.   Att a Co'rt held at mer'chts Hope Jun. 3, 1657
   Present
      mr Thomas Drewe   Capt Rich. Tye
      mr Anth Wyatt   Capt Rob't Wynne

page 100. Abstract. Wm Reines indebted to Tho Rogers 492 lb tobo ordered to pay within 20 days.

page 100.   Whereas John Slayd dec'd left an estate and severall
children the charge and care whereof is claimed by Anthony Tall (as
intrusted to him by the sd deced't) Itt is therefore ordered that the
sd Tall Do bring in and present to the next Co'rt a true and perfect
Inventory of the - sd Slayds estate, so that course may be Legally
taken for admeracon of the sd estate and education of the sd children

page 100. Abstract. Admr of est of Jo: Gallis decd granted Geo. Atkins
"on behalf of the Dece'ts orphanes". Est ordered to "be sold by Outcry
on the 20th Day of this month".

page 100. Abstract. Non suit granted Edd Mosby agt Tho: Turvile

page 100. Ordered that Thomas Peters remayne in safe custody of the Sherr untill he have given good security for his good behavior

page 100. Ordered that the orphanes Co'rt be here held on the 10th of July next and that the Undersherriffe give timely notice thereof to the Inhabitants

page 100. Abstract. Order that est of Wm Burford decd be "attached at suit of the Cor't for 970 lb tobbo and costs". Also attachment agt 2 chairs belonging to the est.

page 101. Abstract. Phillip Ellyott of Spillmans in the parish of Weynoke in Va. binds himself to pay John Dibdall, minister, 1500 lb tobo on 20 Nov. next, being part of 3000 lb tobo in paymt for a man servant named Henry Wentworth. Cattle listed as security, one heifer "now pastureing at fflower duy hundred w'th mr Drewes cattoll". Dated 1st May 1657.
Wit: Signed   Phill x Ellyot
R. Dibdall
David x Goodale
Ack in court Jun. 3. 1657.   Test Anthony Wyatt. Rich Tye
                     Recorded 21 July 1657.

page 102.   At a meeting of the militia of mer'chts Hope
                       Jun. 24th 1657
      Present
        Coll Abra Wood)   Major Wm Harris
        Capt Henry Pery) esqrs Capt Rich. Tye

Ordered that every company of this regim't provide and prepare ten men in readinesse victualled and armed for offence and defense ag'st the Comon enemy upon speciall sumond of the Coll or any by him warr'td or comanded to that purpose, every man haveing one pound of powder and four pounds of shot for each expedicon
    Ordered that Capt Peter Jones have the conduct and comand of the particular company belonging to Coll Abra Wood esqr and exercise the same and the like power and comand as is or shall be Directed by the lawes of this Countrey or the sd Collonell

page 102.   Quarter Co'rt held at James Citty the 11th of June 1657.
            Present   The Governor and Councell
  Lt Howell Pryse is no'inated and appointed sherr for Charles Citty
  Com this ensuing yeare, and to be sworne the next Co'rt there held
                        Test   Tho: Brereton Cl Con

page 102.   In the vacancie of a Co'rt we underwritten do according to
his eleccon and appointmt of the Governor and Councell admitt and Confirme Lt Howell Pryse sherr for this ensuing yeare July 10 1657
                        Anthony Wyatt
                        Rich: Tye
                        Charles Sparrowe

page 103.   April 20th 1657
Recd of Daniell Lewellin the day and yeare above written full satisfaccon (by ord'r and appointmt of my father in Law and my mother mr Wm
Mason and Margaret) for one bill of eight thousand seaven hundred and
fiftie pounds of tobbo and cask made to my sd mother wch is in full of
all accts and reckonings betweene the sd Llewellin and my sd ffather
and mother and my selfe from the beginning of the world to the present
day Witnesse my hand and seale the day and yeare abovewritten
Signed and Delivered
in the presence of   (Signature faded out)
Christopher Woodward
Willm Porter

This is the true copie of that discharge w'ch I have given to my uncle
Llewellin as witnesse my hand
                        Thos Hallam

                    rec Jun: 25, 1657

page 103. Abstract. Abra. Wood binds himself to pay Thos Nothway or
Walte. Deyes of Bristol, merchants, 3200 lb tobo, in Charles City Co.,
10 Oct. next. Dated 4 June 1655. Wit: Henry Randolph, Peter Jones
                    Rec. 21 July 1657

page 104.   Att a Co'rt held at merchts hope Aug 3, 1657
        Present
                    Capt Abra: Wood esqr
            mr Thomas Drewe   Capt Robt Wynne
            mr Anthony Wyatt

page 104.   A comicon of adm'r is graunted to Jane Willma (Williams)
of the estate of Wm Radeway dec'd she giveing Caution &c.

page 104. Mr Tho: Drewe hath proved right to 500 acres of land for importacon of 10 persons as per Indentures produced for w'ch he testifieth no land to have beene formerly taken vidzt

    Edd Lay   Arthur Piece
    Richd Mappin   Archebald Sincluir
    Robt Borne   Hugh - (faded out - possibly 'Caman')
    Wm Gabell   John Mo- (faded out)
    Wm Peck   Henry Macknemore

page 104. Abstract. Mr Stephen Hamelin and Mr Nicholas Perry to settle dif betw Phillip Ellyott and Wm Wilkins. Their award to be final.

page 104. David Jones aged 63 yeares exa'ed and sworne saith That he and Curtis Laud being present when John Jones dec'd desired to devise and dispose his estate did appoint that two cowes and one gunne should be sequestred confirmed and recorded to each of his sons, and to his sister Mary one heyfer w'th calfe named Goodluck, and to his sister Anns child a suite of linnen and wollen to each of his Godchildren one cow calfe as soone as they could conveniently be paid, one cow to James Moore at expiracon of his time and the rest he gave to his wife makeing her ex'erx and further saith not

                                David x Jones

Jur in Cur Aug. 3. 1657
Test Hoel Pryse Cl

Note: As grateful as we are for this old will, still we cannot but regret that there was not more from David Jones - for he could very well remember the times of the settlement at Jamestown. But then again there has been ten thousand times more lost in Davy Jones Locker. B.F.

page 104. Curtis Laud exa'ied and sworne saith and deposeth the like in each particular, and further saith not

                                Curtis x Laud

Jur in Cur Aug. 3. 1657
Test H Pryse Cl

page 104. A probat of the last will nuncupative of Jo: Jones dec'd is graunted to Mary Jones the relict and ex'erx of the sd Decedt

page 105. Capt John Epes present

page 105. Abstract. Charles Tyler ordered to pay Howell Pryse forthwith "one case of Drams".

page 105. Abstract. Attachmt granted Col. Edd Hill agt est of Nichol: Poole for 300 lb tobo.

page 105. Abstract. Rice Hoe confesses Judgt to Col. Edd Hill for 350 lb tobo payable at Merchants Hope.

page 105. Abstract. Thos Hamond ord to pay Col. Edd Hill 220 lb tobo.

page 105. Abstract. Attachmt granted Morris Rose agt the est of fferd: Aston for 2 hhds tobo.

page 105. Ordered that Mathew Chapman shall in considera'con of his present and future maintenance serve mrs Hanna Aston or her assgs untill he shall attaine to the perfect age of 21 yeares.

page 105. Abstract. The dif betw Lt Jo: Howell plt and Curtis Laud deft to next Court.

page 105.
    (Present)
        Capt Henry Perry esqr   Capt Tho. Stegge
        Mr Charles Sparrow   Mr War. Horsmonden
(An abbreviated Latin phrase introduced in the margin here. I cannot read it. B.F.)

page 105. Abstract. Mr Geo. Potter permitted to employ an Indian according to law.

page 105. Abstract. Non suit granted Capt Wm Rothwell agt John Harwood.

page 105. Abstract. In the dif betw Charles Latham and John Stith, Latham ord to pay 500 lb tobe etc and Stith to deliver to Latham "all his goods in his hands or house".

page 105. mr Tho: Drewe is exempted of the levy for six persons runn away before the list taken
    The like is graunted to mrs Peibils for 3 persons escaped

page 105. Abstract. Probate of will of John Lucas decd granted Capt Wm Rothwell.

page 105. Abstract. Claim of Anthony Allen agt est of John Gallis decd for 400 lb tobo allowed.

page 106. Abstract. John Stith confesses Judgt to Capt Tho: Stegge and Mr Stephen Hamolin attorneys of Edd Addenbrooke, Thomas Harrison and Wm Mansfield of London for 12000 lb tobo for future paymt.

page 106. Ordered that Nich Jenkind servt to mr War Horsmonden shall continue and serve w'th his sd master untill he have completed and c-ed the time according to his fathers act under his hand and seale binding him for 9 yeares, and at experacon thereof to be released

page 106. John Stith is publiquely admonished and fined according to law for rash profane sweareing in open Co'rt

page 106. Ordered that a prison howse be forthw'th built for the use of this Com for secureing of such prisoners as shal be in the sherr custody

page 106. Ordered that Edmond Bishopp according to his desire and consent shall serve mrs Elizab: Peibils untill he be 17 yeares old

page 106. Abstract. Admrs of est of Jo. Gallis ordered to pay to Howell Pryse 964 lb tobo for fees

page 106. Ordered that the Com'ers in the severall precincts where Constables are wanting shall chuse sumon and sweare Constables for all such vacant places

page 106. Abstract. Mr Charles Sparrow ord to pay out of the est of Maj. Jno. Westhorpe decd 862 lb tobo to Mr Stephen Hamolin due for levies.

page 106. Ordered that the difference betweene Walter Salter plt and Edd ffitzgarrald Deft be tryed by a Jury

page 106. Abstract. Wm Lambson having confessed Judgt to Wm Bird for 420 lb tobo is ordered to pay.

page 107   Jury intre Salter plt v ffitzgarald
mr Stephen Hamelin foreman   mr James Ward
mr Nicholas Perry   mr Wm Bayly
mr Edd Mosby   mr Antho Allen
mr Wm Short   mr Richd Prise
mr Morgan Jones   mr Cuthbert Wm'son (Williamson)
mr ffran: Redford   mr Walter Brookes

                    Verdict
We find for the defend't the land in question and five pounds of tobbo Damage
Judgm't is graunted by the Co'rt upon the verdict abovesd w'th Damages as per verdict and costs of suite als exec against the plt Salter

page 107.   The Co'rt hath requested impowered and intrusted mr Charles Sparrow to receive and recover the tobbo belonging to the estate of John Gallis dec'd and after Defraying the debts of the deced't to -- remainder equally to the Guardians of the two orphanes of the Dec'dt

page 107.   George Atkins is intrusted and appointed Guardian of Grace orphane of Jo: Gillis dec'd, and Willm Dollin Guardian of John orphan of the sd dec'edt, who are to educate and mainteine the sayd orphanes and give good caution to preserve their estate and render it to them at their full age

page 107.   Howell Pryse hath proved right by testimony produced to 2150 acres of land for importa'con of 43 persons undernamed Vidzt

Henry Peckett	Mary Killinghall	Hugh Jones
Henry Lawrence	Elizabeth Bowyer	Robert Whiteing
Edmond Potter	Mary Ramsey	Bartholomew CrossE
Jo: Mathew	Jone Nelson	Peter Heath
Arthur Coventon	Andrew Keatley	Jo: Smallwood
Louis Beckw'th	Ambrose Parker	John Hancock
Richard Hand	James Wyner	Martha ffryer
Richd Tiller	James Haut (or Hunt)	ffrances Holls
James Harris	Olliner Jewett	Katherine Hart
Tho: Harris	Nicholas Lawrence	Paul Cartrewight
Marmaduke Ladd	Edd Arney	Benjamin Chandler
Jeremya Burdett	Samuell Jeffers	Robert Bigges
Wm Richardson	Richard Lucie	Lawrence Ashpode
Jane Bell	Anthony Burwell	
Rebecca Goldin	Robert Moores	

C 10   85

page 107. Abstract. Judgmt obtained by Edd ffitzgerald agt Walter Salter now suspended.

page 108. The deposition of Wm Justice aged 32 yeares or thereabouts sworne the 8th of Aprill 1657
    Deposeth that being at the planta'con of Jo Gaby then decd in march last was twelve month w'th Edd ffitzgerald and fferdinando Aston the fence of the orchard by the house was downe and further saith not
Wm Justice

Jur Coram me
Thomas Stegge   rec Aug 20 57

page 108. The Deposition of Andrew Neale aged 22 yeares or thereabouts
    This dept saith that at the plantacon of Jo. Gaby the next day after that mr Jones his corne was gathered that he see cattle and hogs w(thin the fence and that so low in some places that it might be stept over and further saith not
the marke of   x   Andrew Neale

Jur Coram me
Thomas Stegge   rec Aug. 20 57

page 108. The Deposition of James Moore aged 22 or 23 yeares
    Saith that at the plantacon of John Gaby the next day after mr Jones his corne was gathered that he did see cattle and hogs in the orchard amongst the trees and the fence in some places very low that it might be stept over
the mark of   x   James Moore

Jur Coram me
Thomas Stegge   rec Aug 20. 57

page 108. Abstract. Bill of Sale. Quaint wording. 3 Aug 1657. Nicholas x Poole sells Maurice Rose 2 cows and 1 black bull.
Recorded 20 Aug. 1657

page 109. January the 25th 1656 then recd upon the accot of mr Thomas Drewe three bills of exchange of the day and date abovesd wherein mr Thomas Stegge becomes debtor the sume of sixtie nine pounds two shillings and tenn pence to the sd Arthur Bayly the bills being drawn on mr John Bird of London, so that mr Thomas Drewe is fully discharged of all Debts and accts to Arthur Bayly, as witnes my hand the sd day and yeare above
Wittnes   per me
Hen: Perry   Robert ffox
Thomas Stegge
No date of record shown.

page 109   Aug: 4. 1657
           present
                   Coll Abr: Wood esqr
           mr Antho Wyatt   Capt Richd Tye
           Capt John Epes   Capt Robt Wynne
           mr Cha Sparrow

page 109. Whereas Lt James Barker who married the relict and admr of Ja: Waradine dec'd hath by his acct produced and app'ved, fully adm'red and cleered the estate and rendered to the severall orphanes their due share and porcon thereof: The Co'rt doth therefore hereby certifie the same whereby a cleere Quitus est may be graunted to him and his wife the adm'rix, from the sd estate.

page 109. Ordered that Antho Tall pay and discharge all the debts of Jo: Slayd decd and give good maintenance education and schooling to the orphanes and at their full age render and deliv'r unto each of them two cowes wth calfs and give caution for the premisses

page 109. I acknowledge to have in my hands custody and possession one heyfer of about 2 yeares old marked vidzt underkeeld on each eare wch was given and bestowed to Jane Rogers the orphane of Wm Rogers dec'd by Robt Killingworth now dec'd and bind my selfe to performe the same w'th her female increase for the use of the sd child giveing yearely acc'ot thereof to the Co'rt and rendering the whole to the sd child at her full age Aug: 4. 1657
                                           John x Chittim
Test Hoel Pryse Cl Cur

page 109. Ordered that James Ward enjoy and possesse the cattell of Winifred Rosser and Mary Townsend, and give Caution to render them the like of age sex and number at their full age (and educate them) according to act.

page 110. Att a Co'rt held at mer'chts hope 8br 3 1657
           Present
                   Capt Abr Wood esqr
           mr Thos Drewe   mr Charles Sparrow
           mr Antho Wyatt   Capt Richd Tye
           Capt John Epes   Capt Robt Wynne

page 110. The difference betweene Geo Barefoote plt vs James Willms defendant is referred to the next Court

page 110. Ordered that - and sattisfacon be given by fferd: Aston to Moris Rose for two hds of tobbo imported to Mavados according to the oath and accot exhibited of the sale thereof wth Costs als execucon

page 110. Sold by me fferdinando Aston one hds of tobo and a halfe of the two (the halfe of one being dammified) belonging to Moris Rose -s carries by me to the Mavados, one of the hds I sold for twelve hundred, the other being repack't was but halfe a hd wch yeelded six guilders - (faded out, 'this' or 'wch') amounting to thirty shillings Mavados pay

          ffer Aston

      rec 8br 30: 57

page 110. Ordered that Edd ffitzgeralds Judgmt obtained the last Co'rt agst Walter Salter proceed and take effect as formerly

page 110. Abstract. Prob. granted Joseph Bradley of Nathan Casby decd proved in Co'rt this day.

page 110. Abstract. Attachmt granted Capt Danl Llewellin agt est of Thos Nothway for 1600 lb tobo "for building at Sherley hundred"

page 110. Ordered that John Adams forthwth pay to Edd Mosby 420 tobo (and) Cask found due per acco of tayloers work, wth costs als exec

page 110. Abstract. Mr Tho Drewe permitted to employ and keep an Indian

page 111. Be it knowne to all men by these presents that I Walter Aston gent of Cawsies care in Charles Citty and have also lately and freely bargained and sold and by these presents do absolutely freely and cleerely bargaine and sell unto John Adams of Westov'r in the Com afore-sd Carpenter a certeine parcell of land called the Levell conteyning a hundred acres of land or thereabouts bounded as foll Vidzt northwest upon the land of Coll Edd Hill East upon the maine pattent tending north upon Essex, the sd land being already marked out by Certeine trees to the Content of both parties: x x In witness whereof I have hereunto sett my hand and seale the 2d of October 1657
Wit: Edw: Hill   Walter Aston the seale
   Edward Hill Junior
       Rec 30 Oct 1657

page 111

Mr Pryor
    I would intreate y'u to Do me that favo'r as acknowledge this Deed of mine in Co'rt to mr Adams, and yu will oblige
        8br this 2d 1657   y'r ser'vt
                                        Walter Aston
            rec 8br 30 57

page 111. Abstract. John Burton ordered to pay Jas Barker 346 lb tobo for the est of Mr Jas Warradine decd.

page 111.   On request of Tho Beedles that probat to Jos. Bradley is rospited and refferred till next Co'rt

page 112.   Be it knowne unto all men by these presents that we Walter Aston and Richd Cook gent do acknowledge to ewe and stand in Justly and duly indebted unto John Adams carpenter the full and whole sume and quantity of twenty thousand pounds of good sound well condiconed m'chtble Virginia leafe tobacco and sufficient good Cask conteyning the same to be pd unto the sd John Adams x x witnes our hands and seales this 26th Day of September in the yeare of our Lord 1657.
    The condicon of this obligation is such that if the above bound Walter Aston, when he shall arrive and attaine to full and perfect age of one and twenty yeares shall and will by himselfe be sufficiently qualified - - assure make good assigne convey and confirm - - the sd John Adams x x x parcell or tract of land purchased by the sayd Adams of the sd Aston x x x.
                                        Walter Aston the seale
                                        Richard Cooke the seale
Sealed and deliv'ed in presence of
Thomas Cocke
Richard Cocke grdn (Guardian)   rec 8br 30. 57

page 112. Howell Pryse hath proved right by testimony and assignmt to 1550 acres of land for the importa'con of

Henry Johnson	Henry Thomson	Ja Morecock
Henry Dawes	Edd Gale	Robt Bradley
Tho: Upham	Alexander Jenkins	Robt Russell
ffranc chester	Tho: Love	Wm Gibson
magdalen Lucie	James Taverner	Tho Waters
Mary Dyer	Timothy Remington	James Parry
Eliz: Harwood	Jo: Penn	Ben: Page
Mary Hart	Jo: Nicholas	Geo. Milford
Martha Curtis	Sam. ffearne	Henry Salmon
Alice Bourne	Walter Henman	
Wm Deacon	Edd Chace	

page 113. Whereas Capt John Wall standeth indebted to mr Tho: Drewe as per severall specialties app'th 1834 lb of picked and culled tobbo and cask and 1300 lb of good merchtble tobbo and cask payable att fflower de hundred, and 8 l. 16 s. 7 d sterl money and one case conteyning three gallons of good wine. It is therefore ordered that the sd Wall make present paym't of all the premisses to the sd Mr Drewe or his assgs w'th interest for the sd 1300 lb tobbo and cask and costs als execuo

page 113. Whereas Wm Gillard exported to the Port of Manados for the use and accot of mr fferd: Aston 20 hds of tobbo for the fraught of 20/s per hd as per agreemt confest appeth: (Aston ordered to pay "according to Manados pay").

page 113. Abstract. Curtis Laud ord. to pay Jo. Hewett 100 lb tobo.

page 113. Abstract. Howell Pryse assigns to Richd Bradford 1/2 of 1200 acres "wch lyeth at the head of Queens Creeke betweene the old tree runn and the ffishing runne". Dated 8br. 3. 1657. Rec. 30 Oct. 1657

page 114. Att a Co'rt held at mer'chts hope
9br. 16: 1657

Present

Capt Henry Pery esqr
mr Thomas Drewe   mr War Horsmonden
mr Antho: Wyatt   Capt Robt Wynne
Capt Richd Tye

Ordered that 47 lb tobbo per poll be forthw'th levied and recd by the sherr of every tytheable person in this Com and payd as foll vidzt

mr Antho: Wyatt for burgesse charge per ord'r	1760
Capt Stegge for 1 wolf	200
Major Rose for 3 wolfes	600
Lt Banister for 1	200
George Browne for 2	400
Sam: Ealle for 2	400
Isaac Hermison for 4	800
Jo. West for 1	200
mr Sparrow for Beckwth for 1	200
mr Holford for 1	200
Ca: Woodleife for 1	200
Morg: Jones for 1	200
Robt Russell for 1	200

(continued)

Charles City County Expenses 16 November 1657 (continued)

```
Tho Reynolds per ord'r for Reynes cure 700 and cask        770
Ja. Parham for 1 wolfe                                     200
Ca Wynne for 1                                             200
Walter Brooke for 1                                        200
Lt Banister for 1 more                                     200
Jo. Hodges for 2                                           400
Tho. Davies and Tho. Bigg for 1                            200
Robert Abernathie for 5 dayes worke                        050
Mrs Peibils for Com service                                240
Dan: Scot for Com service and expence                      400
H Pryse for cop. acts lovy &c                              600
          for Com List                                     500
Lt Banister for boate hire &c                              200
ffor charge of erecting the Co'rt house and prison
          to Capt Tye                                     2650
          to mr Wyatt                                     1878
          to Lt Banister                                  1000
          to Tho: Tanner carpenter                        1600
          to purchase nailes to finish the work           1200
          to mr Drewe to make good so much to Capt Pery   0970
resting due to the Govern'r                               1378
                                                         -----
                                                         20388
                         To sallery                       2038
                                                         -----
                                                         22426
```

page 115. It is ordered that 1064 lb tobbo raised 3 yeares since and pd to Coll Edd Hill esqr to purchase weights and seales for the Com use (w'ch was not performed according to his understanding) be pd and satisfied to the Hono'ble Coll Sam'll Mathews esqr the pre'nt Governor for the use and behalfe of this Countie

page 115. Ordered according to act of Assembly that the satisfaccon and reward for killing wolves be hereafter but 100 lb tobbo per wolfe

page 115. A Comicon of admer'con of the estate of Capt Wm Rothwell dec'd is granted (Cum testamento annexo) to Geo: Potter he giveing Caution as is accustomed

page 115. Abstract. Com of admr of est of Wm Symonds decd granted to Isaac Hermison

page 115. Abstract. Mr Geo Potter admr Capt Wm Rothwell decd, ord to pay Mr Antho: Wyatt 400 lb tobo, also to pay Tho Drewe 1567 lb tobo.

page 115. Abstract. Order that 18 lb tobo per poll for all tytheables on N. side of this Co. be held by sher. until the next Assembly to settle charges for Court House and Prison.

page 115. Abstract. Order that Michael Masters be pd from est of Wm Burford decd 263 lb tobo "for sherr fees concerning the sd estate".

page 116. Itt is hereby Certified and declared that upon the peticon of Capt Geo: Jordan preformed the third of August last agst Robt Rowse for a debt due from the estate of Mathew Lewis dec'd, and exaiacon of the businesse Itt is was (sic) the opinion of the Co'rt that mr Nicholas Perry who had undertaken pay'mt of that debt in Surrey Com Co'rt was lyable to the sd debt (and not Robt Rowse) according to Certificat from Surry Cort aforesd

page 116. The ord'r obteined by Capt Daniell Llewellin late sherr agst the Co'rt for the escape of Elias Webb is reversed and made voyd and the sd escape appe'ing by default and neglect of the sd sherriffs officer mr Charles Sparrow plt agst Webb is left to the benefitt of his proceedings agst the sd sherr

page 116. Howell Pryse hath proved right by testimonie produced in Co'rt to 3850 acres of land for the charge of Importacon of

Richd Price	mr War Horsmonden twice	Mary Binley
Richd Page	Mrs Susan Horsmonden	Elizab: Heyes
Ellinor Abbott	mr Richd Horsmonden	Ann Jenkins
Jo: Cakowne	Mary Jenkins Sen	Geo Walter
Alex Nicholson	Nich Jenkins	Willm Panton
Jo. Makinney	Jo. Stith	Teage ffarnance
Wm Bourne	Jo. Turner	Jo: Penrith
Wm Corinan	Jane Summer	Alex Balfore
Dunken Makaney	Robt Brisley	Wm Buckner
Alex Makinny	Wm - (left blank) -	Wm Bowline
Tho: Jellity	Christian "	Edd ffoster
Dan Macknane	Jane Thomas	Mich Rogers
ffrances Lyelle	Anne - (left blank) -	Margaret Tight
Susan Michell	Richd Curd	Mary Browne
Sam'll Alexander	Henry Wenne	Jone Miller
Margaret Rookesby	Clement Mallin	ffrancis Bland
Christian Dennis	John Codiece (?)	Robt Markham
Geo Day	Robt Jones	Tho: Moody
Jo. Moses	John Look	Elizab: Stevens
Robt Royman	Margaret Reymond	Tho. Callings
Dorcas Jones	Mary Rolfe	Willm Salisbury

page 116. Headrights for 3850 acres of land (continued)

Mary Cooper	Edd Jennings	Andrew Reyne
Mary Dobson	Jos Whaley	Wm Cawdry
Mary Young	Ann Wale	Tho: Ardington
Alles Armson	Jo Lawrence	
Richard Armson	Geo Spell	

page 117. Att a Co'rt held at merchts hope 9br. 17. 1657
    present
        mr Antho: Wyatt   Capt Richd Tye
        mr Charles Sparrow   Capt Robt Wynne

page 117. An attachmt is graunted to Roger Lucas agst the estate of Phillip Mintorne for security of 3300 lb tobbo to be pd in goods at severall rates due to the sd Lucas from the sd Mintorne att a day past wth all costs incident

page 117. Att a Cort held at merchts hope 10br. 3. 1657
    Present
        mr Tho: Drewe   Capt Richd Tye
        mr Antho: Wyatt   Capt Robt Wynne

page 117. Abstract. Tho: Huxe ord to pay Howell Pryse 796 lb tobo from the est of Wm Burford

page 117. mr Antho: Wyat hath produced right by testimony produced to 500 acres of land for importacon of

John Hopkins	Jo: Creasie	Mathew Peter and
Jo Tutchmark	Peter an Irishman	Sam: 3 servts
Isable Jones	Ellinor Harris	Agnis Tomlinson

page 117. Abstr. Wm Short ord to pay Tho: Tanner 1400 lb tobo.

page 117. Abstract. Geo. Potter, admr of Capt Wm Rothwell ord to pay Morris Rose 400 lb tobo. Also to pay Joseph Dunne 297 lb tobo. Also that 3256 lb tobo proved to have been pd from the est, on var bills be deducted from the assets

page 117. mr Sparrowe present

page 117. Abstract. Attach granted Tho. Huxe agt est of Peter Salmon for security of 4367 lb tobo.

page 117. Ca: Pery. Ca Stegge present

page 117. Abstract. Jno Burton confesses Judgt to Mr Tho Drewe "for use of mr Robt Llewellin mercht" for 3820 lb tobo.

page 117. Abstract. Mr Geo Potter ord to pay Coll Edd Hill 499 lb tobo from est of Capt Wm Rothwell

page 118. Abstract. Deed. 3 Dec 1657. Wm Cradock of Sandy point sells to John Epes of Sherly Hundred Island, 50 acres in Sherley Hundred Island, "the w'ch bounds may be made appe by a pattent lying in the hands of Geo Browning wch formerly belong'd to my dec'd father and since properly to me and now in my tenure and possession granted by S'r Geo: Yarlie knt and Governor of Virginia". (sic)
Wit: Signed Wm x Cradock
Jno Richards
                              Rec 10br 10, 1657

Note: Land Office. Book 1. p. 451. grant to Robt Cradock 600 a.
                    "   p. 537.   "   "   300 a.   B.F.
      The name shown above as 'Yarlie' is meant for Sir George Yeardley.

page 118. This bill bindeth me James Lewis x x to pay x unto James Warradine x x 697 pounds x x tobbo x x upon the 10th of October, this tobbo and cask for to be paid at his owne dwelling howse in Sherle hundred Island: witnes my hand and seale this 8 Day July Ano Dom 1654
James Warradine Junr   the mark of x James Lewis the seale
Henry x Barker witnes
                              rec Jan'ry 13, 57   (1657/8)

page 118. Ordered that Lawrence Biggins or Tho: Warren pay to mr Cha Sparrow attor of Marmaduke Beckw'th 1000 lb of good tobbo and cask confessed in Co'rt wth costs als exec agst them or either of them

page 119. Abstract. Deed. 3 Dec.1656. "Rice Hoe of mer'chts hope in the Com of Charles Citty in Virga gent the sonne and lawfull heyre of Rice Hoe late of the place aforesd gent dec'd" sells to Willm Hunt of Buckland, planter, "that the sd Rice Hoe by and with the advice and consent of his mother and guardian Mrs Sara Hee widd", 300 acres in James City Co., bounded Westerly on a Creek formerly called David Jones his Creeke, southerly on the main river, easterly on other land before granted to the sd Rice Hoe decd and since possessed by James Warradine and northerly into the woods extending one whole mile for length from

Deed. Hoe to Hunt (continued)

the main river. This 300 acres granted sd Rice Hoe dec'd by patent
dated 4 June 1639.
Wit   Signed   Sara SH Hoe
Charles Sparrow   Rice Hooe
Hoel Pryse
                          Rec. Janry 10. 1657/8

page 121. Ordered that 764 lb tobo be pd Coll Edd Hill for advance by
him to the Governor.

page 121. Ordered that Mary Light serv't to mrs ffrances Letherland
haveing illegally absented her selfe at times to the number of 350
dayes shall make good the sd time by Doubling the sd service neglected
according to act

page 121. Abstract. Geo. Potter admr Capt Rothwell decd ord to pay Tho
Nothway mercht 600 lb tobo.

page 121. Abstract. Tho: Rands ord to pay Wm Hunt 350 lb tobo from est
of Olliver Hunt dec'd

page 121. Abstract. Tho Huxe ord to pay Mrs Elizab: Peibils 1600 lb.tobo.

page 121. Abstract. Execution for Thos. Tanner agst Wm Short suspended
till next Court.

page 121. Abstract. Execution ord forthwth agt certain est of Phillip
Mintorne attacked at suit of Roger Lucas for 3300 lb tobo.

page 121. Whereas Jone Griffith serv't to Capt Mathew Edloe hath
pet'coned for her freedome alleadging that she had served according
to act, And the Co'rt conceiving in their Judgmt that she was not 16
yeares of age at her arrivall, doth therefore order that she continue
and serve according to act for servts comeing in wthout Indentures

page 122. Abstract. Isaac Hermison admr of Wm Symons' est ord to pay
Richd Baker 400 lb tobo.

page 122. Abstract. Whereas the last Court suspended probate on the will
of Nathan Casby granted to Joseph Bradley at the request of Thomas
Beadles, and Beadles not appearing, the probate is ordered to stand.

page 122.
                        8 br the 3d 1657
I Thomas Clarke aged 33 yeares or thereabouts do declare upon oath that
Wm Radway sending for me from my house, when I came to him I demanded
of him his businesse, he told me that he found him selfe very sick, and
desired me that in case he dyed that I should take notice that he desired to make his will, and did it by word of mouth and further desired
to make it in writing, the wch I did so well as I could, his mother
then replying that if he would give away all that ever he had she was
willing, for she had enough to mainteine her selfe of her owne, and
further saith not
Jur in Cur 8br 3. 57   Thomas Clarke
Test Hoel Pryse Cl

page 122.
                        8 br the 3d 1657
Antho Allen aged 26 yeares or thereabouts doth testifie that Wm Radaway
made his will in writing about 5 dayes before he dyed, and further
saith not
Jur in Cur 8br. 3. 1657   Antho A Allen
Test Hoel Pryse Cl   his mark

page 122. Abstract. Deed. 10th Jany 1654/5. Tho: Morgan sells Edward
Richards (Edd Richds') 1/2 of his land named 'the Ponds'. Acerage and
location not shown in entry.
Wit: Signed   Tho: x Morgan
John Seaman
George x Darnon   Rec. 15 Feby 1657/8

page 123.   Att a Co'rt holden at mer'chts Hope
                    ffebr. 3. 1657
     Present
                 Coll Abra: Wood esqr
       mr Tho: Drewe   Capt Robt. Wynne
       mr Antho: Wyatt

page 123. Abstract. Richd Parker ord to pay Geo Potter 2001 lb tobo.

page 123. Ordered that mrs Elizabeth Peibils forthwth pay to Thomas
Huxe three barrells of good Indian corne at her now dwelling for the
service of his wife, wth costs als exec

page 123.
Present Ca: Perry   Ca: Stegge   )
mr Sparrow. Ca Tye   )   (entered in the margin)
mr Horsmonden   )

page 123. Phillip Ellyot is fined 300 lb tobo for the contempt of his wife in not appearing according to a sumons ag'st her for a witnes on the behalfe of Tho: Hamond And the sd Ellyot is ordered to pay the costs occasioned by the sd Default of appearance

page 123. Itt is ordered that mr Charles Sparrow adm'r of Major John Westhorpe dec'd pay to Ralph Poole 3 barrells of corne out of the sd Doced'ts estate for the service of his wife

page 123. M'd. A Lease of a parcell of land at the head of Samuell Jordans land was let by mr Antho: Wyatt to Howell Edmonds the 25th Day of December Ao Dom 1652 for 19 yeares

page 123. Abstract. Mr Antho: Wyatt ord to have Maj. Wm Harris survey his land at Chapline adj the land of Col. Edd Hill in order to settle differences

page 123. Abstract. Mary West surrenders to Edd Ardington 150 acres at Baylyes Creeke and agrees to confirm this legally. Dated 3 Feb. 1657/8
                                 Signed   Mary M West
                                                      her mark

page 123. Abstract. Mrs Hannah Aston is dismissed from the suit of Mrs Elizab: Peibils wth costs.

page 124. Abstract. Original entries cover five pages in the book. Deed. Dated 17 Sept. 1657. "Elizabeth Hacker late the wife of John Hacker late of Lyme howse in the parish of Stepney als Stebenheath in the Com of Midd planter dec'd for and in the behalf of my selfe and John Hacker my sonne and w'th his - assent and Consent being Co-exer of the last will and testam't of his late father John Hacker w'th me the sd Elizab: Hacker and being Guardian unto my sd sonne John Hacker".
    Elizabeth Hacker and her son John Hacker sell to "Daniell Bandowin of London mercht and George Marshall of London combemaker", for L 25., 150 acres in Virginia, now in occupation of Anthony Allen planter, "given and granted by lrs pattent bearing date 7br the 17th 1645 unto my sd late husband John Hacker decd". John Hacker to confirm sale when 21 yrs of age.

Signed sealed & del'vd in   Signed "E H
the presence of us   the seale affix't
Thomas Grynes. Gabriell Briggs   on a Labell"
the mark CC Cornel' Clements
Henry Briggs the mark of N Nich: Gatley   "John Hacker
& Ellis Pennant scr   the seale affixt
                                                  on a Labell"

Note: The name Grynes may possibly be Gryves or Grymes. B.F.

page 127. A schedule of goods and cattle of and belonging to Elizab Hacker late the wife of John Hacker late of London planter dec'd and by this present deed of bargaine and sale bargained and sold unto Daniell Bandovin of London mer'cht and George (Marshall) Combemaker in man'r and forme foll' according to a schedule sent out of Virginia from mr Cha. Sparrow as foll vidzt

In cattle
    Imprs 7 Cowes. It. 3 steeres. It 1 Bull
    It 3 heyfers of 2 yeares old
    It. 2 steeres of 2 yeares old
    It. 2 steeres of a yeare old a piece
    It 1 heyfer of a yeare old. Lastly 4 Calves

In Hogs
    Impr. 3 breeding sowes
    It 1 barrow of 3 yeares old usely amongst mr Sparrows hogs and
    It 1 small barrow shote of 2 yeares old

In household goods
    Impr. 1 Iron pott
    It 1 small saw. 4 iron wedges
    It 1 brasse kettle conteyning 14 gall
    It 1 drawing knife
    It 1 old bedstead w'th one whole bed cord
    It 1 Coopers addz
    Lastly 1 featherbed bolster pillow and rugg, the tieking all to pieces, and flocks mixt w'th the feathers, and a payre of course holland sheetes

        recorded ffebr. 15. 1657

page 127. Coll Edd Hill hath testified upon oath in Cort that the Judgemt of 755 lb tobbo confest by Lt Coll Walter Aston to Capt Peibils was for the bill now produced in Cort.
Test   Hoel Pryse

page 128.

James Reyner
    My kind love to you remembered and to yo'r wife much wishing that you would become a reformed man and serve God in the first place both of you and then questionlesse things will fall out cleerely upon all accot according to y'r expectacon, and Gods blessing wilbe upon yu. I haveing in hopes of yo'r doing well remitted 1000 lb of tobbo of the 2000 yu should have pd me and do desire yu to pay mr Sparrow the 1000 weight to be sent me home by this shipping either in Read or ffox and

Dame Elizabeth Hacker to James Rayner (continued)

w'th all I request yu to answor this my lre expressely and I have and do hereby give yu all that bedding and household stuffe that I have not express in a schedule anexed to a bargaine and sale I have now sold my land howses and that household stuffe that is exprest in the sd schedule and have requested mr Sparrow to assist yu therein, the parties I have sold them to is Mr Bandovin and Mr Marshall. yo'r wives father is dead but her brothers and sisters are well and this desireing yu to send me word being the request of Mary Lofinghams how Mary Lofingham doth and whether she be liveing, wth my prayers to God for y'r In'st

                                     Yo'r Lo: Dame
7 br 11th 1657   Elizabeth Hacker

Subscribed To her very Lo: frd James Rayner liveing upon uppr Chep Oakes Creek in the parish of Martin Brandon in the uplands of Virga these present
                        Record. ffebr. 15. 1657

Note: Bandovin. Is this the French for Baldwin ? At the end of the letter 'In'st' doubtless is interest.   B.F.

page 128. Abstract. Deed. 27 Dec 1655. Thomas Clarke sells Kidby ffrore 50 acres, late in the possession of John Bromwell, and also certain hogs carrying Bromwell's mark.
Wit: Signed   Thomas Clarke
John x Tompson
Wm x Radaway   Rec. 15 Feb. 1657/8

page 129. Abstract. Deed. 22 Oct. 1655. John Banister sells Richard Jones minister, 100 acres "close by the lower ponds" adj land of sd Jones and James Wards new plantation, "the bredth whereof is bounded nertherly upon the mer'chts land and the length Southerly into the woods toward the old Towne a complete mile as by his pattent app'es".
Wit:
Rice Hoe   Signed   John x Banister
Patrick Jackson

page 129. Abstract. Richard Jones assigns above 100 acres to Morgan Jones. 20th 9br 1656.
Wit: Signed   Richard Jones
Patrick Jackson
George Cubbidge   rec. 5 Feb. 1657/8

page 129. Abstract. Geo. Brewer admr of Jno. Devall ord to pay Capt. Tho: Stegge 800 lb tobo.

page 129. Abstract. Hugh Evans confesses Judgt to Mr. Tho. Drewe 700 lb tobo.

page 129. Abstract. Ord. that 1 bbl corn be pd to Jno. Wilson from est of Capt Wm Rothwell decd.

page 129. Mr John Dibdall minister and his family not exceeding six persons is exempted from all publicke dues according to order of Assembly

page 129. Abstract. Jos Bradley exor of Nathan Casby decd ord to pay Mr John Dibdall minister the tythes of tobo and corn due for this past year.

page 129. Abstract. Jo. Drayton ord to pay Howell Pryse for Wm Burford's est, 15 lb tobo foe fees.

page 130. Abstract. Quietus est granted Geo Potter for est. of Capt Wm Rothwell decd, he having pd beyond the assets.

page 130. Abstract. Walter Salter ord to pay 1000 lb tobo for nonperformance of terms of lease granted by Mr Wm Lawrence "to Edward ffitzgerald who married the relict of the sd Lawrence".

page 130. Absent Coll Wood

page 130. Abstract. Cornelius Clemence ord to pay Daniell Murrayne "resting due for wages 1000 lb tobbo and two barrels of corne".

page 130. Abstract. Daniell Scott confesses judgt to Robt Rowse for 305 lb tobo.

page 130. Abstract. Richd. Parker confesses judgt to Mrs Frances Letherland for 408 lb tobo.

page 130. Abstract. Robt. Rowse confesses judgt. to Tho Turvile for 620 lb tobo pd by Turvile to Jo: Hodges for Rowse.

page 130. Oswan Hall aged 40 yeares or thereabouts exa'ed and sworn saith That he heard Capt Wm Rothwell in his life time say that John Lucas did by his last will and testamt give and bequeath unto Milliscent Rothwell the Daughter of the sd Capt Rothwell two cowes, and that one

The deposition of Oswan Hall (continued)

cow more called Mully, he sayd, belonged to his sd daughter and further saith not
Jur in Cur ffebr. 3. 1657   Oswan ◊ Hall
Test Hoel Pryse

page 130. Daniell Holicresse aged 22 yeares or thereabouts exaed and sworne saith That two cowes given by John Lucas to Milliscent Rothwell were acknowledged by her father to belong to the sd Milliscent, as also one heyfer and one female calfe, and two heyfers and a bull calfe being the increase of the Cowe Mully, and further saith not
Jur in Cur febr. 3. 1657
Test Hoel Pryse Cl   Daniell Holicresse

page 130. Abstract. Richd Parker confesses Judgt to Robt Rowse for 1178 lb tobo.

page 131. Ordered that the cattell belonging to Milliscent Rothwell according to testimony of Oswan Hall and Daniell Holicresse be del'red unto John Huntley who married the sd Milliscent or such of them as are now extent

page 131. Itt is ordered that Jane Wms widd do at the next Com Co'rt produce and present to the Co'rt the last will and testam't of Wm Radway.

page 131. Thomas Sharpe and Samuell Phillips ingage themselves in Co'rt to deliver to Elizabeth the orphane of John Gibson decd att expiracon of her time one cowe w'th calfe in consideracon of a steere belonging to the sd Gibsons estate w'ch the Co'rt ordereth them to possesse and enjoy

page 131. Abstract. Wm Greene confesses Judgt to Mr Tho. Drewe for 1511 lb tobo.

page 131. Abstract. Fine imposed on Phillip Ellyott for his wife's default is remitted.

page 131. Abstract. Thos Huxe to have possession of half part of a sloop belonging to Peter Salmon at his suit, he giving security.

page 131. Abstract. John Burton ord to pay Howell Pryse 386 lb tobo found due

page 131. Abstract. Est. of John Lucas ord to pay Tho: Bridges 400 lb tobo.

page 131. The Co'rt hath bound Mary the orphane of Jo: Minter dec'd unto Ralph Poole to serve him untill she shalbe fifteen yeares of age, and ordered that the sd Poole do give good caution to educate and mainteine her dureing that time, and deliver her estate w'th cloathing and other necessaries according to law at expiracon of the sd time

page 132. Capt Llewellin his agreemt w'th mr Tho: Nothway
One roome four lengths of boards to be joyned to a howse weh was then standing, and a store of four lengths of boards at distance from the howse, weh building was to be finished w'thin one yeare. Mr Nothway then paying of him so much tobacco as it should cost the sd Capt Llewellin, the sayd mr Nothway enjoying the howses and land then belonging to them the tearme of seaven yeares paying for the last six yeares five or six hundred pounds of tobbo yearely
Jur in Cur ffeby 3. 1657
Test Ho: Pryse Cl   John Sloeman

Referred to mr Antho: Wyat and Capt John Epes to examine and view the building and perpar'acon, and give report to the next Cort thereof

page 132. Howell Pryse hath proved right by testimony and assignemt granted unto him for 3950 acres of land for the importacon of

John Clay	Ann Towne	Richd Thorne
Jo. Norman	Margaret Jeanes	James Hall
Jo Parker	Mary Batts	Theoph: Parker
Wm Luck	Mary Dawson	Wm Horner
Robt Gaskin	Isabell Rayner	Judeth Mayle
Ann Colchester	Geo fforby	Robt Wallis
Willm ffloriday	Robt Marsh	Walter Browne
David Robts	Robt ffavell (ffanell ?)	Tho: Brooke
Gregory Nash	Hugh Evers	John Hewett
James Rownds	James Thornton	John Mercer
ffreder Hanley	Peter Wrench	Cha: Burdett
Tho: Gunning	Patrick Garret	James Harrison
Ralph Watts	Denis MacDonell	Wm Mosse
Tho: Hancock	Wm Cartwright	Sam Baynard
Jo. Harwell	Wm Hause	Alexander Hayes
Richd Gilbert	Jo. Berry	James Swanley
David Crosse	Geo Rand	Jo Thompson
Richd Wright	Antho Watlington	Ben: Claxton
James Cocker	Robt ffarr	Edd Wenne
John ffoy	Andrew Guyer	Tho Baycock
John Perrott	John Savill	Geo Hertford
Wm fflawne	Tho. Atkins	ffranc: Greene
Wm Richardson	James Cale	Alice Greene
Nich: Quaile	Robt Meares	Rebecca Greene
Robt Moore	Alton Ramsey	Wm Platt
Jane Hawley	Peter Jackson	Edd Aylesworth
	Sam Andrews	

page 133. Att a Cort held at mer'chts hope ffebr 9. 1657
Present
mr Thomas Drewe
mr Antho: Wyatt   Capt Tichd Tye
mr Charles Sparrow   Capt Robt Wynne

page 133. Itt is ordered that Moore Morayne ser'vt to mr James Barker after expiracon of her time of service give good caution to appear at the next Com Co'rt to answer what shall be objected ag'st her

page 133. Ordered that Christopher Woodward be allowed and paid his share of the crop made at Capt Llewellins planta'con according to his Coven't

page 133. Ordered that the land in controversie between George Barefoot plt and Jane Williams defte be recorded and confirmed to the children, according to Wm Radwayes will, after the Decease of the sd Jane Wms and that she proceed to adm'or'con according to her Comis'on

page 133. mr Charles Latham being 62 yeares of age is exempted from all publick services and taxes for the future

page 133. Abstract. The diff. betw. Thos. Tanner and Nicho: Perry to be settled by Mr. Tho. Drewe.

page 133. Daniell Scott indebted to Howell Pryse by assignment of Mich: Master 770 lb tobo.

page 133. Ordered that Robt Rowse pay to mr Thomas Drewe 1500 lb tobbo and cask for the use of S'r John Pawlet knt for a yeares rent of land and howse at Westov'r, due that he and Tho: Turvile repair the orchard fence according to Lease, wth costs, als exec.

page 133. The Co'rt hath granted and allowed to mr's Margery Masters widd out of her late husbands estate, freely w'thout accompting for the same her bedding and furniture two Iron potts w'th pott hookes and hangers, three barrells of corne and three pewter dishes

page 133 Capt Edloe non suite Richd Bradford wth costs accustomed
Id non suite Howell Pryse wth costs accustomed
A non suite is granted to Sam: Smith against Walter Salter wth costs, als exec.

page 134. Abstract. Lt John Banister and James Ward to settle dif. betw Wm Short and Tho: Tanner concerning tobacco.

page 134. The Co'rt hath permitted Tho: Rande on his request and peticon to relinquish the will and estate of Olliver Hunt dec'd.

page 134. Mr Antho: Wyatt Mr Charles Sparrow and Capt Robt Wynne are humbly presented and no'iated to the Hono'blo Governor and Counc'll according to act, whereof one may be elected sherr for the ensuing yeare

page 134. Abstract. Quietus est granted Tho. Tanner of the est. of Jno. Letherland, he having overpaid.

page 135.   Att a Co'rt held at mer'chts hope Apr 3. 1658
      Present
              mr Tho. Drewe
    mr Antho Wyatt   mr Charles Sparrow
    Capt John Epes   Capt Richd Tye

page 135. Abstract. Ord. that Tho. Coale and Tho. Hamond settle their dif., each paying own charges.

page 135. Abstract. Dif. betw Tho. Stevenson and Walter Salter to next Court.

page 135. Abstract. Curtis Laud sworn in Court (age not shown) says Tho Stevenson has sold certain land and wants his note of Walter Salter Salter having lost the note is nevertheless ordered to produce it in Court.

page 135. Abstract. Order that Mr. Antho: Wyatt be pd 450 lb tobbo and the tythe corn by the securities for Jordans Parish.

page 135. Abstract. Order that Robt Rowse pay Mrs Elizab Peibils 404 lb tobo due from Jo. Greenhough, being his security. Attachmt granted Rowse agt Greenhough.

page 135. Abstract. Wm Lambson conf. judgt. to Mr Tho. Drewe for 400 lb. tobbo.

page 135.   Antho: Allen sworne saith
That he went along w'th Martin Quelch to receive a hhd of tobbo from Benjam Cartwright and that the sd Quelch demanded the Country Levies of the sd Cartwright and the sd Cartwright sayd he would not pay him the tobbo in the cask but the sherr should follow him and receive it where he had it oweing him and behanged if he would, and further saith not

page 135. Abstract. Court adj. to 20th this month. All causes referred to that date.

page 136. Whereas Mr Henry Isham and Lt Jo Howell wholly reffered all differences between them to the award of mr Tho Drewe and mr Antho Wyat who having determined therein that the sd Howell shall enjoy the 150 acres of land and howseing in the controversie according to the Lease x x and pay rent accordingly x x x.

page 136. Robt Coale sworne saith That Ann Mascall comeing to goodman Staddors did say to his sister Jone Thomas that she should have a care what she did do w'th mr Owen for he was a married man and had a wife in Engl'd, and further saith not

page 136. Peter Harris sworne say'th that Ann Mascall comeing to goodman Staddors did say to his sister Jone Thomas - etc, as above.

page 136.   Abstract.   Mr Antho: Wyatt certifies 100 lb tobbo due Edd Mosby from levy for a wolves head.

. . . .

The next entry, on page 137, shows record of a Court held at Merchants Hope on the 20th of April 1658.

INDEX

Abbott, Ellinor 91
Abernethy, Robt. 40. 77. 90
          Sara 77
Adams, John 57. 87. 88
Addenbrooke, Edd 83
Alexander, Saml. 91
Allcock, Richd 24
Allen, Anth: 45. 31. 66. 83,
          84. 95. 96. 104.
      Danl. 64
      Edd. 29
      Symon 78
Allester, Mark 78
Allin, Jno. 10
Allison, Edmond 64
         Jno. 23
Ameson (?) Edd 54
Anderson, Tho. 64
Andrews, Roger 39
         Sam. 101
         Tho. 64
Apomattooks 25
Arden, Jas. 33
Ardington, Edw. 2. 96
           Mrs. Edw. 2
           Tho. 92
Armson, Alles 92
        Richd. 92
Armstrong, Andrew 34. 38. 40
           Danl. 33
           Geo. 38. 40
           Jno. 34
Arner, Tho. 61.
Arney, Edd. 84
Arnold, Arthur 29
        Eliz. 33
Arrow, Jno. 15
Ash, Richd. 12
Ashby, Phil. 78
Ashley, Danl. 64
Ashpode, Law. 84
Aste, Jno. 44. 57. 68. 73
Aston, Ferdinando 26. 85. 87. 89
       Mrs. Hanna 45. 49. 50. 59
              66. 76. 82. 96
       Col. Walter 3. 13. 14. 16
              17. 24. 28. 33
              36. 45. 49. 57
              59. 87. 88. 97
Atkins, Geo. 19. 66. 78. 84
        Jo 78

Atkins, Richd 24
        Tho. 101
Aylesworth, Edd 101
Ayres, Mary 29

Bailey, Arthur 74. 75
Baker, Christopher 64
       Dorothie 49
       Josua 64
       Richd 13. 94
       Syl 39
Baldwin, Danl. 97
Balesman, Wm. 78
Balford, Alex. 91 (?)
Balfore, Alex. 91
Ball, Jno. 64
Ball-, Leon 74
Ballance, Wm. 38
Bandovin, Danl. 96. 97. 98
Bannister, Jno. 6. 17. 33. 50. 57
           58. 63. 89. 90. 98
           103.
           Robt. 64
Banks, Hen. 37
Barber, Jo 38
Barefoote, Geo. 86. 102
Barker, Henry 8. 93
        James 50. 63. 86. 88.
               108
        Tho. 29
        Wm. 31
Barnes, Ralph 46
        Robt. 24
Barnett, Richd. 64
Bartlet, Sir Wm. 59
Barwick, Antho. 33
Bates, Roger 64
Batesman, Wm. 78 (?)
Batte, Capt. 13
       Henry 76
       Mathew 53
       Susanna 13. 60
       Tho. 76
       William 60. 76
Battin, Jno. 39
Batts, Mary 101
Batty, William 33
Baugh, Wm. 4
Baycock, Geo. 64
         Tho. 101

Bayle, Mathew 38
Bayley, Capt. Arthur 61, 68,
      69, 70, 71, 74, 75,
      85
    James 54
    John 64
    Luke 78
    Philip 29
    Richd 19
    Wm, 6, 9, 19, 84
Bayleyes Creek 96
Baylies Creeke 20 25
Baynard, Sam 101
Beadles, Tho. 35, 72
Beale, Tho. 29, 33, 78
Beare, Jas. 78
    Richd. 64
Beckwith, - 89
Beckwith, Louis 84
    Marmaduke 93
Beedles, Tho 88, 94
Bell, Jane 84
    Margt. 39
    Roger 33
Bennet, Jone 29
Bennett, Gov. Richd. 5, 14,
      25.
Benson, Ellis 29
Bentley, Jane 24
Berkeley, Sir Wm. 14, 69
Berry, Andrew 29
    Jo 101
Best, Tho. 64
Bigg, Tho. 90
Bigges, Robt. 84
Biggins, Lawrence 93
Bingley, Jas. 54
Binley, Mary 91
Bird, Ja. 78
    John of London 85
    Walter 24
    William 37, 83
Bishopp, Edmond 83
    Mrs. Eliz. 50
    Capt. John 1, 6, 12,
      16, 21, 34, 39, 42,
      48, 51, 54.
Blackman, Henry 64
Bland, Francis 91
    Richd. 55
    Theod: 38, 39, 47, 48,
      49, 55.
Blanes, Jane 24
Blankes, Tho. 50, 57

Bolling see Bowline
Bond, Geo. 68
Borne, Robt. 81
Bourne, Alice 88
    Edd 78
    Wm. 91
Bouy, Robt 29
Bowles, Christopher 1.
Bowline, Wm. 91
Bowyer, Eliz. 84
Boyee, Cheney 13
    Tho. 13
Bradford, Richd. 35, 46, 51, 89,
      102.
Bradley, Jos. 87, 88, 94, 99
    Robt. 88
Braine, Thos. 46
Brereton, Tho. 80
Breward, Geo. 5
Brewer, Frances 64
    George 98
Bridges, Tho. 101
Brier, Robt. 10
Briggs, Gabriel 96
    Henry 4, 96
Brisley, Robt. 91
Bristow, Jas.
Bromwell, Jno. 22, 98
Brooke, Robt 39
    Tho. 101
    Walter 90
Brookes, Marmaduke 14, 24, 62
    Mary, 64
    Walter 31, 57, 84
Broome, Tho. 35
Browne, Amie 33
    Geo. 21, 28, 55, 89
    Jno. 1
    Mary 91
      29 Peter
    Susan 46
    Symon 64
    Walter 101
Brownes, Geo 38
Browning, Geo. 93
Buckner, Wm 91
Bull, Fran: 46
    John 9
Burdett, Cha. 101
    Jeremya 84
    Kath: 29
Burford, Wm. 17, 32, 33, 34, 40,
      44, 48, 54, 56, 64, 77,
      79, 91, 92, 99.

C 10

Burford, Wm. Illness of 52
Burgiss, Robt. 25
Burley, Edd 24
Burton, Geo. 39
       John 1. 9. 88. 93. 100.
       Sam. 78
Burwell, Anthony 84
Bury, Alice 64
     Susan 24
Butler, Jas. 64
Byham, Gervase 11

Cakowne, Jo 91
Cale, Jas. 101
Calle, Sam 17
Callings, Tho. 91
Carey, Jno. 46
Carter, Richd. 19
Cartie, Hugh 24
Cartrewight, Paul 84
Cartwright, Benj. 104
       Wm. 101
Casby, Nathan 57. 87. 94. 99
Cawdry, Wm 92
Cawsies Care 87
Chace, Edd 88
Chandler, Benj. 84
Chandler see Chaundler
Chaplins Choice 25
Chapman, Sam 64
Chappell, Thos. 26
Chapman, Mathew 82
Charington, Edd 29
       Susan 33
Chatterton, Wm 46
Chaundler, Wm. 64
Clarke, Michaell 64
Clayton, Robt. 64
      Roger 78
Clemence, Theoph: 53
Chepakes brook 3
Chester, Franc. 88
     Phill. 29
Chiles, Col. Walter 14. 18
Chirurgeon's apprentice 37
Chittim, Jno. 86
Citty Creeke 16
Claiborne, Col. Wm. 14
Clanton, Marmaduke 39
Clark, Tho. 22. 95. 98
Claxton, Ben 101
Clay, Jno. 19. 101
    Wm. 19. 42

Clemence, Corn: 19. 37. 52. 54. 55. 56. 58. 63. 96. 99.
Clayes Clossett 19
Cleark, Tho. 22
Clover, Edmund 67
Coale, Robt. 104
    Tho. 9. 103
Coaleman, Robt. 14
    Tho. 29
Cocke, Richd. 88
   Thos. 88
Cocker, Jas. 101
Codiece, Jno. 91
Colchester, Ann 101
Cogan, Jno. 19
Colbrooke, Richd. 32
Coleman, Nich: 39
    Wm. 38
Colsey, Richd. 16
Comings, Jno. 29
Cooper, Edd 33
   Mary 92
   Philip 59
   Wm. 29. 64
Corbett, Richd. 64
Cord, Richd. 78
Corey, Wm. 33
Corinan, Wm 91
Cotes, Jo 78
Covell, Geo. 53
   Jacob 19
   Jno. 39
Coventon, Arthur 84
Covey, Francis 33
Cowley, Wm. 15
Coxe, Jas. 24
   Richd. 46
Cradock, Hester 42
   Jono 42
   Robt. 42. 93
   Wm. 6. 8. 93
Crane, Peter 64
Crauford, Tho. 64
Crawley, Jno. 46
Creasie, Jo. 92
Crewe, Mary 64
Crewes, Jas. 19. 35. 36. 37. 41. 44. 45. 46. 47. 49. 53. 54. 57. 60. 65. 68.
Cromer, Wm. 64
Crosby, Nath. 53
Croshaw, Judith 33
Crosse, Crook 19

Crosse, Barth: 84
    David 101
    Wm. 64
Cubbidge, Geo. 98
Cubisho, Sara 77
Culmer, Tho. 41
Curd, Richd. 91
Curtis, Martha 88
Dallison, Tho. 39
Darnell, Jno. 33
    Capt. Tho. 21. 35
Darnon, Geo. 95
David Jones Creek 93
Davids, Hugh 33
Davies, Tho. 78. 90
Davison, Chas. 53
    Patrick 39
Dawes, Henry 88
    Jas. 39
Dawson, Jane 53
    Mary 101
Day, Geo. 91
Deacon, Wm. 88
Delabore, Richd. 48
Dennis, Christian 91
    MacDonell 101
Denny, Jane 39
Derwas, Evan 20
Deyes, Walt. 80
Dibdall, Rev. John 6. 9. 18.
    19. 22. 24. 31. 42
    49. 72. 76. 79. 99
    Richd. 32. 36. 54. 61
    72. 79.
Diggs, Gov. Edw. 26
Ditty, Wm. 5. 20. 25. 54
Dixon, Francis 64
    Hannah 24
    Tho. 40
Dobson, Mary 92
Dod, Tho. 64
Dolling, Wm 55. 84
Dorman, Jno. 64
Douglas, Tho. 34
Downes, Mrs. Ann 21
    Arthur 54
    Ford (or Ferd) 78
Drayton, Jno. 8. 14. 24. 36. 62.
    99.
Drinker, Tho. 6. 8. 15
Drewe, Thos. 1. 6. 7. 8. 9. 11
    12. 16. 17. 18. 19. 21
    24. 29. 32. 33. 35. 38
    41. 42. 47. 48. 50. 53
    57. 61. 64. 65. 66. 78
    79. 80. 81. 82. 85. 86

Drewe, Tho. 87. 89. 90. 91. 92
    93. 95. 99. 100.
    102. 103. 104
Dunne, Dr. 62
    Joseph 32. 36. 92
Dunning, Tho. 78
Dunninger, Edw. 68
Dutton, Alex: 46
Dyer, Mary 88

Eallo, Saml. 60. 72. 89
Eals see Eells
Eallo, Sam. 11
Edea, Tho. 11
Edloe, Capt. 6
    Mathew 36. 59. 60. 94.
    102
Edmonds, Howell 37. 96
    Wm. 78
Edwards, Mr. 22
    Peter 24
Eells, Jno. 10
Elam, Robt. 60
Eley, Jas. 64
Ellis, - 58
Ellyot, Jo 29
    Philip 22. 46. 79. 81
    96. 100
Epes, Capt. Fran: 57
    Mrs. Mary 4
    John 1. 4. 12. 16. 24. 26
    33. 35. 47. 53. 57.
    81. 85. 86. 93. 101
    103
    Tho. 57
Erreene, Joseph 38
Essex, 87
Evans, Hugh 99
    Jno. 57
    Pond 58
    Reginald 39
Eveling, Mr. 55
Evers, Hugh 101

Fairepoint, Jos. 53
Fanel, Robt. 101
Farnace, Teage 91
Farnham, Richd. 29
Farr, Robt. 101
Farrar, Capt Wm. 16. 28. 31
Farrell, Alic 29
Farrington, Robt. 64
    Tho. 33
Favell, Robt. 101

Fearne, Sam 88
Fecknham, Tho. 78
Fenner, Ferd: 64
Ferne, Robt. 78
Fisher, John 72
  Wm. 24. 36. 37. 41. 44.
   50. 54. 61. 62. 72.
   76.
Fishing Run 89
Fitzgarald, Edd 51. 83. 85. 87.
  99.
Fitzgarrett, Edw. 40. 42. 45. 63
Flawne, Wm. 101
Fletcher, Cuthbert 78
  Marmaduke 64
  Michael 34. 48. 60. 66
Floriday, Wm. 101
Flower, Jno. 14. 20
Fockwell, Mary (the name is prob.
  Hockwell, but seems so like
  this in the original that it
  must be indexed thus) 10.
Fones, Tho. 4. 12
  Mrs. Tho. 4
Foord, Francis 64
Forby, Geo. 101
Forshaw, Danl. 55
  Eliz. 45
  Henry 46
  Hugh 22. 45. 46. 55. 77
Foster, Edd 91
Four Mile Creek 16
Fowler, Ellinor 29
  John 11
Foy, Ales 39
Fox, Capt Robt. 61. 85
Foy, Jno. 101
Frame, Rebecca 38
Freaton, Wm. 29
Freme, Ann 32
  Arther 32
  James 32
  John 7. 12. 16. 18. 19.
   28. 31. 40.
  Jonne 32
  Mrs. Mary 18. 19. 21. 25.
   26. 28. 31. 32.
  Sara 32
  Wm. 32
Frere, Kidby 22. 98
Fry, Jas. 11
  Wm. 6. 7. 8
Fryer, Jno. 11
  Martha 84

Fuller, Mrs. 10

Gabell, Wm. 81
Gaby, Jno. 26. 38. 58. 85
Gale, Edd 88
Galer, Tho. 46
Gallis, Grace 84
  Jno. 66. 78. 83
  Jno. Jr. 84
Garret, Patrick 101
Gasgazones (personel memo) 72
  (B.F.)
Gaskin, Robt. 101
  (Gasgoine - see Pepys re.
  origin of this name in the
  British court circle)
Gates, Marg: 53
Gatlet, Nich: 96
Gayler, Wm. 78
George, Jno. 20. 25
Gibbs, Mr. 57
  John 1. 7. 16. 18
Gibson, Eliz. 100
  John 45. 51. 72. 77.
   100.
  Joshua 78
  Wm. 88
Gilbert, Richd. 101
Gilham, Jno. 4. 57
Gill, Wm. 33
Gillard, Wm. 89
Gilnutt, Tho. 60
Goldin, Rebecca 84
Goodale, David 79
Goodheart, Jas 46
Gorton, Andrew 64
Gray, Jasper 33
Greene, Alice 101
  Fran: 101
  Herbert 29
  John 66
  Peter 39
  Prudence 33
  Rebecca 101
  Tho. 15. 16
  Wm. 31. 40. 100
Greenhough, Jo 103
Greenhow see Grinehow
Gregory, Cha. 10. 18
  Francis 29
  Jane 32. 56
  Tho. 15. 32. 41. 44.
   54. 56.

Grey, Francis 18, 20, 21, 24
              29, 62, 63
      Mary 64
      Richd. 29
      Roger 78
Griffith, Jane 29
        Jone 94
Grimes, Jno. 1
Grinshow, Jno. 59
Grymes, Thos. 96
Grynos, Thos. 96
Gummic, Richd. 10
Gunning, Tho. 101
Gayer, Andrew 101
Gyles, Robt. 54
      Tho. 78

Hacker, Eliz. 40, 96, 97, 98
      Jno, 96, 97
Haines, Geo. 64
      Lancel 39
      Robt. 11
Hall, Edd 29
      Jas. 101
      Jo. 39
      Oswan 99, 100
      Symon 53
Hallam, Ann 71
      Mrs. Margaret 68, 70
                       73, 74
      Robt. 67, 69, 71, 72
              73, 74
      Thos. Jr. 43, 44, 67
      Thos. Sr. 43, 44, 67
                68, 72, 73, 74
                80
      Wm. 43, 44, 67, 68
            69
Hally, Dr. Jno. 38
      Margaret 29
Hallywell, Bernard 29
Ham, Hieromo 14
Hamelett, Richd. 1, 50, 58
Hamelin, Stephen 16, 17, 19
            21, 28, 49, 51, 54
            63, 81, 83, 84
Hamond, Edd 37, 39, 40, 50
          52, 54, 55, 56
      Tho. 17, 21, 60, 82
          96, 103
Hancock, Jeromy 64
      Jno. 84
      Tho. 101

Hand, Richd. 84
Hanett, Wm. 6, 8, 15
Hanley, Fred 101
Harahan, Geo. 40
Harlston, Roger 24
Harper, Henry 78
Harris, Ellinor 92
      Jas. 84
      Peter 104
      Robt. 64
      Roger 64
      Tho. 84
      Wm. 3, 5, 16, 79, 96
Harrison, Grace 39
      Jas. 101
      Jno. 10, 38
      Jos. 21
      Mathew 29
      Thos. 83
Hart, Henry 29
      Isaac 39
      Kath: 84
      Mary 88
Harwell, Jo: 101
Harwood, Eliz 86
      Jno. 82
      Jos. 35, 37
      Phill 78
      Wm. 64
Harvey, Sir Jno. 25
Hatcher, - 4
Hatley, Jo 63
      Simon 46
      Wm. 39
Hause, Wm 101
Haut, Jas. 84
Havit, Wm. 59
Hawkins, Henry 1.
Hawley, Jane 101
Hay, Tho. 11, 64
Hayes, Alex. 101
Hayslwood, Tho. 38
Hayward, Tho. 10
Heads, Ellinor 11
Heath, Eliz. 38, 45
      Peter 84
      Richd. 33
Henman, Walter 88
Herdman, Robt. 55
Hermison, Isaac 57, 63, 89, 90
                   94
Hermy, Kath: 39
Herrin see Erreeno
Hertford, Geo. 101

Hewett, Jo 89. 101
    Myles 64
    Robt. 24
Heyes, Eliz. 91
Heyward, Jas. 29
    Wm. 15
Hide, Jno. 10
    Roger 29
Hiden, Mrs. Martha Woodroof 13
Hienders, Wm 21
High Peake 5. 20. 25
Hill, Col. Edward 1. 3. 4. 5.
    6. 7. 12. 15. 16. 17. 19
    24. 26. 27. 29. 31. 33.
    34. 41. 45. 47. 49. 52.
    53. 57. 59. 64. 76. 82.
    87. 90. 93. 94. 96. 97.
    Edward, Jr., 76. 87
    Wm. 15
Hiller, Martha 33
    Wm. 64
Hinson, Paul 39
Hobs, Richd 36
Hockwell, Kath: 10
Hodges, Jno. 39. 63. 90. 99
Hoe, Rice 1. 5. 6. 7. 8. 12. 15
    16. 21. 32. 45. 47. 56
    59. 82. 94. 98.
    Rice, Sr. 93
    Rice, Jr. 21. 93
    Mrs. Sara 16. 21. 26. 27.
    28. 30. 56. 59. 63.
    72. 76. 77. 93. 94.
Holder, Tho. 24
Holdsworth, Martin 54
    Walter 63
Holford, - 89
    Tho. 17. 30. 39. 45. 50
Holicresse, Danl. 100
    Jas. 53
Holland, Gabriel 1
    Robt. 64
Holliman, Wm. 10
Holls, Frances 84
Holman, Wm 24
Holmes, Elias 2. 4.
Holmwood, Jo 43
Hooke, Capt. Edd 19
Hopkins, Jno. 92
Horner, Wm. 101
Horsmonden, Richd 91
    Susan 51. 91
    Warham 7. 8. 12. 15.
    21. 22. 24. 49. 82.
    83. 89. 91. 95.

Hoster, Robt. 11
How see Hoe
Howell, Jno. 9. 19. 73. 82. 104
Huberd, Robt. 14
Huckes, Jas 11
Huckes see Huxe
Hughes, Jane 29
    Mathew 78
    Peter 33
    Richd. 54
Hugnet, Jas. 13
Hull, Francis 29
    Mary 10
Humfreyes, David 29
Hunt, Jas. 84
    Jane 33
    Olliver 94. 103
    Wm. 93. 94
Huntley, Jno. 100
    Wm. 24
Huson, Jno. 10
Huxe, Tho. 14. 26. 40. 46. 92.
    93. 94. 95. 100.
Hyde see Hide

Indian Invasion 47
Ingelton, Mr. 12
Isham, Henry 19. 104

Jackson, Patrick 20. 46. 98
    Peter 11. 101
    Randoll 33
    Rebecca 24
    Sam 64
Jacob, Jno. 76
James, James 10
    Mary 33. 53
Jay, Alex'r 64
Jeanes, Margarett 101
Jeffers, Hugh 11
    Saml. 84
Jenkins, Alexr. 88
    Ann 91
    Mary Senr. 91
    Nich: 83. 91
    Tho. 29
Jennings, Edd 92
Jett, Tho: 29
Jewett, Olliner 84
Johnes see Jones
Johnson, Mr. 46
Johnson, Abra. 78
    Diana 39

Johnson, Dorothy 64
    Edd 78
    Henry 88
    Richd. 24
    Symon 29
    Wm. 4. 74
Jollitz, Tho. 91
Jolly, Jas 39
Jones, Mr. 85
    Ann 81
    David 35. 37. 81. 93
    Dorcas 91
    Hugh 84
    Isable 92
    John 81
    Mary 24. 81
    Morgan 11. 22. 26. 63. 84. 89
    Capt. Peter 79. 80
    Rev. Richd. 10. 20. 26. 28. 31. 57. 98.
    Robert 24. 63. 91
    Thos. 4
Jordan, Geo. 91
    Saml. 96
Joyner, Edmond 38
    Jas. 29
Jugle, Tho. 46
Justice, Wm. 38. 85

Keatley, Andrew 84
Keble, Wm. 10
Kent, Humphrey 4
    Joseph 29
Keybler, Marmeduke 29
Killinghall, Mary 84
Killingworth, Robt. 28. 86
King, - 58
Kirbie, Jas. 29
    Robt. 29
Knightley, Tho. 78
Knolls, Walter 64

Lacie, Sara 29
    Wm. 24
Ladd, Marmaduke 84
Lambson, Wm. 1. 36. 83. 103
Land. The name shown in these Abstracts as Curtis Laud may very well be Curtis Land.
Lancaster, Wm. 78

Lane, Mary 64
Langham, Phill 29
Langman see Longman
    Robt. 20. 25
Lansdale, Mr. 4
Latham, Charles 82. 102
Laud, Curtis (this name may be Land) 4. 9. 20. 21. 26. 36. 58. 81. 82. 89 103
Lawes, Jeremy 24
Lawrence, Ann 38
    Arthur 38
    Henry 84
    Jo. 92
    Mary 38. 40
    Nicholas 84
    Richd. 29
    Sarah 38
    Timothy 33
    William 38. 40. 99
Lay, Edd 81
Lea, Wm. 46
Lee, Peter 47
Lee, Rich. 38
    Wm 24
Letherland, Mrs. Frances 94. 99
    Jo. 58. 61. 103
    Robt. 9. 20. 25. 31. 49. 54
    Mary 31
Leveine, Mr 59
Levell, The 87
Lewis, - 56
    Ann 32
    Jas. 24. 93
    Mathew 91
    Morgan 78
    Philip 2. 3. 10. 32
Light, Mary 94
Linton, Margery 39
Lister, Humphrey 59. 60
Llewellin, Capt. Danl. 6. 9. 13. 16. 19. 34. 44. 49. 57. 58 60. 61. 62. 63. 67. 68. 69 70. 71. 73. 74. 75. 77. 80 87. 91. 101. 102
Llewellin, Robt. 11. 93
Lucas, Jno. 58. 82. 99. 100. 101
Lucio, Sam 72. 75
Luck, Magdalen 48
    Wm 101
Luderas, Dav. 42. 44. 50. 66

Lock, Jno. 91
Lodge, Eliz. 64
Long, Marmad: 78
Longe, Michaell 29
Longman, Mary 32. 36
   Robt. 32. 36
   Mary, Jr. 36
Love, Tho. 88
Lucas, Edmond, 53
   Jno. 21
Lucie, Magdalen 88
   Richd. 84
Ludeons, David 38
Lyelle, Frances 91

Mabbett, Jane 29
MacCraw, Archebald 29
MacDonnell, Jas. 24
Mackerell, Peter 9
Macknane, Dan 91
Macknemore, Henry 81
Madder, Tho. 41. 75
Madrin, Tho. 33
Mahne, Jas. 53
Major, Alex 58
   Edw. 35. 59
   Eliz. 24
   Rebecca 29
   Susanna 13. 35. 36. 59
Makaney, Dunken 91
Makinny, Alex 91
Makinney, Jo 91
Male, Jas. 53
Mallin, Clement 91
Malmo (?) Jas. 53
Malory, Phillip 76
   Thomas 36. 76
Man, Tho. 29
Manados 89
Mansfield, Wm. 83
Mappin, Richd. 81
Marble, Fran: 46
Margerom, Herbert 10
Markeham, Jno. 53
Markets 15
Markham, Robt. 91
Marks, Richd. 64
Marler, Geo. 10
Marsh, Robt. 101
Marshall, Capt. 59
   Geo. 96. 97. 98
   Jo: 51. 55. 60. 75
   Robt. 25

Marshall, Capt. Roger 43
   Sam 64
Marston, Jno. 78
Martin, Richd. 25
   Tho. 64
Martins Brandon, Bequest to Vestry
   62
Mascall, - 58
   Ann 104
Mason, Edd 39
   Henry 29
   Jno. 64
   Margaret 80
   Wm. 44. 64. 70. 71. 80
Mastehooks (Indians) 47
Master, - 58
   Margaret 42. 102
   Michaell 8. 17. 28. 31. 35
    36. 42. 51. 91.102
Mather, Tho. 63
Mathew, Capt. 8
Mathewes, Capt. Edd 63
   Jno. 38. 84
   Gov. Saml. 90
   Tho. 33
Mavados 87
Maw, Tho. 29
Maxwell, Mrs. Eliz. 27
May, Cornelius 33
   Ja: 39
Maylan, Francis 11
Mayle, Judith 101
Meaner, Eliz. 24
Meares, Robt. 101
Meldrom, Andrew 20. 21
   Isabel 33
Mercer, Jno. 101
   Alice 29
Meredith, Mary 39
Michell, Ales 38
   Dorathie 53
   Susan 91
Midleton, Peter 11
   Wm. 23. 51
Milford, Geo. 88
Miller, Erasmus 39
   Henry 25
   Jone 91
Milles, Robt. 64
Minter, Eliz. 5. 11
   Jno. 5. 11. 101
   Mary 101
Mintorne, Phill 14. 23. 28. 92. 94
Molesworth, Col. Guy 31. 51. 53

Monfort see Munford
Monnace, Luke 46
Mont, Alex 78
Montfort, Jane 33
Moodye, Tho. 16. 55. 91
Moore, Jas. 81. 85
    Richd. 29
    Robt. 101
    Wm. 64
Moores, Robt 84
Morayne, Moore 102
Morecock, Ja. 88
Morgan, Tho. 19. 95
Meris, Hugh 29
Morley, Chas. 29
    Wm. 10
Morris, Eliz 29
    Mary 10
Mosby, Edd 6. 61. 63. 75
    79. 84. 87. 104
Moses, Jo. 91
Mosse, Andrew 39
    Wm 101
Mothley, Geo. 29
Moyles, Eliz 37. 43
    Peter 10. 37. 43
Munford, Jas. 11
    James' children 11
Munson, Jeffrey 39
Murrayne, Danl. 99
Murrey, Tho. 78
Myles, Jo. 64

Nash, Bernard 33
    Gregory 101
    Jas. 46
Neale, Andrew 85
    Jas. 78
    Pru: 39
Nelson, Fran: 38
    Jno: 29
    Jone 84
    Mich: 64
    Thos: 64
Newcome, Arthur 33
    Henry 57
    Wm 53
Newsham, Margar: 64
Nicholas, Anthony 49
    Jo 88
    Richd. 17. 22. 42.
        49. 51. 52.

Nicholls, Wm 53
Nicholson, Alex 91
    Robt. 22
Norman, Jo. 101
North, Richd. 29
    Wm. 28
Norton, Eliz: 39
    Roger 10
Nothway, Tho. 26. 30. 39. 49. 58
    73. 75. 80. 87. 94
    101

Okams, Henry 15
Oneale, Bryon 64
Orphan's Court, notice 79
Orton, Mich: 78
Osborne, Dorathie 75
    Francis 75
    Jane 75
    Jenkin 1
Owen, Mr. 104
    Edd 64
    Mary 26
    Phill 57
Oxenden, Roger 46

Pace, Geo. 4
    Richd. 4
Paddam, Jas. 25
Page, Ben 88
    Judith 24
    Richd. 91
Paine, Humphrey 29
Panton, Tho. 78
    Wm. 91
Parham, Jas. 2. 4. 23. 25. 32. 90
Parke, Ann 40
Parker, Ambrose 84
    Jo 101
    Mary 68
    Richd. 37. 38. 48. 52.
        68. 95. 99. 100
    Theoph: 101
Parry, Jas. 88
Parsons, - 58
    Mrs. Jane 56
    Joseph 1. 6. 16. 17. 20
        21. 25. 41. 42. 50
        52. 54. 61. 63.
Pawlet, Sir John 102
Paydon, Hum: 33

Peach, Jo 60
Peake, Nicholas 33
Peck, Wm. 81
Peckett, Henry 84
    Jno. 64
Peibils, Capt. David 1. 5. 6.
    7. 8. 12. 16. 18. 19. 22. 23
    24. 27. 28. 29. 30. 31. 33.
    34. 35. 37. 38. 41. 43. 45.
    46. 47. 50. 53. 57. 64. 65.
    66. 97
Peibils, Mrs. Eliz. 82. 83.
    90. 94. 95. 96. 103
Penn, Jo. 88
Pennant, Ellis 96
Penrith, Jo 91
Penton, Thos. 10
Perkins, Mary 48
    Nichol 52
Perrott, Jno. 101
Perry, Capt Henry 1. 5. 6. 11
    12. 17. 18. 19. 21. 31. 33.
    34. 35. 41. 42. 45. 46. 47.
    50. 52. 53. 55. 64. 65. 68.
    79. 82. 85. 89. 90. 93. 95.
Perry, Nich: 15. 22. 28. 48.
    51. 60. 81. 84. 91. 102
Peter an Irishman 92
Peters, Tho. 14. 26. 79
Phillips, Saml. 100
    Wm. 38
Philpot, Jo. 78
Piece, Arthur 81
Pierson, Thos. 15. 17
Pike, Jno. 46
Platt, Gilbert 31. 39
    Wm. 101
Play, Roger 29
Playce, Edd 78
Plumer, Peter 26. 38
    Roger 78
Pollard, Mrs. Jas. Claiborne 13
Pond, Tho. 29
Poole, Eliz: 30
    Nich: 2. 23. 43. 66. 82.
    85.
    Ralph 30. 39. 96. 101
Porter, Wm. 80
Potter, Edmond 84
    Geo. 30. 59. 82. 90. 91
    92. 93. 94. 95. 99
Powell, Jas. 50
    Jno. 42
Powell's Creek 1. 16

Poynton, Wm 29
Pratt, - 58
    Jno. 57
    Walter 33
Preston, Jas. 29. 64
    Roger 69. 74
    Thos. 78
Price, Edmond 29
    Howell (Hoel Pryse) 1. 2.
    4. 5. 7. 8. 9. 10. 11.
    12. 14. 15. 16. 17. 19
    20. 22. 23. 24. 27. 28
    30. 33. 35. 36. 38. 39
    49. 51. 53. 55. 57. 58
    64. 65. 66. 76. 78. 80
    81. 83. 84. 86. 89. 90
    92. 94. 95. 97. 99. 100
    101. 102.
Price, Jno. 4. 54
    Richd. 31. 45. 84. 91.
    Wm. 5. 38
Prise, Mr. 62
    Ann 54
Prison 83
Pryor, Mr. 88
Pryse, Ann 28
    Wm 28

Quaile, Nich: 101
Queens Creek 89
Quelch, Martin 104

Radeway, Wm. 16. 80. 95. 98. 100
    102.
Radford, Ja. 46
Ramsey, - 58
    Alton 101
    David 17. 57
    Mary 84
Rand, Geo. 101
    Tho. 103
Randolph, Henry 8. 51. 80
Rands, Thos. 4. 35. 94
Rawlins, Richd. 48
Ray, Geo. 33
    Sam 64
    Walter 29
Rayner, Isabel 101
Read, Capt Abra: 21. 23. 37. 65
    John 46
    Robt. 78
Redford, Fran: 37. 55. 63. 72. 76. 77.
    84.

Remington, Timothy 88
Reyman, Geo. 78
Reymond, Ann 53
  Margarett 91
Reines, Wm. 45. 78
Reyne, Andrew 92
Royner, Jas. 41. 54. 97. 98
Reynes, - 90
Reynolds, Tho. 16. 54. 90
Richards, Edd 19. 95
  Jno. 26. 31. 32. 36
   37. 45. 93
Richardson, Wm. 84. 101
Richohockans 47
Rickahocks 47
Rixe, Richd. 51
Roberts, David 10. 101
  Jas. 78
Robeson, Jas. 74
Robinson, Martha 29
  Morgan Poitiaux 13
Rodes, Robt. 33
Rogers, Jane 86
  Mich: 91
  Tho. 64. 78
  Wm. 86
Rolfe, Mary 91
Rookesby, Margaret 91
Rose, Major Morris (Maurice) 58
  82. 85. 87. 89. 92
  Robert 64
Rosse, Danl. 39
  Jo. 64
Rosser, Mary 29
  Winifred 86
Rothwell, Milliscent 99. 100
  Wm. 10. 31. 63. 82
   90. 91. 92. 93.
   94. 99.
Rownds, Jas. 101
Rewse, Hen 39
  Robt. 32. 55. 91. 99
   100. 102. 103
Royes, Antho. 29
Royman, Robt. 91
Royston, Phillip 64
Russell, Jno. 46
  Robt. 88. 89

Sacker, Jno. 64
Sadler, - 30
  Mr. Jo 56
Saines, Richd 64
Salisbury, Wm. 91
Salmon, Mr. 59
  Henry 88
  Jas. 20. 50. 54
  Peter 28. 60. 61. 93. 100
Salter, 59
  Franc 11
  Robt. 78
  Symon 78
  Walter 14. 26. 27. 31. 58
   65. 83. 84. 85. 87
   99. 102. 103
Sambeck, Jas. 58
Sanders, Jno. 56. 64
  Wm. 63
Sanson, Walter 10
Sands, Jane 11
Savill, Jno. 101
Scott, Danl. 23. 34. 50. 55. 57
  60. 61. 90. 99. 102
  Danl. Jr. 23
  Elizab. 23
  Isaac 78
  Robt. 34
Seamon, Jno. 95
Seale, Wm. 29
Seares, Henry 11
Seines, Law: 33
Senior, Tho: 29
Shap, Jno. 15
Sharpe, - 59
  Ralph 78
Sheffield, Jo. 64. 78
  Wm. 63
Shell, Henry 46
Shorborn, Hugh 67
Sherwood, Mary 38
  Peter 29
Shipley, Mr. 9
  Humfrey 14. 37
  Mrs. Mary 37
Shorer, Hen: 11
Short, Math: 39
  Wm. 17. 30. 41. 57. 59.
   84. 92. 94. 103
Simpson, Edd 46
Sincluir, Archebald 81
Slaner, Jas. 33
Slaney, Tho. 46
Slayd, Jno. 78. 86
Slee, Roger 53
Slitt, Barnaby 11

Sloman, Jno. 75. 101
Smallwood, Jo 84
Smeed, Jno. 10
Smith, Edmond 36. 59
 Edd 46
 Fredk. 64
 Mary 24
 Richd. 78
 Robt. 29
 Sam. 18. 37. 102
 Mrs. Temperance 32
 Tho. 75
Smart, Tho. 64
Smurt, Tho. (?) 64
Snealls, Edd 78
Sneath (?) Edd 78
Sparchett, Edd 50
Sparrow, Mr. Charles 1. 4. 5
 23. 29. 30. 33. 35.
 41. 47. 51. 57. 62.
 63. 65. 77. 80. 82.
 83. 84. 86. 89. 91.
 92. 93. 94. 95. 96.
 97. 98. 102. 103.
Speed, Henry 29
 Hulda 33
 Jeffrey 11
Speeding, Tho. 15
Spell, Geo. 92
Spire, Jno. 78
Spires, Edw. 11
Spring Gardens 76
Staddors, 'Goodman' 104
Stafford, Wm. 29
Stagg see Stegge
Stegge, Capt. Thos. 3. 7. 34.
 35. 36. 37. 41. 46.
 47. 48. 50. 51. 53.
 55. 57. 62. 64. 65.
 66. 82. 83. 85. 89.
 93. 95. 98.
Sterne, Hen: 78
Stevens, Eliz: 91
Stevenson, Andrew 29
 Tho. 103
Stith, Jo. 44. 57. 60. 61. 62
 63. 82. 83. 91.
Stokes, - 59
Stone, Rebecca 33
Strood, Wm. 78
Summer, Jane 91
Swan, Col. Tho. 9. 14. 24
Swanley, Jas. 101

Symmons, Roger 78
Symonds, Symon 13
 Wm. 90. 94

Talbott, Henry 78
 Mich: 54
 Wm. 46
Tall, Antho: 78. 86
Tanner, Eliz: 29
 Thos. 61. 90. 92. 94.
  102. 103
 Wm. 78
Tate, Jno. 38
Tatham, Nath: Jr. 57
Tavener, Jas. 88
Tawney, Alice 29
Taylor, Edmond 24
Thomas, David 64
 Hugh 53
 Jane 91
 John 57
 Jone 51. 104
 Wm. 17. 33. 51. 56
Thomson, Henry 88
Thompson, Jo. 101
Thorne, Jno. 11
 Richd. 101
Thornton, Hen: 39
 Jas. 101
Tight, Margaret 91
Tiller, Alex 33
 Richd. 84
Tinker, Ann 54
Titbury, Nich: 11
Tobacco Adulterated 34
Tomlinson, Agnis 92
Tompkinson, Tho. 55
Tompson, Jno. 98
Toms, Fran: 62
Tonstall, Mr. 26
Towne, Ann 101
Townsend, Mary 86
Trenser, Chris: 64
Trevett, Jno. 53
Tunstall see Tonstall
Turkey Island Creek 16
Turner, Jno. 15. 91
 Robt. 46
Turvile, Tho: 79. 99. 102
Tutchmark, Jo. 92
Tye, Capt. Richd. 6.12.13.16.18.
 26.30.33.41.47.48.50.53.57.65
 78.79.80.86.89.90.92.95.102.
 103.

Tyler, Charles 49. 63. 81
     Jno. 78

Upham, Tho: 88

Viccars, Wm. 35

Wale, Ann 92
Walker, Jno. 11
     Robt. 29
Wall, Capt. John 17. 27. 55.
     57. 89
Waller, Mich: 24
Wallis, Robt. 101
Walter, Geo. 91
Ward, - 59
     Jas. 17. 57. 84. 86. 98
     103
     Jeremy 64. 78
Ward's Creek 3. 16
Warradine, Mrs. Eliz: 18. 25.
     Jas. 6. 11. 17. 18
     20. 25. 39. 45
     50. 51. 86. 88
     93.
     Jas. Jr. 93
     Sara 50
Warnham, Thos. 78
Warren, Sam: 78
     Tho. 93
Waterford, Mich: 11
Waters, Tho. 88
Watlington, Antho: 101
Watts, Bryon 29
     Ralph 101
Web, Mr. 16
Webb, Elias 10. 63. 75. 91
     Steven 64
Webber, Jas 11
Wells, Barth: 64
     Richd. 10. 51
     Wm. 29
Wenne, Edd 101
     Henry 91
Wentworth, Henry 7. 14. 79
West, Jno. 33. 89
     Joseph 29
     Mary 96
     Wm. 53

Westhorpe, Major John 30. 33. 37.
     38. 39. 51. 58. 62. 75
     83. 96.
Weston, Henry 78
Weynoke, King of 47
Whaley, Jos. 92
Wheeler, Robt. 78
     Wm. 19. 47
Whethall, Thos. 53
Whitby, Wm. 74
White, Jno. 22. 46. 54
     Phillip 64
     Steven 29
     Tabitha 53
Whitehead, Barth: 20. 24. 29
Whiteing, Robt. 84
Whitter, Tho. 38
Whittier, Tho. 38
Whittingham, Wm. 29
Wilkins, Wm. 81
Wilkinson, Jervis 78
Wilks, Wm. 64
Willard, Jas. 64
Williams, Mr. 51
     Eliz: 54
     James 29. 86
     Jane 11. 80. 100. 102
     Wm. 25
Williamson, Cuthbert 84
Wills, Mich: 78
Willyard, Austin 55
Wilson, Edd 54
     Jno. 99
     Nich: 78
     Ralph 46
Wishert, - 59
Wood, Mr. (salter) 71
     Ann 71
     Major Abraham 1. 3. 6. 7.
     12. 16. 24. 26. 35.
     40. 47. 58. 79. 80.
     86. 95. 99.
     Tho: 29. 64
Woodleife, Capt. Jno. 1. 2. 3. 10.
     12. 53. 89
Woodward, Christopher 80. 102
     Sam 4. 26
Woolfe, Rice 59
Worsuham, Geo. 27
     Wm. 27
     Wm. Jr. 27
Wray, John 78

C 10

Wray, Thos. 64
Wrench, Henry 29 (Heavens knows what he looked like but he had a
             name with an edge. B.F.)
Wrench, Peter 101 (And he even more so. B.F.)
Wright, - 59
        Jno. 64
        Richd. 101
Wyatt, Antho: 1. 2. 5. 6. 7. 9.   (All this concerning my
             11. 12. 14. 15. 18. 19.   reputed ancestor - and yet I
             21. 22. 24. 25. 26. 27.   am no wiser. More distinguished
             29. 33. 35. 41. 46. 47.   but no more certain descendants
             49. 50. 57. 59. 64. 65.   please take warning.   B.F.)
             78. 79. 80. 86. 89. 90.
             91. 92. 95. 96. 101. 102
             103. 104.
Wyat, Geo. 46
Wyes, Robt. 54
Wyner, Jas. 84
Wynne, Robt. 34. 35. 47. 50. 53
             57. 58. 64. 65. 77
             78. 80. 86. 89. 90
             92. 95. 102. 103.

Yates, Austin 64
Yeardley, Sir Geo. 93
Young, Capt of the Adventure 43
       Mary 92

VIRGINIA COLONIAL ABSTRACTS

Vol. XI
Charles City County
Court Orders   1658 - 1661

Abstracted by
Beverley Fleet

Southern Historical Press, Inc.
Greenville, South Carolina

This volume was reproduced from
A 1941 edition located in the
Publisher's private Library

All rights reserved. No part of this publication may be reproduced, stored in a retrieval system, transmitted in any form, posted on to the web in any form or by any means without the prior written permission of the publisher.

Please direct all correspondence and orders to:

www.southernhistoricalpress.com
or
SOUTHERN HISTORICAL PRESS, Inc.
PO Box 1267
375 West Broad Street
Greenville, SC   29601
southernhistoricalpress@gmail.com

Originally published: Richmond, VA. 1941
ISBN #0-89308-368-2
All rights Reserved.
Printed in the United States of America

Preface

When lost in a tangle of faded and involved lines and impossible abbreviations, Mrs. James Claiborne Pollard, of the Archives Division of The Virginia State Library, is my final Court of Appeal. It was she who called my attention to the fact that the preface for this volume had been written as far back as 1823. It follows:

Statutes at Large
William Waller Hening. 1823.
Vol. 1. Preface XXI.
"In a work so laborious as the present, where the characters in which the laws are written are as difficult to decypher as the Greek language would be to a person who had never learnt the alphabet, it is impossible to avoid the committing of many errors. The effect upon the eyesight, too, has been incalculably injurious. To this cause may, doubtless, be ascribed some of the mere literal errors which have escaped my utmost diligence. "

If you don't believe it, try it.

                Beverley Fleet.

June 25th 1941.

CHARLES CITY COUNTY
Court Order Book

page 137

Att a Co'rt held att merchts hope Apr 20, 1658
Present
     mr Thomas Drewe
 mr Anthony Wyatt   Capt Robt Wynne
 Capt John Epes   mr James Barker
          mr ffran Epes

page 137. mr James Barker and mr Francis Epes sworne Com'rs

page 137. Abstract. Hugh Evans ord. to pay Tho. Hamond 435 lb. tobo. Also Wm. Greene ord. to pay Hamond 300 lb. tobo.

page 137. Abstract. Geo. Atkins ord. to pay Robt. Rowse two cows in ten days.

page 137. Ca: Stegge present

page 137. Abstract. Upon petition of Walter Salter agt. Tho. Stinson "it apper'eth to the Co'rt that the sd businesse is a vexatious turbulent cause allready judged and decided severall times" – therefore dismissed. John Stith for the plt. appeals to next Quarter Court.

page 137. mr Stephen Hamelin sworne Com'r

page 137. Abstract. Receipt, 17 Feb. 1657/8 for 8 hhds tobo from Mr. Anthony Wyatt for sale.
Wit: signed Thomas Nethway
Robt Wynne   (or Nothway)
Thomas Crane
"Tho: Nethway at mr George Lauds a mer'cht in Horse Street Br'o"
    recorded 20 April 1658

page 138.
Samuell Smith aged 36 yeares or thereabouts sworne sayth
 That Walter Salter about the beginning of Janry last sayd to the Dept, what will you not come to Co'rt and side w'th me about this land ? the Dept answered I have nothing to say in itt. Salter replyed, well if you will not, I will make some body suffer as well

The deposition of Samuell Smith (continued)

as I, Ibeleeve it will fall upon Scotch Thom: I told him I had lost his note and he doth not know to the Contrary; but I have it here in my pockett, and showed to the dept the note: Likewise the sd Salter told the Dept that ffitzgarret should have an ord'r ag'tt him, and then he would have the same ag'st the Scott, he would make som body suffer as well as himselfe and so it will runne to the end of the Chapter;   And further sayth not
                                                Samuell Smith
Jurat' Coram me March 29th 1658
     Charles Sparrowe
                                   Rec. 23 April 1658

page 138. Abstract. Deed of Gift. 18 Feb. 1657/8. James Rayner gives "unto my sonn John Reyner" a brindled heifer, 3 years old with calf, "wch heyfer was bequeathed to me (when she was a calfe) by the last will and testamt of my late master John Hacker decd, and caused to be Del'red the 10th of June last by mr Charles Sparrow"
                             signed   James x Rayner

page 138. Abstract. Order that Peter Salmon pay Mr. Antho: Wyatt 1000 lb. tobo.

page 138. Abstract. On confession of Beniain: Cartwright, he is ord. to pay Tho. Drewe 415 lb. tobo.

page 139. Abstract. Order that Joseph Dunne, security for Richd. Parker, pay to Geo. Atkins 2 cows according to Judgt. against him at suit of Robt Rowse.

page 139.   mr Cha: Sparrow present

page 139. Abstract. Order that Wm Harrison pay to Wm Wheeler a cow according to bargain.

page 139. Abstract. Comm. of Admr. of est. of Thos. Walls dec'd granted Mr. John Dibdall "on the behalfe of the relict of the sd deced".

page 139. Abstract. John Greenhough ord. to pay Mrs. Eliz. Peibils 230 lb. tobo.

page 139. Abstract. Attach. granted Capt John Wall agt. est. of Peter Salmon, for certain tobo., half to be pd Mr. Wyatt.

page 139. Abstract. Wm Short ord. to pay Tho. Tanner 900 lb. tobo. to settle diff.

page 139. Abstract. Ord. that Joseph Dunne, security for Richd. Parker, give caution to Geo. Atkins for pmt. of 1700 lb. tobo.

page 139. Abstract. Order that Jane Williams pay Thomas Reynolds 485 lb. tobo. in full of bill under her hand.

page 140. Abstract. Order that John Daniell, George Midleton and Richd. Pace shall pay Wm Short 300 lb. tobo. each, "according to the ord'r recorded agst the sd Short by Tho: Tanner".

page 140. Abstract. Order that Thos. Tomlinson pay Tho: Clearke (sic) 350 lb. tobo. due by bill.

page 140. Abstract. Order of Court agst. the Sheriff reversed in the case of Jo: Greenhough who has now appeared and answered the suit against him.

page 140. Whereas Ben: Cartwright is arrested to this Co'rt and convict by evidences for opprobrious language uttered agst the sherr in contempt of his office and consiquently of the authority whence it derives: Itt is therefore ordered that the sd Cartwright be imediately punished w'th two lashes on his bare sholders for his sd abuse, and pay all costs occasconed in the suite agst him, als exec.
  Upon request and intercession of Howell Pryse and recantation and submission of Ben: Cartwright the Co'rt is pleased to remitt and release the corporall punishm't adjudged and to be inflicted on the sd Cartwright.

page 140. Capt Tobt Wynne sworne sherr according to eleccon
           Robt Rowse sworne Undersherr

page 140. Abstract. Mr. Stephen Hamelin granted judgt. agt. Howell Pryse, late sheriff, for 2057 lb. tobo. and 29 shillings Sterl. for nonappearance of John Drayton merchant. Attachmt granted Pryse agst est. of Drayton for foregoing.

page 140. Abstract. Tho. Drewe and Antho. Wyatt ordered to audit levy a/cs of Howell Pryse on May 10th next and report to the Court, so he may be discharged of responsibility.

page 141. Abstract. Nonsuit granted Richd. Mascall agst Bartlet Owen.

page 141. James Salmon confesses Judgt to Capt Richd Tye for 414 lb tobo.

page 141. Abstract. Quietus est to Isaac Hermison admr est of Wm Symonds decd, he having pd beyond the assets.

page 141. Abstract. Mr. Tho: Ligon sued by Howell Pryse at last Court, for the escape of one Thurgood Pate a prisoner in his custody, for 695 lb. of tobo., of which he pd 345 lb., requests remission of bal of 350 lb. This refused and he is ord. to pay by 10th Nov. next.

page 141. Abstract. Nonsuit granted Robt. Rowse agst Tho: Sharpe with costs.

page 141. Abstract. Nonsuit granted Wm. Vaughan agt ffran Grey with costs.

page 141. I John White do hereby give and freely give unto Charles White for consideracons rec'd in hand of the sd Charles White of London mariner, One hundred acres of land lying and being neere the falls upon distance of three miles from the falls beginning upon my first entry upon the first Survey. Witnes my hand this 13th Day of Aprill 1658

Test
John Posled   (sic)
Christopher Batt
Walter Holdsworth

being my owne land
per me John White

Recognit in Cur April 20. 1658 per Edd Mosby and John White suprad't

Recorded 12 May 1658.

page 142.
                          1657
Cha: Citty
     To pay for 479 persons 17 per poll is   8143
To Coll Wood for his accomodation is   1666
to the Appomattock Indians for 8 wolves   700
to Sr Willm Berkeley   3000
to Coll Morrison   2037

                                                 7403
                    To sallery   740   8143

                    Test Tho: Brereton Cl Con
                    rec May 12 sequ

page 142. Abstract. Receipt to Howell Pryse, dated 19 Dec. 1657,
(1657) for 1666 lb. tobo. for this years levies and 700 lb tobo.
due out of the levies to Appomatock Indians for killing 8 wolves.
                    signed Ab: Wood
                    rec May 12. seq

page 142.   Mr Pryse pray make paym't of 610 lb of tobbo and cask
to Henry Randolph out of the tobbo due to me in yo'r Com and the rest
to Capt Stegge and this w'th their receipt shalbe yo'r discharge
from   Yo'r frd to serve yu
8ber 25. 1657   Francis Moryson

Rec'd of mr Howell Pryse full satisfaccon of this note witnes my
hand this 27th of october 1657
                              Henry Randolph
                    rec May 12. 58

page 142.   1657 Howell Pryse is debt'r   tobbo
Per ord'r of Sr Wm Berkeley for so much due out of the
     publick levy of this Com   3000
Per ord'r of Coll Morison for so much Due out of the Levie 1367
Per ord'r for a wolfe killed   0200
Per tobbo to be Deposited in my hands per ord'r 18 lb
     per poll for 214 persons   3852
Per 1 hhd tobbo appointed, unrec'd   0368

                                                            8787

Rec'd full paym't of these severall sumes of Howell Pryse this 22th
Day of ffebr 1657   (1657/8)
                         per me
rec. May 12. 58   Thomas Stegge

page 142. The Co'rt hath exempted from the lists and levies two old negr women belonging to Coll Guy Molesworth esqr, who are proved to be past yeares and abilities of laboring and consequently of being taxed for the publick and County Levies

page 143.
      Charles Citty Com Cred'r
1657 By 17 lb per poll assessed by the Co'r and Counc'll
   on 479 persons is   8143
   by 47 lb tobbo per poll assessed by the Com Cor't is 22513

                    30656
          rests to ball   01250

                    31906

      Charles City Com is Debtor per Contra
1657 Charles City Com is Debtor per Contra by tobbo pd
   per ord'r to Sr Wm Berkeley knt   3000
   to Coll Wood 2366 to Coll Moryson 2037   4403
   to mr Wyatt 1760 to Capt Stegge 200 to Moris Rose 600   2560
   to Lt Banister 1600 Geo Brewer 400 Sam: Ealls 400 2400
   to Hormison 800 Jo West 200 mr Sparrow 200
   mr Holford 200   1400
   to Capt Woodleife 200 Morgan Jones 200 Robt Russell 200   0600
   to Tho: Reynolds (inpart of 770) 412 James Parham 0612
   to Capt Wynne 200 Walt: Brooke 200 Jo. Hodges 400 0800
   to Tho: Davies 200 Abernathie 50 mrs Peibils 240 0490
   tO Daniell Scott 400 Howell Pryse for list & acts &c 1100   1500
   to Capt Tye 2650 to mr Wyatt 1870   4520
   to the carpenter Tho: Tanner 1600 to purchase nailes 1200   2800
   to the Honoble Gov'ner 1378 to Mr Drewe 970 2348
   To Sallery of the whole Levie   3065
   ffor exempted departed and insolvent persons 1408

                    31906

May 10, 1658   Hoel Pryse   improvicer

According to request and ord'r of the last Cor't we have examined this acco't, and found it fully proved, and do therefore discharge Howell Pryse the late sherr from his bond and trust of his late place and ord'r and appoint that 1250 lb tobbo the ball' of acco't above-mencconed be pd and satisfyed to the sd Pryse at the next Levy
                       Thomas Drewe
rec: May 12, 58   Anthony Wyatt

page 143.

    At a Q'r'l Cort held at Ja: Citty the 20th of March 1657
                Samuell Mathewes esqr go'vr
       Coll Tho. Pettus   Capt Hen: Pery
       Coll Obed: Robins   Coll Geo Read
              Coll Abr. Wood

Capt Robt Wynne is elected sherr for Cha. Citty Com this ensuing yeare and to be sworne at the next Co'rt there held
                      Vera Copia
                      Test
                          Tho Brereton Cl Con

page 144.

Sr
  I shall Desire yu to send the acco't what tobbo yu rec'd the last yeare and what is behind, for I have given mr Price ord'r to pay yu what remaines. I will not dispute whether the tobbo mr Ligon paid yu for the two servts were part of this Debt, but leave it to yo'r selfe who can best Judge of itt. S'r if yo'r boate comes downe I would Desire yu to send the Salt sellers w'th itt, pray present my service to yo'r Lady
                              Yo'r humble Servant
Subscribed   William Berkeley
ffor my honored ffriend mr Thomas Stegge
           these
rec May 21. 1658

page 145
        Att a Co'rt held at merchts hope Jun: 3. 1658
    Present
             mr Tho: Drewe   Capt Richd Tye
             mr Antho Wyatt   mr James Barker
             mr Cha: Sparrow

page 145. Abstract. Nicholas Poole conf. Judgt. to Mr. Thos. Drewe for 437 lb. tobo.

page 145. Abstract. Tho. Rands impowered to collect debts due the estate of Olliver Hunt deceased.

page 145. Ordered that the Constables (in each precinct) w'th assistance of one more to be appointed by the next Com'r, take care for fitting building and repayring all high wayes passages and bridges (according to act) w'th the joint helpe of the Inhabitants proporconably. And where any other charge then labo'r shalbe requisite, that to be defrayed by levie on that precinct.

page 145. Abstract. Persons possessed of intestates estates in the County ordered to give accounting.

page 145. Abstract. Order that non-residents shall pay fees in money at 2 d per lb. tobo.

page 145. Abstract. Order that Edw. Fitzgerald pay to Francis Redford in right of his wife 2 ewe lambs according to the will of Mr. William Lawrence.

page 145. Attachmt is granted to Tho; Tanner against the estate of the King of Weynoke for security of ffifteene pounds of beaver w'th all costs incident

page 145. Abstract. Curtis Laud (or Land) conf. Judgt. to George Barefoote for 400 lb tobo.

page 146. Abstract. Order that John Lash pay Wm Odian, mariner, for imp. of 2 servts, L 12. Sterling. John Lash appeals to Quarter Court and is ordered to give bond.

page 146. Abstract. Dif. betw. Mr. Jno. Dibdall plt and Mr. Theod. Bland refered to next Court as also that betw. Rev. Dibdall and Mr. Jo: Holmwood. Also the dif. betw. Jane Wms plt and Tho: Reynolds deft. to next Court.

page 146. Abstract. Nichol: Perry conf. judgt. to Mr. Wm. Baugh for 1000 lb tobo.

page 146. Abstract. Order that "James Crewes for Capt Dan: Llewellin pay to mr Richd Cook attorn' for Arthur Bayly mariner" 1000 lb tobo.

page 146. Abstract. Richd. Parker conf. Judgt. to Mr. Tho: Loveing for 1600 lb. tobo.

page 146. Mr Hamelin present

page 146. Abstract. Com. of Admr. granted Milliscent Huntley on est. of Jo: Huntley decd.

page 146. Abstract. Exec. granted Capt. Jno. Wall agst certain est. of Peter Salmon at his suit for 8000 lb. tobo.

page 146. Mr Horsmanden present.

page 146. Abstract. Com. of Admr. granted Jo. fflower of the est of Walter Daux dec'd. John Flower having married the relict of sd Daux.

page 146. Abstract. Dif. betw. Peter Plun'er plt and Jo. Turner deft to next Court.

page 147. Abstract. Deed. 3 June 1658. Thos. Tanner sells to Howell Pryse a bay gelding formerly bought of Wm. Bird. The horse delivered to Walter Holdsworth for use of Pryse.
Wit: signed   Thomas Tanner
James Barker
Robert Wynne

page 147. Abstract. Non-suit to Jo: Marshall agst. Theod: Bland.

page 147. Abstract. Antho: Allen ordered to pay Wm. Bird 635 lb tobo due on 2 bills.

page 147. Abstract. Tho. Sharpe ord. to pay Howell Pryse 381 lb tobo.

page 147. Abstract. 200 lb. tobo. to be allowed Robert Nicholson for killing 2 wolves.

page 147. Abstract. Mr. Nichol: Perry ord to deliver forthwith to Edd Ellis, 2 cows and all the hogs belonging to Edd Greenwood, Ellis giving bond to preserve sd property for the estate.

page 147. Abstract. Anthony Wyatt and John Epes certify that the building betw. Capt. Llewellin and Mr. Tho: Nothway is not according to agreement and is val. at 400 lb tobo.

page 147. Abstract. Thomas Huxe, by his attor. Robt Rowse, conf. judgt. to Howell Pryse for 864 lb. tobo.

page 148. Abstract. John Flower "for and in consideracon of marriage w'th Mary the relict of Walter Daux decd, and in consideracon of my love and affection to the children of the sd Mary Daux now my wife" gives unto John Plaine "the son of the sd Mary by her former husband Robt Plaine decd", 2 steers, a bed and other furniture and household stuff. "Also unto Ann Daux", 3 cews, certain furniture. Also to Susan Daux cattle, household furniture etc. The land descended from Robt. Plaine to his heirs. Dated 24 May 1658.
Wit: signed   John fflower
John Stith
Howell Pryse.   Rec. 25 June 1658.

page 148.
Debts pd out of the estate of Jos Parsons
```
     To mr Edenborough                              12000
     to mr Hamolin                                  02500
     to mr Hamolin for a bill turned over
          from mr Prise                             02280
     to Capt Pery                                   01309
     to Capt Stegge                                 01600
     to Jo Harris                                   00060
     to mr Wms                                      00090
     to Ralph White                                 00330
     to mr Crewes     49/s
     to mr Horsmonden                               00380
     to mr Price                                    02170
     to mr Bland                                    00540
     to Roger Rawlins for 3 dayes work              00060
                                                   -----
                                                   23319
```
                       Rec. Jun 25. 1658

page 149. Abstract. Nicholas Perry confesses judgt. to Jno. Richards merchant, for 6300 lb tobo and 30/s Sterl. money. Payments extended to 1659. Security "a young filly w'ch wilbe at the time of paym't about two yeares old, and a flea bitten horse and two cowes".

page 150.
          Att a Cort held at Westov'r Aug: 3. 1658
present
          mr Tho: Drewe   mr James Barker
          mr Antho: Wyatt   mr Steph: Hamelin
          Capt John Epes   mr ffran Epes

page 150. Abstract. Abstract. Several dif. betw. John Sloeman, gent., plt. and Capt. John Epes, Mr Francis Epes and Mr Tho. Epes Defts., to next Court.

page 150. Abstract. Dif. betw. Francis Redford and Edd Fitzgerald to next Court.

page 150. Abstract. In suit Jane Williams plt. agt. Tho. Reynolds deft., he is ord. to pay 1570 lb. tobo. less certain discounts.

page 150. Abstract. Order that Theod: Bland be pd exp. incurred in "intering &c of Tho: Walls deed" according to a/c by Mr Jno. Dibdall.

page 150. Abstract. John Turner ordered to pay Peter Plumer 1000 lb tobo now in dispute. And that 2 hhd tobo at the house of Edd Fitzgerald to belong to Turner.

page 150. Abstract. Nich: Perry conf. Judgt. to Mr. Thos. Drewe for L 5: 17: 2 Sterling.

page 151. Abstract. "This Indenture made the third day of Aprill in the yeare of o'r Lord God 1658 Betweene Mary West of Appamattock in the Com of Henrico widd formerly the relict &c of Jo: Butler chirurgeon decd of the one part and Edd Ardington of Jordans in the Com of Charles Citty of the other part". Mrs. West sells Ardington 150 acres at Baylyes Creek in the par. of Jordans. Bounded northerly by the creek, westerly by land of Wm. Reynes, southerly into the woods and easterly "on the land late in the tenure and occupacon of Wm Worsuham", "wch sd land did formerly belong to Mr Thomas Bayly and was purchased of him by the sd John Butler decd".
Wit:
Tho: Holford   Signed   the mark of Mary West
John West
James Warradine

"Recognit in Cur Aug 3. 1658 by Joh'om West for Mar' West present"

Recorded 5 August 1658.

page 152. Abstract. Diff. betw. Capt. Tho: Stegge, plt., and ffran: Grey, deft., to next Court.

page 152. Whereas Capt Wm Rothwell decd stood indebted to Willm Edwards as assigne of Henry Basterd attorn' of Seger Dekem mercht 800 lb tobbo and cask per obligacon, for wch the sd Edds haveing arrested the adm'r, Itt is therefore ordered that Geo Potter admr of the sd Decedts estate Do pay out of the sd estate unto the sd Edds the sd sums w'th costs, als exec.
(Note: this name possibly 'Dehom')

page 152. Abstract. In the diff. betw. Mr. Jno. Dibdall and Mr. Jno. Holmwood, by consent of both parties, John Adams is to estimate the value of the work and Mr. Dibdall to pay on that basis.

page 152. James Hardway is no'iated and elected Constable for Westov'r precinct

page 152. Mark Avery is released from his bond for the yeare wherein he was obliged w'th security on the complt of Jane Reynolds, the Cor't finding no cause to continue the same

page 152. Abstract. Mr. Anthony Wyatt and Capt Robt. Wynne app. to settle diff. betw. Milliscent Huntloy, widow, and Wm. Vaughan.

page 153.
    Mr Drewe
          I recd a subpena from yu but the company of friends hinders me from comeing to Cor't to testifie my knowledge in the difference betweene mr Cook and mr Barker I shall in this paper declare as much as I am able, that is, In the yeare when Mr Bayly tooke twelve hds fraught in Capt Odean I offered him fraight, and he told me he had tobbo enough, this to the best of my rememberance I am ready to Depose
                                Yor frd to serve yu
Aug. 3. 1658   Hen: Pery

                    rec 7br. 18. 58

Note: Now what is this ? Captain Henry Perry appears on page 143 of the original and on page 7 of these Abstracts as a member of the Council. And here as of "the company of friends". It looks to me as though God had once sat in high places, or at least had an ambassador there.   B.F.

(see next page)

page 153.

The Deposition of Jo White aged 48 yeares or thereabouts
    Saith   That being aboard the ship planter Capt Wm Odean comd'r w'th Capt Henry Pery, Capt Odean told Capt Pery he was to ship 12 hds tobbo for the acco't of mr Arthur Bayly wch mr Waradine was to ship, wch mrs Waradine after her husbands Death could not performe, so Capt Pery did reply he would make the fraight good. Capt Odean denyed and sayd he had fraight enough below. And further the dept saith not, nor never heard of any protest made
                                    per me Jno. White

Jur in Cur Aug 3. 1658
Test H Pryse Cl   rec 7br 18. 58

page 153

Worp'll Gent
    Whereas I am sumoned to appe' before yo'r worp's at the suite of one fflower these are to certifie you that it hath pleased God to visit me w'th sicknesse that I am not in a capacitie to appe before yu my earnest request to yo'r wor'ps is, yu will please to graunt me reference untill the next Co'rt, and God willing I shall not faile to wayt on yu, so I rest
                Yo'rs to serve yu   William Odian
Aug. 2. 1658
                        rec 7br 18 seq.
Subscribed
    To the worp'll Com'rs of Charles City Com
        these present

Note: Certainly the foregoing letter is worthy of any gentleman at any time. Would that the Captain could know, that at this late date we admire his style.   B.F.

page 153. Abstract. Moris Rose ordered to dispose of the est. of Wm Wheeler, dec'd., and give a/c to the Court. Nichol: Perry and Capt. Jno. Wall to make appraisal.

page 153. Robt Murray haveing this day in Cor't given accot upon oath unto Wm Bird of two hds of tobbo consigned w'th him for Holland is therefore acquitted and dismist from the suite and obligacon ag'st him for the same

page 153. Abstract. Diff. betw. Howell Pryse and Mr Richd Cook, attor of Arthur Bayly to next Court.

page 154.

Inquisicon made this 18th Day of June Ano Dom 1658 before me Charles Sparrow (by us whose names are here underwritten being thereunto sworne) upon the bodies of Wm Wheeler and Edd Lee being found Drownd in Wards Creeke on the 17th Day June last past whose verdict is as foll
Charles Sparrow
We whose names are here subscribed after exa'con of ffeba Rose and Jos. Harard and finding by them that there were no differences betwixt she and will Wheeler, nor betwixt she and her serv't boy, nor betwixt Wm Wheeler and the boy but that the sd Wm Wheeler and the boy went forth of the house w'th no other intent by her perceived but to wash themselves in the Creek, her husband Morice Rose being then from home. We find and retourne in our verdict that they both accidentally came to their ends, and not willingly by the sd boy nor Wm Wheeler intended.

    Thomas Reynolds Richd x Bayley
    Austin x Willyerd Hugh x Gubbens
    Richd x Hamlet   James Drysdall
    George Marshall John x Griffis
    Henry Briggs   Clement x Sholl
    James Reyner   Ellias Osborne
    Jos x Taylo'r

     rec 7br 26. 1658

page 154.
   Att a meeting at merch'ts hope 7br 13. 1658 present mr Thomas Drew and mr Antho: Wyatt
  Ordered that mr Charles Sparrow and mr Steph: Hamelin satisfie and pay to the sherr for the use of the Co'rt each of them 300 lb of good mercht'ble tobbo as a fine according to act for their absence and non attendance this day after notice of this meeting and Co'rt als exec.

page 154. John Pratt hath ord'r to imploy an Indian under the hands of mr Drewe and mr Wyatt

page 155

          Att a Cort holden at merchts hope 8br. 4, 1658

Present   mr Tho: Drewe
     mr Antho: Wyatt   mr Steph Hamelin
     mr Cha Sparrow

page 155. Abstract. Order that Court meet 18th Oct. re. levy.

page 155. Abstract. Edw. ffitzgarrald appeals to next Quarter Court Nov. 4th from suit agt him concerning the est. of Arthur Lawrence dec'd. Ordered to give bond.

page 155. Ordered that Edward ffitzgarrall forthwth render and deliver unto ffrancis Redford for the use of Tho: Moody orphane nine breeding sheepe and one young ramme belonging to the sd Moody, wth costs als exec.

page 155. The opinion of the Cort is that the personall estate of Arthur Laurence orphane dec'd should Descend to be divided amongst his surviveing brothers and sisters and his Lands to his eldest brother onely

page 155. Ca: Epes present

page 155. Abstract. John Cleark appeals to next Quarter Court from suit of Wm Hunt. He to give bond.

page 155. Abstract. Order that a constable be appointed for Merchants Hope precinct and then Thos. Hamond to be released from that office.

page 155.
Mr John Holmwood is sworne Com'r for this Com
Tho: Calloway sworne Constable for Weynoke parish
mr Rice Hoe sworne Constable for mer'chts Hope precinct

page 155. The differce betweene Capt Richd Tye plt and Wm Sandors and Jone his wife defts is refferred to the next Cort.

page 156. Abstract. John Adams reassigns to Mr. Walter Aston a deed. Dated 8br 4, 1658. Signed Jo: x Adams. Walter Aston acquits John Adams of above. Signed Walter Aston.

page 156. The Court binds Robt Rothwell and Wm Rothwell orphans of Capt Wm Rothwell decd and Tho: Ludson an orphan to serve Geo Potter until 21. he to educate and clothe them

page 156. Upon comp'lt and prosse* of Edd ffitzgarrald and his wife of some opprobrious words and languages uttered to them by Ann the wife of ffrancis Redford, Itt is ordered that the sd Ann shall on her bended knees acknowledge the sd offence before her mother the sd Mrs ffitzgarrald, and begge forgivenesse for the same, and that the sayd Redford pay all Costs of suite als exec.

* 'prosse' - process.
Note: Alas ! Ann was not the first, nor yet the last, who failed in the appreciation of motherhood. My mother-in-law was a saint. Yet my own wife, at the age of 3, spit in her face and called her a devil. Shame upon our family. No remarks from us concerning this independent Ann.   B.F.

page 156. Abstract. Order that Capt. Wm Odeon render affidavit re. shipping 2 hhd. tobo. to Eng. for Walter Daux, "or otherwise satisfie to John fflower who married the relict of the sd Daux" of the full value.

page 156. Abstract. Dif. betw. Robt Murray plt and Thomas Stinson to next Court.

page 157. Abstract. Bond. "I Richd Bayley do acknowledge to owe to his Highnesse the Ld Protector", 10000 lb. tobo., to be pd out of his estate forthwith. 8ber. 4. 1658., re an "accusacon of the suspic'on of fellony moved agst Thomas Till", to be brought before the Quarterly Court at James City.
                               Signed   Richd x Bayley

page 157. The Cor't hath ordered that Tho: Huxe Barbara Huxe Nichol Marsellis Bridgett Willyard Ann Townsend and Jane Bayley shall personally appe at James Citty the 2d day of this present Quarter Cor't before the Gov'r (and) Councell then and there to give evidence, viva voce, on the behalf of his Highnesse the Ld Protector agst Tho Till a person then and thare to be tryed for the suspecon of fellony and in case of their failing to forfeit and pay to his Highnesse the Ld Protector each of them 2000 lb of good marchtble tobbo and cask als exec.

Note: Now historians and genealogists may skip the items to follow. Just a great excitement over a few scratches. All of this is not your business and not my business, but I doubt if any of us would have missed this Quarterly Court had we had an opportunity to be there.
                                                             B. F.

page 157. The Cor't finding by the evidences agst Tho: Till that the suspicon and accusacon agst him are high and criminall doth therefore ordr and require the sherr of this Com to convey and deliv'r the sd Till a prisoner, according to act, to receive his tryall before the Honorble Co'rt and Counc'll this present Quart'l Co'rt.

page 157. We Jone Thomas and Jone Banister midwives and John Jacob chirurgeon being appointed com'anded and sworne to view the body of ffortune Bayley and give our report thereof, do declare upon our oathes aforesd (to the best of our Judgmt and discouv'ry) that there hath beene no penetracon of the body of the sd ffortune, nor any force or injury by violence of any man acted to her privie parts, nor no apperance of any such matter, except some sinds of scratching or the like.   8 br 4. 1658

                               John Jacob
                               Jone x Thomas
Jur in Cur   Jone x Banister
Test Hoel Pryse
                    rec 8 br 27

page 158. Ordered that all possessers of orphanes estates shall give such security for the same as the Cort shall think suffic't, or else that such estates be sold at an Outcry and deposited into such sure hands as the Co'rt shall appoint.

page 158. Abstract. Wm. Beaseley servt to Mr Jno. Dibdall, for frequent illegal absences, to serve his master 2 years from this date according to act, and the Rev. Dibdall to give him one cow and calf at end of service.

page 158. Abstract. Nichol: Perry confesses Judgt. to Wm Hill for 473 lb. tobo.

page 158. Abstract. Mr. Richd. Nicholas and Antho: Tall are fined 200 lb. tobo. each "for their absence and nonattendance being sumoned on the Jury"

page 158. Ordered that Walter Darnham who married the relict of Tho: Chappell decd satisfy and pay unto the decedts orphanes their severall dues and porcons according to law and the nuncupative will of the Decedt testified by mr Edd ffitzgarald and mr fferd: Aston and that he maintaines and educate them till their full age, and give good Caution for performance thereof

page 159. Be it knowne unto all men by these presents that I Richd Parker haveing exchanged one cowe called Rose w'ch belonged to Elizabeth the orphane of Nichol' Perkins dec'd and del'red the same unto Capt Otho Southcott for the use of Robt Rowse, w'ch I hereby confirme unto him and his heirs ex'rs adm'rs and assigns for ever w'th all increase, Do therefore x x in liew x x and for the better breed proffitt and increase for the sd orphane give x x for the use of the sayd orphane one cow called Gentle x x and one cow calfe that came of her of the same mark: As also unto Lydia Perkins one heyfer of about two yeares and a halfe old named Coale x x To have hold and enjoy the sd cattell w'th all increase proffitt and produce thereof unto the sd children x x wittnes my hand 8br qr. 1658
Wit: Rich Parker
Wm ffisher

        Recognit: in Cur 8br. 4. 1658
        rec 8br 27. sequ

Note: '8br qr. 1658'. October 4th 1658. 'qr.' for quarter - fourth.
                                                                          B.F.

page 159. Edd ffitzgarald exa'ed and sworne sayth That shortly before the death of Tho: Chappell the dep't was at his house, and the said Chappell sent for mr fferd: Aston and before him and the dep't Declared, as his last will, that he gave and bequeathed to each of his children two breeding cattell, and his lands to his eldest son and his heires for ever and the rest of his estate to his wife, and in case of misuse of the children the sd mr Aston was to be overseer of them and their estates and further sayth not
                                            Edward ffitzgarrald
Jur in Cur 8br. 4. 1658
Test H Pryse Cl

page 159. Ferdinando Aston ex'aed and sworne saith and deposeth the very same in each particular, and further saith not, onely that the sd Chappell the day before his death sent againe for the dept and desired his care of the sd children and their estates
                                                  ffer: Aston
Jur in Cur 8br 4. 1658
Teste Hoel Pryse Cl
                rec 8br 27 sequ.

C 11

page 160.
Att a Co'rt held at merchts hope 8br. 18. 1658

Present   mr Tho: Drewe
     mr Antho. Wyatt   mr War Horsmonden
     Capt Tho: Stegge   mr Steph: Hamelin
     mr Cha. Sparrowe   mr ffrancis Epes

Ordered that 27 lb tobbo for each tytheable person in the Com be forthwith levied and Collected by the sherr and pd as foll' viz't

Tho: Tanner per ord'r ass'd by Coll Hill	0825
Capt Wynne for burgesss charge &c	3520
mr Horsmanden per do &c	2860
Howell Pryse per ball' last yeares acc't per ord'r	1250
mr Mosby for 2 wolves	0200
Robt Nicholson for 2 wolves	0200
John Mayes for 1 wolfe	0100
To Robt Coalman sen'r for 1	0200
mr Drayton for his boate 10 dayes	0100
Howell Pryse for arreares	0748
to him for Cop acts &c	0750
mr Wyatt for arreares occasioned by charges	0121
The sherr per list	0500
to him to satisfie 4 mens labour 4 dayes	0240
to him to satisfie 4 men for 15 dayes a piece	0900
	12314
to sallery	1231
	13545

And that 18 lb per poll be levied by the sherr on the tytheables of the South side of the Com in particular and pd as foll vidzt

To Capt Tye for arreares and other charges	1002
to mr Wyatt for charges	1122
to Tho: Tanner for worke cr	1210
to Patrick Jackson for work	0600
to be Deposited to purchase nailes &c	0600
to Robt Rowse for accomodacon	0300
	4834
to sallery	483
	5317

Ordered that Howell Pryse shall present on behalfe od the Co'rt and Com agst Mrs Hannah Aston for certeine arreares of the Levy and other collec'con in 1655 in the shorriffalty of her late husband Lt Coll Walter Aston decd.

page 161. Contracted and agreed by and betweene the Co'rt of this Com and Lt John Banister that the sd Banister shall fall mall and bring in place and readinesse all such timber as shalbe usefull and necessary for the finishing and fitting of the two howses belonging to the Com, and in consideracon thereof shall have the use and benefitt of the sd 2 howses for hanging and cureing of tobbo for the space of three or four yeares, he secureing and repayring the sd lofts

page 161. Ordered that certeine clothing sent into Virginia by Jane Prince intended to her son Tho: Prince late the serv't to mr Tho: Drewe be valued by mr Cha: Sparrow or by his appointmt

Note: Here is verification of the feeling in England that he who took the trip to Virginia came to his death. This simple entry carries a tragedy that intensifies the absurdity of the petty Court quarrels and differences shown in these records. B.F.

page 161. Abstract. The sheriff ordered to collect 696 lb tobo from tytheable persons of Jordans Par., and pay it to Mr Antho: Wyatt, "who hath satisfied that sum for them".

page 161 Abstract. The sherr. ordered to seize any of the estate of Tho: Till "lately a criminall person" to pay expense of imprisonment and trial.

page 161. Ordered that Coll Guy Molesworth esqr give an exact list of his tytheable people to the sherr or Cleark and satisfy according to publiq' assestemts or otherwise that he be taxed double the sume according to act.

page 162.
    Att a Cort holden att mercht hope 10br: 3: 1658
Present   mr Tho: Drewe
  mr Antho: Wyatt mr ffran Epes
  mr Charles Sparrow

page 162. Abstract. Order that Benj. Cartwright pay Howell Pryse 350 lb tobo according to bill.

page 162. Abstract. Order that Wm Hill be pd for collecting levies of Jordans Par., to reimburse Mr. Antho: Wyatt for advances.

page 162. Capt John Epes present

page 162. Abstract. Capt Jo: Woodleife and Mr Geo Potzer app. to examine dif. betw. Capt Robt Wynne for the est of Mr John Sloeman dec'd and Mr ffrancis Epes and Mr Tho: Epes and report to next Court.

page 162. Abstract. Michaell ffletcher ord. to pay Sam: Lucie 370 lb. tobo. due by bill.
    Samuell Lucie ordered to pay Michaell ffletcher "three quarts of drams (for w'ch he hath past a bill recovered agst him wth costs" etc.

page 162. Present Capt Stegge, mr Holmwood and mr Hamelin

page 162. Whereas Richd Parker hath disobeyed a wart sent to him by mr John Holmwood w'th some contemptuous slighting Language added : Itt is therefore ordered that the sd Parker shall remaine a prison'r in the sherriffs custody Dureing pleasure of the Co'rt, who will deliberate what further censure to inflict on him for the sd offence

Note: 'wart' - warrant. While Dr. Parker was in jail for the 'contemptuous slighting Language added' we cannot but wonder what became of the Charles City ladies having babies, the hypocrondiacs, the really ill, etc.   B.F.

page 163. Capt Henry Pery esqr hath proved by testimony produced to eleven hundred acres of land for importacon of

    John Polson   Mary Wilson
    Rich. Plaine   John Roaffe
    Rich. Donnalls   Wm ~~Roaffe~~ Moris
    Jo: Will'ms   Wm Horsley
    Sam: Hoxsteed   Jo: Sparrow
    John Osman   Daniell Heriman
    Sara Dawdin   Robt Heynet
    John Lewis   Rich'd Shepard
    Ralph Blessing   Bernard Tyns
    Basil Allcock   Steph: Hall
    Tho: Wilkinson   Robt Sanders

Dated 3 Dec. 1658.
Sworne before us
Thomas Stegge
John Holmwood
Step: Hamelin

C 11

page 162. Richd Parker and Wm ffisher have in open Co'rt reciprocally acquitted each other of all services and other claimes w'tsoever, onely the sd ffisher is to receive and have all his cattell and cloathing and goods w'tsoever that are in the sd Parkers custody or knowledge howsoev'r due, and all bookes formerly given him by the sd Parker or others, w'th costs als exec to issue or.

page 162. Mr John Dibdall hath proved right to 400 acres of land for the charge of importacon of 8 persons vidz't

        Mrs Sara Dibdall   Willm Bryans
        Timothy White   ffran: Cooke
        Rowland Lurs   Agnes Buck
        Susan Bourcher   James Haines

page 163. Ordered that John Flower give bond and caution to Will'm Odeon marin'r for the fraught and other charges of two hds of tobbo sent and consigned by Walter Daux dec'd to his father Richd Daux of London, the sd hds being proved to be delivered according to form'r order.

page 163. Abstract. Mr. Charles Sparrow to settle disputes re. est. of John Gallis decd.

page 164. Abstract. Capt Thos Stegge and Mr. Steph: Hamelin to settle dif. betw. Edw. Fitzgerald and Francis Redford.

page 164. Abstract. Richd Parker conf. Judgt. to John Stith for Mr. Tho. Loveing for 200 lb. toho. due from former Judgt.

page 164. Abstract. Robt. Abernethy ord. to pay Capt. Thos Stegge for estate of Geo. Armstrong dec'd., 340 lb tobo. due by bill.

page 164. Abstract. Howell Pryse ord. to pay Ja: Crewes 1002 lb tobo by 5th Feb. next.

page 164. Abstract. James Crewes, attor of Capt Dan Llewellin ord. to pay Mr. Cha. Sparrow 420 lb tobo "recovered by former ord'r for non appereance of Ellias Webb, wth costs and inter als exec".

page 164. Abstract. Thos. Huxe ord. to pay Mr. Antho: Wyatt 600 lb. tobo.

page 164. Abstract. Daniel Murrayne ordered to pay John Sterage 400 lb. tobo.

page 164. Abstract. George Brower admr. of Jo: Devall ordered to pay Capt. Tho. Stegge 800 lb. tobo.

page 164. "A probat of the last will and testamt of Capt Richd Tye dec'd, this day proved in Co'rt is granted to mrs Joyce Tye the widdo and Ex of the sd will"

page 165. Mr Thomas Drewe mr Antho: Wyatt Capt Tho: Stegge and mr Steph: Hamelin are hereby requested and appointed to prize and value the estate of Capt Richd Tye dec'd as it shalbe proposed and presented unto them on munday the 13th day of this present month of December and Devide the same according to law and the decedts will

page 165. Abstract. Charles Gregory ordered to pay John Sterage 290 lb tobo due by bill.

page 165
    To the worp'll the Com'ers of Cha: Citty Com
    The humble peticon of Rich Parker
Humbly sheweth
    That whereas your pet'nr standeth now comitted by your wor'ps ord'r for not obeying mr Holmwoods warrt, for the w'ch offence yo'r petn'r is extreamly sorry, and doth promise for the future never to be found tardy in the like offence or any other agst the power of magistracie, and
    Yo'r petn'r doth humbly implore yo'r worps that yu wilbe pleased to pardon yo'r peticonr for his first offence
        and yo'r petn'r shall ever pray
            Rich Parker
Test Hoel Pryse Cl

page 165. Upon the humble peticon and submission of Richd Parker extent under his hand w'th publick recognicon of his offence in disobeying mr Holmwoods warr't and his sorrow for the same, The Co'rt is pleased to release him from his imprisonm't or any other censure for the sd offense

page 165. Ordered that all the members of the Jury of inquirey impanelled that have absented themselves are amerced and adjudged to pay to the sheriffe as a fine for nonattendance each of them 200 lb tobbo to be levied by distresse (if needfull) except Walter Holdsworth who hath submissively made the just cause of his necessary absence knowne to the Co'rt, And that the full Jury be impanelled and prepared to receive their oath and charge at the next Co'rt the third day of Jan'ry next

page 165. The Co'rt is adjourned to the third day of Jan'ry next.

page 166. Know all men by these presents that I Elizabeth Barker widd do hereby give and bequeath my sonne James Barker unto my brother Henry Barker and Margarett his wife or the longer liver of them, by them to be brought up and imployed as they shall think fitt, and I do hereby bind my selfe that neither I nor any one that I shall or may marry nor any other on my behalfe shall molest or trouble my brother and sister or either of them for or concerning the sd child. In wittnes whereof I have hereunto sett my hand this 23th Day of 8br 1658

Wittnesses   the mark of M Elizab Barker
the mark of B Jo Burton
the mark W Jone Banister
R Dolbens

Recognit in Cur 10br 3. 1658 per Elizab: Barker present
                       Test Hoel Pryse   Cl
rec 10br 7. sequ.

page 166.
      The Deposition of Wm Justice aged 35 or thereabouts
      Saith
That being at the howse of Edd ffitzgarald about the beginning of 7ber last did heare Edd. Mosby say that he gave his man the taylour Satterdayes in the afternoone for himselfe the first yeare he came in, and for w't he got that yeare it made a sum when ships came in and the saylours layd it out wth his master Charles White that brought him in and gott dimity for it and made drawers w'th it and other things Edd Mosby saith that for this that was his owne he gave him leave to trade w'th, and further yo'r Dept saith not

                       Wm Justice
Jur in Cur 10br 3. 1658
Test Hoel Pryse   rec 10br 7.

page 166.
      The deposition of Wm Justice aged 35 or thereabouts
      Sayth
That being at the howse of Edd ffitzgarald about the beginning of 7br last did heare Robt Rowse say that he would prove that Edd Mosby

gave his man the taylour toleracon to trade and further yo'r Dep't saith not

Wm Justice

Jur in Cur 10br 3. 1658
Test Hoel Pryse Cl

rec. 10br 7. sequ

page 167.

The deposition of John Lash aged
50 yeares or thereabouts exa'ed
and sworne
Saith

That he was on board a sloope belonging to Capt ODeons ship (wherein was 27 hds of tobbo) and came to anchor by appointm't in Jordens bay, at w'ch time the sd sloope was in indifferent serviceable condi'con, onely a little leaky but shortly after the sd sloope being there frozen in was so wrung and impaired by the violence of the ice that not w'thstanding the utmost endeavour of the Depon't and another that was with him, the sd sloope sunk, together w'th her sd loading, irrecov'ably for the time by reason of the hard weather, whereby also the depon't and his mate were in danger of perishing: and further saith not

the mark of
John X Lash

Jur 10br. 14. 1658
Coram me Anthony Wyatt

William Hopper aged 22 yeares or thereabouts exa'ed and sworne saith and Deposeth the very like in each particular as is above expressed by John Lash, the dep't being all the while w'th him in the sd sloope, and further that shortly before the sd sloope sunk the depont saw the sterne boards open from the sterne post that he could have runn his hand betweene quite through

the mark of
Wm X Hopper

Jur 10br 14. 1658
Coram me Anthony Wyatt

page 167

The deposicon of Thomas Coolish aged 29 yeares or
thereabouts ex'aed and sworne
Saith

That rideing at anchor in Jordens bay in a sloope belonging to Capt ODeones ship, neere wch rid another sloope belonging to the sd ship wherein were 27 hds of tobbo the Dep't heard the men that were in the sd sloope calling and saying the sloope wherein they were was so

wrung and pressed w'th ice that she would suddenly sink: whereupon
the dept cherished the men and admonished them to bayle what they
could, they answered they did their utmost endeavo'r, but (sayd they)
the tobbo (page 168) is ready to floate in her, and we shall not
be able to keepe her above water, or to that effect, calling to the
dep't for helpe, the depon't and another man w'th him trying the
ice adventured to their succour but found the sd sloope halfe full
of water, where upon finding no hope of preserving any of the goods
the Dept advised the men to run a shore, if possible w'th their
sayle, w'ch they attempted to do till they mett w'th thicker ice
where the sd sloope was stopped w'th the strength thereof, and there
sunk, whereupon we unrig'd the sd sloope and conveyed the rigging
on board the other sloope, and betooke our selves to perserve her
that was but in danger, w'ch (w'th Gods helpe, and hard endeavo'r)
we through Difficulty performed by breaking the ice and haling her
neere the shore, and there secured and fastened her, and further
saith not

         Thomas Coolish

Jur 10br. 14. 1658
Coram me Anthony Wyatt

page 168.
    Tho: Crane aged 30 yeares exa'ed and sworne
  Saith
That on sunday the 12th of this instant 10ber he walked w'th Geo:
Harris mer'cht to the rivers side to see how the sloops lay that
were frozen in Jordens bay, and heard the men that were on board one
of the sloopes (wherein was some hds of tobbo) calling to mr Harris
and saying the sloope was extreame leakie that they could not keepe
her free, to w'ch the sd Harris answered that they should pumbe And
the day following in the afternoone the dept walking downe againe to
the waters side saw the sd sloope sunk and the men on board the other
sloope labouring and endeavouring her safely w'ch w'th much Difficulty
they performed by breaking way through the ice and haling and setting
her to the shoare and further saith not

         Thomas Crane

Jur 10br. 15. 1658
Coram me Anthony Wyatt   rec 10br 16 sequ

page 169.
We Anthony Wyatt and Capt Robt Wynne do hereby testifie affirme and
declare (and shalbe ready to depose being lawfully required) that
on Sunday the 12th of this present December we Walked down to the
river side neere where lay two sloopes belonging to Capt ODeons ship
and then imployed by Geo: Harris mercht, and saw one of the sd
sloopes Droven by violence of ice and weather from her anchoring
and the Seamen, that were aboard her Labouring and endeavouring the

preservacon of the sd sloope, but haveing no helpe or accesse of
any boate or cannow could not prevaile agst the weather, not that
we could discov'r, wittnesse our hands this 15th Day of December
1658

        Anthony Wyatt
        Robert Wynne

rec. 10br 16. sequ.

page 169. Abstract. Rec'd 23 Sept. 1658 of Henry Perry, 8435 lb tobo
"And is for Mary Stokes Daughter of Capt John Bishopp dec'd as also
all the cattle due to her".
Wit: signed Sylvanus x Stokes
John White
Thomas Turvile   Rec. 17 Dec. 1658

page 170. Abstract. Power of Atty. 25 Aug. 1658. Major John Harper,
Capt Thomas Morgan and Robt Dessell, Citizens of the City of Bristol
to John Cogan of the City of Bristol "but now resident in Virginia
aforesd chirurgeon", to receive certain properties belonging to
Margarett Bird. "Whereas Margarett Bird of the sd Citty of Bristoll
widd (admr'ix of the goods and chattells that were of Capt Rich'd
Bond late dec'd sometimes of the Citty of Bristoll but dyed in the
Countrey of Virginia) hath constituted and appointed as her attor-
neys concerning the mill plantacon stock goods merchandizes and debts
w'ch were of the sd Capt Rich'd Bond as may apper'e"
Witnesses:
Richard Price
John Osborne
ffra: Yeamans Junr   Recorded 31 Janry 1658/9.

Note: This entry may be more important than we think. I tried to be
particularly careful in regard to the names 'Bird' and 'Bond'. B.F.

page 171. Howell Pryse hath proved right by testimony produced to
3850 acres of Land for the charge of importacon of

James Duckett	Ben: Alsop	Richd Morgane
Roger Heywood	Roger Gerey	Tho: Price
Robt Ward	Elizab: Tompkins	ffran: Osborne
Dennis MacBryon	David Wynne	John Younge
Daniell Cormack	Edd Jones	John Dodford
Hugh Berry	Margarett Barker	Tymothy Rosse
Ralfe Perkinson	Luce Johnson	Wm Harwell
Seth Dobson	Isaac Badger	Ralfe Lacie
John Denne (sic)	Wm Sadler	Humfrey Mallard
Tho: Barton	Robt Sheffield	James Tofte

      (continued on next page)

List continued from page 27.

Theoph: Baston	Benefield Atkins	Ellinor Tucky
Richd Polson	Joseph Muces (?)	Martha Lloyd
Susan Herman	Rebecca Harrison	Edd Benfield
Bernard Hall	Jane Elcock	Peter Gibson
Steph: Halsey	Jerem: Perkins	Math: Taylour
Geo Wilkinson	Tho: Glasbery	James Greene
Sam Sanders	Tho Pollard	James Rushworth
Tho: Heynes	Richd Toke	Hen Matchett
James Shepard	Robert Wells	Gabriell Hart
Nichol Marsh	Henry Webster	ffranc Thwayt
Sam Collett	Josias Wilkins	James Barriss
Geo Hayes	Wm Arwood (sic)	James Lee
Wm Leonard	Walter Sedgrave	Gregory Webb
John Andrews	Phill: Armore	Henry ffarmer
Jo: Pryor	Mary Tame (?)	Robt Seaward
Roger Case	Johanna Rogers	

page 172.
Present   Att a Co'rt holden at merchts Hope ffebr: 3, 1658
        mr Thomas Drewe
    mr Antho: Wyatt   mr John Holmwood
    Capt John Epes   mr Steph: Hamelin
    mr Cha: Sparrowe

page 172. A Comicon of admr'acon of the estate of Sam'll Woodward dec'd is graunted to Sara Woodward the relict of the sd decedt, she giveing caution as is accustomed

page 172. A Comicon of adm'racon is graunted to Robt Hide sen'r of the estate of Robt Hide Junr Chirurg decd he giveing caution as is accustomed

page 172. Abstract. John Harwood ord. to pay Mr. Tho. Drewe 500 lb tobo due by bill

page 172. Abstract. Com. of Admr. to Mary ffitzgerrald widdo of the estate of her late husband Edward ffitzgerrald decd.

page 172. Abstract. Com. of Admr. to Tho: Calloway of est. of Andrew Armstrong decd.

page 172. Upon comp'lt of Edward Mosby that Robt Rowse hath sold drink to and trucked w'th Thomas Turnour serv't to the sd Mosby, The Co'rt hath fined the sd Rowse to pay to the use of the Co'rt 300 lb tobbo and cask and Ordered that the sd Turnour for his disobedience and neglect be forthwth punished w'th five lashes inflicted on his bare sholders.

page 172. Abstract. Robt Nicholson ord. to pay James Crewes mercht., 860 lb tobo "for wch he confesseth to have subscribed to his booke"

page 172. Attachm't is graunted to mr Antho: Wyatt ag'st the estate of Joseph Dunne chirurg' for 760 lb tobbo and cask pd him for a cure not yet performed, and all costs incident.

page 173. Abstract. Geo. ffarley conf. judgt. to Jno. Drayton merchant for 200 lb tobo.

page 173. Abstract. Rice Hoe ord to pay Tho: Cuerton 420 lb tobo confessed due

page 173. Ordered that Rice Hoe satisfie and pay to Capt Robt Wynne for Joseph Dunne chirurgeon 350 lb tobbo and cask Due by Contract under his hand, w'th costs als exec.

page 173. Abstract. Dif. betw. Martin Quelch plt and Richd Mosby deft, by absence of witnesses for plt referred to next Court.

page 173. Abstract. Mrs Sara Hoe and Rice Hoe ord to pay Thos. Drewe 4518 lb tobo "of the best sort cleere from ground leaves w'th cask" according to specialty.

page 173. Abstract. Nonsuit granted Jno. Stith agt James Crewes merchant.

page 173. Itt is ordered that John Stith satisfie to James Crewes mercht or his ass'gs 2 1 9 s 9 d sterl in goods according to specialty wth costs als exec

page 173. Abstract. Mrs Hanna Aston ord. to pay Jo: Howell 435 lb tobo per bill.

page 173. Mr ffrancis Epes present

page 173. Abstract. Sam: Lucie ord to pay Lawrence Biggins 380 lb tobo due by bill.

page 173. Whereas it appeareth by receipt of major John Westhorpe dec'd and the oath of Wm Bird here declared that his note to John Bird cittizen of London to pay 3 l sterl was in lieu of a specialty of that sume yet extent among the sd Maj'r Westhorpes writings; The Co'rt doth therefore order and appoint that the sayd bill be rendered up to the sd Willm Bird

page 173. Whereas Capt John Woodleife hath assaulted and threatened Mr Antho: Wyatt whereby he is in perill of his life: Itt is therefore ordered that the sheriffe require and take good suretyes of the sd Woodleife for the peace and good abeareing, and for his personall appereance to answer the sd mr Wyatts complt at the next Co'rt the 25th of this present ffebr

page 173. Abstract. Capt Robt Wynne ord to pay Jo: Stith 1000 lb tobo according to Richd Parker's bill or produce sufficient est of sd Parker to answer the sum

page 174. Abstract. The present sherr. ord. to produce the person or sufft est of Richd Parker to pay Mrs ffrances Letherland's debt or pay it himself.

page 174. Abstract. The jury impannelled ord to app at next Court or be fined 200 lb tobo each

page 174. This present Co'rt is adjourned and removed to the 25th day of this instant ffebr.

page 174. Abstract. Judgt Jno Howell agst Mrs Hanna Aston respited till next Court.

page 174. Abstract. The sherr ord to seize all est of John fflower or Walter Daux dec'd till exact a/c be subm to Court of Daux est.

page 174. Abstract. Rice Hoe ord to pay Elizab. Barker relict of Michaell Barker 300 lb tobo due her late husband's estate.

page 174. Abstract. Capt John Epes of Cha: C. Co sells Tho Rands of Wyanoke, for 2000 lb tobo payable 10 Nov next, 60 acres at Wyanoke formerly belonging to Mr Humfrey Kent dec'd which he lived on in his lifetime, "As in fol 4 and 5 of his booke is fully recorded and confirmed".

  Rands assigns right of above to Ham'on Woodhowse. Dated 14 August 1658.
Wit: signed Thomas Rands
Wm Justice
       Recorded 17 Feb. 1658/9

page 175. Abstract. John Burton of Cha. City Co., planter acks. himself indebted to Lt John Banister of Merch. Hope 4160 lb tobo. This payable 340 lb on 10th of Oct next, and two hhds containing at least 800 lb each year thereafter until pd. Banister holding 2 Judgts agt Burton assigned to him by Mr Tho: Drewe and Mr Antho: Wyatt

  Burton therefore mortgages to Banister "one plantacon at Bonaccord wch I hold by Lease for thirteene yeares, or upwards, to come, one cowe wch I rec'd of Richd Braine, and all my crops of corne and tobbo wch (by Gods blessing and my owne endeavour wch I promise and bind my selfe shalbe just faithfull and industrious) I shall attaine to make and plant untill the sd paymts be fully accomplished and performed". Dated 12 Janry 1658/9
Wit:
Robert Wynne   signed John x Burton
Tho: Crane and
Howell Pryse Cl   Recognit in Cur Feb 3. 1658
         Recorded 17 Feb 1658/9

page 177.
    Att a Co'rt holden att merchts Hope ffebr. 25 1658
Present   mr Thomas Drewe
    mr Antho: Wyatt mr War: Horsmonden
    Capt John Epes mr Steph: Hamelin
    Capt Tho: Stegge

page 177. Abstract. Judgt agt Geo. Brewer for 800 lb tobo to Capt Thos Stegge confirmed and renewed

page 177. Abstract. ffrancis Redford ord to pay Wm Gillard 350 lb tobo per bill.

page 177. Abstract. Dif betw Edw Ardington plt and Capt John Woodleife dft to next Court. Capt Robt Wynne and Mr Geo Potter to exam and report.

page 177. The orphane of Wm Olliver Dec'd is hereby intrusted and placed w'th John Hodges to be by him kept and educated Dureing his minority; and the sd Hodges to take care of w't estate doth or shall belong to the sd orphane, and give acco't of and render the same unto him at his full age according to law, and give bond for performance.

page 177. Ordered that 509 1 tobbo be pd to Morgan MacKenny out of the estate of Wm Olliver Dec'd by Jo: Hodges trustee for the sd estate

Wm Olliver Dr

for 6 months Dyett for himselfe and his boy	600
for makeing of 4 shirts	040
for a winding sheete	040
for 120 wt of tob pd Phill: the negr' at mr Blands for him	120
for 32 w't of tobbo pd mr Dibdall for his tythes for him	032
for 19 1 of tobbo that I pd him over and above his rent	019

	851

Allowed 509

rec Apr 25. 59

page 178. This bill bindeth me ffrancis Radford my heirs or ass's to pay or cause to be pd unto Willm Gillard or my appointm't the just quantity of three hundred and fiftie pound of good merchtable tobbo and cask Due to be pd on the 10th Day of November next att my now dwelling ffor performance I have sett my hand this 15th Day of July Ano 1657

ffrancis Redford

Teste James Powell

ffebr the 1st 1658   (1658/9)

James Powell aged 62 or thereabouts Deposed that this above menconed was the bill of ffra: Redford made for three hundred and fiftie pounds of tobbo. &c according to the contents of the said bill
Jurat Coram me   War. Horsmonden

rec. Apr 25. 1659

page 178. Abstract. Howell Pryse granted Com. of Admr on est of Mr Jas Barker decd on petition of the relict.

page 178. Howell Pryse hath proved right per assign'mt and
testimony produced to 2350 acres of Land Due for importa'con of

Mr James Barker	Tho: Jackson	Elias Porter
John Lanier	Lewis Jones	Julian Heath
Lucrece Lanier	Robt Rice	Marg: Wray
Jo: May	Wm Thorne	Peter Waller
Joice Annis	James Bayly	Rich Mayor
Robt Burgesse	Jone ffarley	Hen: ffenn
Elizab: Smith	Henry Maine	Robt Hookes
Martha Honney	Rich: Browne	Robt Covell
Tho: Ashwin	Wm Peters	Tho: Dyer
Math: Moore	Timothy Hinton	Ellinor Blyth
Jo: Wickerson	Jane Wilson	Jane Wharton
Amy Davies	Rebecca Rhodes	Tho: Wigge
Rich Twyford	James Hackett	Robt Haines
Moore Marrone	Isaac Key	John Hunter
Wm Hampton	Tho: Key	Joseph Love
Ro: Gay	Wm Reeves	

page 179. "Know all men by these presents, and witnesse that I Richd
Pace sonne and heire apparent of mr Geo Pace of the Com of Charles
Citty att Mount March in Virginia, and sonn and heire as the first
issue by my mother Mrs Sara Macocke wife unto my aforesd father
(being both dec'd) Do hereby by these presents ffor my selfe my
heirs ex'ors adm'rs and ass's for ever absolutely confirme and allow
of the sale of eight or nine hundred acres of land being neere unto
Pierces hundred, als fflowrday hundred, sold by my dec'd father mr
George Pace unto mr Thomas Drewe as per bill of sale bareing date
the 12th Day of October Ao 1650 may more large app'e " x x (Richd
Pace further confirms sale to Thos. Drewe) x x. Dated 25 February
1658/9

Wit: Signed   Richard Pace
Anthony Wyatt
Thomas Stegge
Hoel Pryse C1   Rec. 19 May 1659.

page 180.
              Att a Co'rt holden att merchts hope Jun: 3: 1659
Present   mr Tho: Drewe
        mr Antho: Wyatt   mr Cha: Sparrow
        Capt Tho: Stegge   mr Steph: Hamelin

page 180. I John Dibdall minister do freely and of my own accord
and good will give and bequeath unto John Dibdall my grand child the
sonne of Richd Dibdall one bay mare filly of a yeare and three
monthes wch shalbe marked for his use wth JJD w'th her increase both

male and female forever. Also I give unto him, one black two yeare old heyfer called Neger Nose marked w'th a swallow fork and an under keile on the right eare, and a crop w'th a slitt in the crop and an overkeeld and an underkeele on the left w'th her increase both male and female for ever. Also one Ewe Lambe wth a black foot marked w'th the same mark x x his father to be his guardian and overseer x x to take care of them for his sons use till he come to the Age of eighteene yeares or be married w'ch shalbe soonest, and if the stock proceeding of the increase of the mare heyfer or ewe shalbe burthensome to be kept by reason of their number then my will and pleasure is that he sell of their increase so many as he seeth convenient converting them into plate for the profitt and use of his sonne, delivering the same unto him at the time before menc'oned, he reserving still six cowes and a bull four mares and twentie ewes, if God shalbe pleased to blesse them so to him, as a constant stock surviveing for his use aforesd, of my sd son not giveing an acco't of the sd filly heyfer ewe lambe or their proffit and increase to any Co'rt or Corts person or persons w'tsoever, not doubting but he will demean himselfe conscionably herein for the advantage of the child of his bowells: And further my will and pleasure is that if my son Richd Dibdall should Dept this Countrey to live in England and shall se it conven't to carry his sonne w'th him and convert this estate given to him into money or tobbo for the better adeance thereof I do hereby impower him so to do he entring into bond to my selfe or my wife Jone Dibdall, if then liveing to give an accot thereof at the time herein expressed for the use of his sonn as aforesd: But if the sd Richd Dibdall should dye, then I do hereby appoint Sara Dibdall his wife to take care and charge of the estate aforesd, she giveing security to my selfe or wife if then liveing, or if dead to the Cor't of Westover for the delivery of the same in kind to her son at the age aforesd, takeing onely on the sd estate the sum of eight hundred pounds of tobacco yearely for his mainteynance and education.

Provided that if the sd John Dibdall my Grand child should dye before the time expressed wherein the sd estate should come into his hands, then I hereby give the same in Specie to the next child Sonne or daughter of my sonne Richd Dibdall, and in case of default thereof unto the sd Richd Dibdall as my guift unto him, any thing conteined herein notw'thstanding, And for the better assurance hereof I acknowledge this deed in Co'rt this third of June 1659

            John Dibdall

This deed is acknowledged in Cor't the third day of June 1659 and desired to be recorded according to act
        per John Dibdall

Test Hoel Pryse Cl
    rec Jun: 4. 59

page 181. Abstract. Ellin Varnham, widow of Geo. Varnham decd., granted com. of admr. on his estate.

page 181. Abstract. Attachmt granted Capt. Jno. Wall agt est. of Capt Wm ODeon for 1 hhd tobo.

page 181. Mr ffran: Epes present.

page 181. Abstract. Robt. Evanes gr. com. of admr. of est. of Mr. John Gibbs decd.

page 181. Capt John Wall, mr David Jones, mr fferd: Aston and mr ffrancis Redford are required and appointed to apprise the estate of mr John Gibbs dec'd on the 10th of this instant month.

page 181. Abstract. John Thompson gr com of admr of est of Christofer Greenfield decd.

page 182.
Newport on Rhoad Island this 31 of Jan'ry 1658
Know all men to whom this present writing shall come that we whose names are here Underwritten Robt Potter Agent unto mr George Potter of the Virginia being mer'cht of the Barq' Black bird and Mathew Bunne marrin'r and m'r of the aforesd Barq' and we wanting effects to carry on our designe to retourne unto Geo: Potter of Virginia mer'cht, in regard we wanted sails rigging cables and ancho'rs as also provi'con for our voyage and money to pay Seamens wages, And we finding so much favour w'th mr Wm Breuton that he was pleased to furnish us w'th one hundred thirty and six pounds nineteene shillings sterl' for w'ch aforemenconed sum of 136l. 19s. 00 we have ingaged mr George Potter w'th the aforemen'coned Barq' Blackbird w'th our selves personally and Jointly to make paymt unto the aforesd Breuton according to our ingagemts w'ch then we hoped might have beene performed soone after this time, but the sharpnesse of the winter proveing contrary to expectation, and our provision being spent, and we being in want of more provision, and also in want of some cloathing and being relieved by the aforesd Breuton w'th thirty one pounds tenn shillings sterl more and to the end the sd Breuton may be secured, we in behalfe of our Imployer mr George Potter have wholly and absolutely sold unto Wm Breuton mer'cht all the right title and interest whatsoever the aforesd Geo: Potter formerly had and now hath in the Barq' called the Blackbird w'th w'tsoever is or doth belong unto her in any kind and also w't goods is now aboard that did or doth belong unto either of us as Agents unto the sd George Potter; Giveing and granting unto the sd Breuton full and peaceable possession of the sd Barq' and goods for him and his peaceably to enjoy

for ever, provided that in case the sd Barq' Blackbird do safely arrive at Virginia that the sd George Potter w'thin two dayes after her ariveall do putt in suffic't securitie unto the sd Breuton or his assgs to the value of three hundred pounds sterl to make paymt in kind and at the time that Robt Potter and Mathew Bunne have given ingagemts to performe in the behalfe of the sd Geo Potter and themselves, and to make good paymt but the sd Breuton or his assgs according to agreem't w'th them then the sd Blackbird w'th what then shall belong unto her and what goods or provicons that doth then belong unto her, is to be delivered into the hands and possession of the aforesd Geo: Potter or his ord'r peaceably to possesse and enjoy as his owne proper right   But in case security be Denyed and refused to be given by the sd Geo: Potter as is above expressed then the abovesd Wm Breuton him or his heirs ex'rs admrs or assgs is quietly and peaceably to enjoy the aforesd Barq' Blackbird and goods for ever w'thout any trouble or molestacon from the aforesd Geo: Potter or any under him or by his meanes or any that doth or shall apperteine unto him

    In wittnes whereof we have hereunto sett our hands and seales the day and yeare first written

Wit:
John Gibbs
Roland Moes
Tho: Parram (Perram)
Peleg Sanford

                           Robert Potter
                                     the seale

page 183. Abstract. Ackm't made by "my Agents" to Mr Breuton and assignment endorsed to "Mr Hatcher, Mr Randolph and my self". "Howell Pryse to acknowledge the same in my name". Dated 14th Mar. 1658/9.

                          signed George Potter

                    Recorded 4 June 1659.

Note: Index shows "Buns sale of a barq' "

page 184. Abstract. Mathew Bunne, Agt. for Mr. Wm. Breuton of "Rode Island merch't", assigns to Geo. Potter, Wm. Hatcher and Henry Randolph, all right in the vessel 'Blackbird'.

Wit:
Rich Webley
Ho Pryse Cl
John fflowers

                     signed   Mathew Bunne

Howell Pryse authorized to confirm above.

                         signed   Mathew Bunne

                  Recorded 4 June 1659.

page 184. These are to testifie whom it may concerne that upon the 23rd day of Aprill 1659 a stray black filly w'th her two hind feet white about the age of one yeare old as is conceived came in to ffort Henry, if any man can lay just claime to her, paying for the takeing her up, may fetch her away

Ab: Wood Jr

rec Jun 4, 1659

page 185. Abstract. Order formerly granted Capt Thos Stegge agt Geo Brewer admr of Jno Devall decd recinded.

page 185. Abstract. Jno. fflower conf. judgt. to Howell Pryse for 2635 lb tobo.

page 185. Itt is ordered that on performance and paymt of 24 dayes work by Denis Kigan to Wm Egbrough, the sd Egbrough pay to the sd Kigan three barrells of Indian corne and cloathing accoustomed, for his service, wth costs, als exec.

page 185. Capt Jno Epes present

page 185. Itt is ordered that mr John Cogan who married the relict and exer'x of Capt Richd Tye dec'd pay to mr Tho: Drewe the sum of 1313 lb of good tobbo and cask and 71: 17s: 8d sterl money found due by acc'ot assigned from Howell Pryse wth costs, als exec.

page 185. The Cort hath bound and intrusted John the orphane of Jo: Slaid decd apprentice to Wm Edwards cowper untill the sd orphane be 21 yeares of age, And ordered that the sd Edwards educate and teach the sd child w'th his best endeavour in the sd trade or profession of a cowper, and give caution for performance thereof by himselfe or his sonne.

page 185. Abstract. Phill Elliott ord to pay Mr Jno. Drayton 1073 lb. tobo. ack'd due.

page 185. Abstract. Dif betw James Warradine and Edward Wolverton referred "to the sole and full determinacon of mr Antho: Wyatt".

page 185. Edd Hill present.

page 185. Ordered that the sherr' do sumon by vertue hereof the personall appearance of Richard Parker to answer at the next Co'rt concerning the maintenance of James Wihhert (Wishert) w'ch he hath not performed according to agreemt.

page 186. The Co'rt on behalfe of the parish of Westover have contracted and agreed w'th John fflowers to keepe and mainteine James Wishert dureing his life w'th Dyett washing lodging and attendance according to his condicon, for performance whereof he confesseth Judgemt in Cort, in consideracon whereof Itt is ordered that the vestrey of the sd parish or any of them pay to the sd fflowers or his assgs 1500 lb of good legal tobbo and cask the 20th of 8br next in some conven't place in the sd parish, als exec and costs.

page 186. Mr Edward Hill sworne Com'r according to eleccon of the last Assembly

page 186. Lt John Howell is hereby authorized to seize and distreine the estate of Wm Short in this Com for paymt of 247 lb tobbo parish dues

page 186. Abstract. Thos. Batts gent ord to pay Jno. Drayton mercht 1357 lb tobo per bill assg from Mr Henry Randolph.

page 186. Ordered that Nicholas Perry give by a Copie hereof to any person or persons interessed in the state of Edward Greenwood to appe' at the next Co'rt for this Com. And bring and present an Inventorie of the sd estate, att w'ch time ord'r shalbe for disposall of the sd estate as the Co'rt shall find just cause.

page 186. Abstract. Capt Tho. Stegge ord to pay Tho: Mather 200 lb tobo.

page 186. The Co'rt doth hereby tolerate Lycence permitt and allow Robt Rowse onely to keepe a publick Inne or ordinary in any the Co'rt howses of this Com and to sell drink of any sort, And ord'r that he enter into bond to keepe good ord'r and sell according to rules to be hereafter sett downe according to law

page 187. Abstract. Dif betw Wm Lea and Rice Hoe to next Court.

page 187. Mr Stephen Hamelin is sworne sherr according to elecoon of the Governor and Councell, for whom Capt Thomas Stegge hath promised and undertaken in Co'rt to be security for due execucon of the place according to Law.

page 187. Samuell Smith sworne undersherr

page 187. mr Richard Cock hath declared and testified in this Co'rt that on the first day of June last he saw a search made in the records of Henrico Com for an ord'r at the suite of Capt Tho: Stegge agst the admir'or estate of John Devall dec'd, and that no sucper (sic) ord'r was found in the sd records

page 187. Upon the peti'con of Tho: Batts gent and a probability that his brother mr Wm Batts is dead, The Cort hath ordered that all the cattell belonging to the sd Tho: Batts and his brother Henry Batts be delivered unto him the sd Thomas, he giveing good caution to keepe the Co'rt harmlesse, And that the male cattell belonging to the sd Wm Batts shalbe and remaine in the hands and custody of his attorn' mr Tho: Holford.

page 187. Whereas Capt Richd Tye att a Co'rt holden in August last at Westover Did freely give to the use of this Com halfe an acre of land at merchts hope for ever (according to his title and tenure) inhereon to build and continue a Co'rt house and prison for the Com use, as by testimony of divers gent of the Comicon doth appe', upon wch land the Co'rt haveing gratefully accepted the sd offer and guift, hath caused to be erected two howses for the uses aforesd; This Co'rt doth therefore continue and establish the sd Donacon to be and continue to this Com use as aforesd.

page 188. Itt is ordered that 1500 l tobbo be raised at the next Levie of this Com, and paid to mr Steph: Hamelin for mr Wm Drum'ond for an arreare of the publick Levie since the yeare 1656

page 188. Capt Robt Wynne and Howell Pryse are hereby requested and appointed to prise the estate of Walter Daux, decd, and divide the same to the relict and his two children according to Law.

page 188.
To the right worp'll the Com'rs for the Com of Cha: Cittie
   These presents witnesse that I Anthony Tall haveing in my custodie the orphanes of John Slayd, have thought it good to place one of the orphanes named John Slayd w'th Wm Edwards cooper, provided the said Wm Ed's wilbe bound to learne the sd orphane his sd

trade of a Cooper and withall to bestow upon him suffic't learning for the mannageing thereof, all woh I reffer to the Discreeon of this worp'll Cort whether they think it fitting so to better the sd orphane untill he comes to the age of 21 yeares or else to let him remaine as he is w'th me

  As witnesse my hand this 4th of March 1658 (1658/9)
         The mark of T
Test   Anthony Tall
Tho: Stevenson
      rec Jun: 15. sequ.

page 188.
      April the 4th 1659
Elizabeth Brewer widd confesseth Judgem't to James Parham for 2500 lb of tobbo and cask in consideracon of 1800 lb and cask woh the sd Parham is bound for
       Thomas Drewe
       Anthony Wyatt

     rec Jun: 15. 59

page 188. The deposition of Martin Quelch being about the age of 23 yeares sworne and ex'aed Saith that about Jan'ry last was in the presence of mr Chamberlin and goodman Madard saith that he heard the sd Madard ask the aforesd Chamberlin whether he couk make a perfect cure of his wife and daughter and the aforesd Chamberlin replying that if he did not he would not have a pound of tobbo for his paines, the aforesd Madard replying that he should think his 2500 lbs of tobbo well bestowed, and further y'r dept saith not

        Martin Quelch
Jur. Coram me 8br 26 Ao. 1658
  Thomas Drewe
     rec. Jun. 15. 59

Note: 'he couk make' sic, meaning of course 'he could make'. B.F.

page 189.
  Att a Cort holden at the house of Majr Harris
     Aprill the 1st 1657
Present
     mr Richd Cook
 mr Xpofor Branch mr Henry Isham)
 mr Richd Ward   mr Wm Worsuham) Com'rs
 Capt Wm ffarrar   )

Itt is ordered that George Brewer have a Comicon of admer'acon upon the estate of John Devall he appeering to be the greatest Creditor
      Ver Cop.
         Teste me Jos Tanner Clk

page 189.
  Att a Cor't holden at Curles Jun: the 1st 1657
Present
     mr Richd Cook
 Maj'r Wm Harris Capt Wm ffarrar)
 mr Rich'd Ward   mr Henry Isham) Com'rs
 mr Wm Worsuham mr Tho: Branch)

Itt is ordered that Jo: Coxe and Nichol: Webb have each of them 60 lb tobbo for appraising the estate of John Devall
      Ver cop test me
        Jos: Tanner Cl

page 189.
  Att a Cort holden at Curles Aug: the 1st 1657
present
     mr Rich'd Cook
 Maj'r Wm Harris mr Richd Ward
 mr wm Baugh   mr Tho: ligon
 Capt wm ffarrer mr wm Worsuham
 mr Xpofer Branch

Whereas Geo: Brewer admr of the estate of Jo: Devall dec'd had in his possession the sum of 2332 lb of tobbo and by acc't exhibited hath pd 2076 out of the same, Itt is ordered that the sd Brewer be responsible for the surplus Payd, and then to have certified for Quietus est.
  Ver. cop teste me Jos: Tanner Cl C

    (see next page)

page 189.

      Att a holden at Curles Aprill the first 1657
Present
                  mr Richd Cook
     mr Xpofer Branch   mr Henry Isham)
     mr Richd Ward   mr Wm Worsuham) Com'rs
     Capt Wm ffarrar

Itt is ordered that Rich'd Clarke shall have five hundred and sixtie pounds of tobbo out of the estate of John Devall for his buriall and other charges by him expended

                Ver cop teste me Jos. Tanner Cl Cur
              rec Jun: 15 59

page 190.

   Recd by me Geo Brewer out of the estate of John Devall   tobo
the sume of   2332

Disbursed by me George Brewer out of the sd estate
   To Richd Clark by ordr of Cort   560
   To the appraisers by ord'r of Co'rt   120
   To me by specialty   865
   To the Clearke for fees   251
   To my selfe for trouble in Takeing the Inventory   280

                                                               2076
   to charge in adm'racon   256

                                                               2332

                        rec Jun: 15, 1659

page 190.

The deposition of Antho: Allen taken and sworne this 25th day of 8br 1658 aged 28 yeares or thereabouts
     Saith
That whereas there was an agree'mt made betweene Wm Chamberlin surgeon and Tho: Madder about a cure w'ch the sd Chamberlin was to performe on the wife of the s'd Madder and also his daughter, he being there at the sd Madders house heard the agreemt, wch he saith was that the sd Madder was to give the sd Chamberlin 2500 lb of tobbo in case the sd Chamberlin did make a perfect cure on the afore sd wife and daughter of the sd Madder. And if he did not make a perfect cure the sd Chamberlin Did say he would have nothing. And further saith not

                                    the mark of
Jur Coram me   Antho: X Allen
Thomas Drewe
                  rec Jun: 15. 59

C 11   43

page 191.
            Att a Cort holden att Westov'r Aug. 3. 1659
Present
                        Coll Edward Hill esqr
        mr Thomas Drewe   mr Edward Hill
        mr Anthony Wyatt   mr Jo: Holmwood
        Capt Robt Wynne

page 191. Abstract. Jno. Howell allowed to employ an Indian

page 191. "Jo Stith nonsuite Rowse w'th costs accustomed"

page 191. Ordered that the sherr' seize and cause to be Legally
valued such cattell of ffrancis Redford as shall satisfie the debt
for wc'h the sd Redford is imprisoned at suite of Wm Gillard and
all costs thereof appending, and thereupon release the person of
the sd prisoner

page 191. Capt Stegge present

page 191. Abstract. Mr Jno. Drayton allowed to employ an Indian.

page 191. Whereas Richd Parker hath contrary to Law lent a gunn
to an Indian, by the force of wch transgressed law he hath incurred
the penaltie of 2000 lb tobbo halfe to the inform'r and halfe to
the Com.
    Itt is therefore ordered that the sd Parker shall pay to the
Com of Charles Citty 1000 lb tobbo And to Lt John Howell who in-
formed and presented the premises 1000 lb tobbo and all costs of
the suite, als exec.
    Lt Jo: Howell hath released and remitted in Cort the sd 1000
lb tobbo Due to him as inform'r of the premisses

page 191.   July 4. 1659
I Wm Greene confesse Judgmt to mr Tho: Drewe for 2000 lb of good
tobbo pick'd and cull'd according to act wth suffic't Cask conteyn-
ing the same to be pd to the sd mr Drewe or his assgs in one intire
paymt at my now dwelling wth costs als exec
                                sign
                                William x Greene
Recognit Coram nobis
Robert Wynne
Anthony Wyatt   rec Aug. 6. 1659
                          per H Pryse Cl

page 191. Itt is ordered that Richard Parker do forthwth give Caution to discharge the parish of Westov'r from 1500 lb tobbo and cask w'ch they are to pay for the necessary sustenance of James Wishert whom the sd Parker obliged himselfe to keepe but hath not performed w'th costs als exec.

page 191. John fflowers sworne Constable for sherley hundred precinct.

page 192. Abstract. Lease. "This indenture made the second day of August in the yeare of our Lord God 1659 Betweene Richd Parker of the pa'ish of Westov'r in the Com of Charles Citty in Virginia chirurgeon of the one part and John Beauchamp of the place aforesd mer'cht". Parker sells Beauchamp "his planta'con at Digges his hundred in the parish aforesd", 110 acres. Certain agreemts re live stock.
Wit: signed Rich Parker
Edward Hill Junr
Thomas Stegge
Jno Holmwood
Howell Pryse Cl Cur pre'dt   rec. Aug. 6. sequ.

page 193. Ordered that mr Jo: Cogan keepe and mainteine Jos: Reynolds till the next Co'rt w'th all necessary Dyett Lodging and endeavo'r of cure according to contract at wch time further course may be taken for the necessitie of the sd poore impotent person.

page 194. Be it knowne unto all men by these presents that I Wm Edwards of the Com of Cha: Citty in Virga cowper for and in consideracon of marriage contracted and solemnized w'th Margaret the relict of Wm Stadword decd, and for and in consideracon of my love and affeccon to Wm and Joice the orphanes of the sd Stadword and for their better subsistance hereafter do hereby freely clerly and absolutely give graunt and bestow unto the sd children vidz: unto Wm Stadword one black cow called Starr about five yeares old and one heyfer about a yeare old both marked w'th a fflower de Luce on the left eare and a slitt in the right eare. And unto the sd Joice Stadword one black white faced cowe called Lilly about four yeares old, one heyfer about halfe a yeare old and one cow calfe all marked wth a fflower de Luce in the left eare and two slitts in the right eare To have hold enjoy and possesse x x x And in case of mortality of either of the sd children dureing their minority the sd whole stock w'th increase as abovesd to Divolve and come to the surviv'r x x In wittnesse whereof I have hereunto sett my hand and seale this second day of July 1659.
Wit:
Jone x Cordell   the m'k and seale of
Howell Pryse   Wm XI seale Edwards

Indors: Recognit in Cur Aug 3. 1659 (etc). Rec Aug. 6. sequ.

page 195. Abstract. Dif betw Mr Anthony Wyatt and Mr Jas Crewes to be settled by Coll Edd Hill and Capt Thos Stegge

page 195. Abstract. Mr Theod: Bland and Mr Ferdinando Aston mutually conf. judgt. for 10000 lb tobo for final settlement of dif betw them by Coll Edd Hill and Mr Warham Horsmonden

page 195. Abstract. Order that Richd. Taylor pay Mr Warham Horsmonden 659 lb tobo due.

page 195. Dan: Murraine nonsuite w'th costs accoustomed

page 195. Abstract. Mary Ast widow to give bond to protect Court and County of Cha: City from trouble concerning estate belonging to her children by descent from their late father John Ast dec'd. Also that the estate "be legally prised".

page 195. Abstract. Dif betw Mr Lea and Mr How to be tried by a Jury. This name doubtless Hoe – see item to follow.

page 195. Abstract. Rice Hoe ord. to pay Wm Lea 4 cows and 1 heifer.

page 195. Abstract. Two nonsuits granted Robt Evans agst Mr Jno Cogan.

Note: Dr. Cogan must have expressed his opinion. See below. B.F.

page 195. Ordered that mr John Cogan enter into bond w'th good Caution for the good abeareing before he Dep't the Co'rt.

page 195. Itt is ordered that mr John Cogan and mr Rice Hoe or either of them shall by the end of the next Com Cort pay to Lt John Banister for Thomas Tanner fifteene pounds of good beaver for w'ch they ingaged themselves for appeance of the King of Weynoke, wherein he failed, and all costs incident to the proceedings of Thomas Tanner ag'st the sd King of Weynoke, als exec agst them or either of them and costs.

Note: To w'ch the King of Weynoke probably remarked 'Ugh' – if anything. B.F.

page 196.

Know all men by these presents that I Samuell Woodward heire to Christppher Woodward dec'd do assigne over to mr Anthony Wyatt his heires and ass's for ever four hundred and fiftie acres of Land lying in the South side of Appomattock bounded as is expressed in my pattent of six hundred acres the sd four hundred and fiftie acres to be next adjoyning to my hundred and fifty. Witnes my hand this 8th of October 1650.

Wit:
Simeon Trenser
Robert Burgis

       Samuell x Woodard
       his mark

rec Aug. 8. 1659

page 196. Abstract. Dif betw Capt Henry Perry esqr and Willm Lambson to next court

page 196. Abstract. Order that Edw. Greenwood's est. in this Co be delivered to Edward Ellis for use of sd Greenwood's child.

page 196. Ordered that there be pd and allowed to Coll Edd Hill esqr at the next Levy 700 lb tobbo for wch he is to cause to be sufficient-ly Covered the Co'rt howse at Westov'r And find timber nailes &c w'thout publiq' charge: And that 3800 lb tobbo be then levied and pd to John Stith for wch he is to finish and complete the sd Co'rt house w'th seeleing dawbing windows new locus posts and all things necessary according to agreem't w'th the Co'rt

page 196. Abstract. Mr Jno. Holmwood permitted to employ an Indian according to law.

page 196. Abstract. Dif betw Capt Tho. Stegge and Francis Grey to be settled by Mr. Thos. Drewe at his house by 10th Sept next.

page 197. The first day of September next is appointed for the orphanes Co'rt to be held at mer'chts Hope

page 197. Abstract. Capt Jno Epes, Mr Charles Sparrow and Mr Francis Epes each fined 300 lb tobo for absence from Court. Sheriff to collect.

page 197. Abstract. Power of Atty. Capt Henry Pery esqr "now by Gods permicon bound for England" to "my trustie and welbeloved friend" Stephen Hamelin of Cha. City Co., gent., to collect debts and transact other business. Dated 7 Feb 1658/9.
Wit:
Will Mumford   signed Hen: Pery
Ste: Hamelin Jn'r
                 Rec. 8 Aug. 1659.

page 198.
        Att a Co'rt holden at mer'chts hope Sept: 1. 1659
present   Mr Thomas Drewe
          Mr Anthony Wyatt   Mr Edd Hill
          Capt John Epes

page 198. The Co'rt hath graunted and allowed unto Jo: fflowers out of the estate of Walter Daux decd in consideracon of his wifes bedding 1000 lb tobbo and cask w'thout accot of assetts for the same

page 198. Mr Sparrow present

page 198. Abstract. Com of admr gr Mr Jno Drayton of est of Wm Robinson

page 198. Ordered that Robt Cradock have a full and equall share of the crop made this yeare by his father in law and his mate and himselfe, and be at his owne disposall for his endeavo'r and accomodacon, and have liberty to Comitt his stock of cattell to the care of some trusty friend, but not to be disposed before his full age.

page 198. Ordered that Wm Smith who married the relict of Tho: Blanks be hereby impowered to require recov'r and receive of Mr Richd Nicholas one cowe or any other estate belonging to the orphane of Robt Jones Dec'd and give caution for the sd orphane and her estate   (sic)

page 198. Abstract. Capt Thos. Stegge, Capt. Robt Wynne and Mr Jo: Holmwood fined 300 lb tobo each for absence from Court.

page 198. Mr Antho: Wyatt and Capt Robert Wynne are hereby requested and intrusted to appraise the perishable estate of the orphanes of Capt David Peibils and mr Roger Booker, and the estate of Edmond Bishop as shalbe presented unto them

page 198. Abstract. 1500 lb tobo to be pd Ho: Pryse for making up levy for Westover parish.

pages 199 - 200 - 201. Abstract. Power of Atty. 23 Sept 1658. Roger Welsteed otherwise Roger Walter of the City of Bristoll (England), marriner to John Cogan of Charles City Co.Va. to settle a/c with Phill: Ellyot "late of the Citty of Bristoll shipwright now resident in Virginia". Concerns an obligation dated 21 Oct 1648 for six pounds. (L. 6.). Refers to "the good ship called the Amity of Bristoll of the burthen of 100 tunnes or thereabouts, whereof one Richd Bond went Master, and then bound on a voyage from Bristoll to Virginia"
Wit:
Arth ffarmer   signed   The mk of
Nick Warren   Roger R Welsteed
Joh: Watkin
Christopher x Taylor
Tho: Baylie Sr

Note: Arthur Farmer, Mayor of Bristol 1658.   B.F.

page 201. Abstract. Order that Symon the orphan of Symon Symonds decd be bound to Howell Pryse till full age. He to educate and feed him, etc. "except he be otherwise legally bound to wm Short dec'd, whereof the sd Shorts relict is to make proofe at the next co'rt for this Com haveing warning to appeare by a copie hereof"

page 201. Abstract. Mr Stephen Hamelin given Quietus est of est of Robt fferdinan decd.

page 202. Abstract. Power of Atty. 25 Aug. 1658. John Evans, senr., of the City of Bristol, England, sadler, to John Cogan of Charles. Cittie Com in Virg'a., gent., to settle accounts with "Phillip Ellyott late of the sd Citty of Bristol shipwright now resident in Virginia or wheresoever he can or may be found". "And of and from James Ramage late of the sd Citty of Bristoll Barber chirurgeon", or either of them. Refers to bond dated 22 Sept. 1658 "wherein they the sd Phillip Ellyott and James Ramage stand Jointly and severally bound to me", in the sum of six pounds (L 6.). Also refers to the

ship John of Bristol of 100 tons burden, having gone to Virginia
and returned.
Wit: signed   John x Evans
Thomas Morgan
Robert Deffell (or Dessell)
Ann Dunne
Richard Price
John Osborne
Thomas Baylie   Rec. 8 Sept. 1659

page 203. Whereas I Charles Sparrow and Capt Richd Tye late decd form'ly tooke up by a Joint pattent 2500 acres of land scituate and being at the old Towne neere merchts hope whereof I acknowledge the sd Capt Tye pro'v'd rights for 1000 acres of the sd land. And in his life time drew a crosse line betwixt the 1500 acres of land for wch I prov'd rights to and the 1000 acres due to him; And though by Law all of the sd land by the decease of him the sd Tye of right belongs to me the sd Sparrow, I out of my owne free will do by these presents give deliv'r and make ov'r all my right and title unto the aforemenconed 1000 acres of land being part of the pattent for 2500 acres of Land unto Elizabeth Tye the eldest daughter of him the sd Richd Tye Late dec'd for ev'r according to the right I hold it by pattent and shalbe ready upon request to acknowledge this my act in Co'rt

In witnesse whereof I have hereunto put my hand and seale this 7th Day of July 1659
                                        Charles Sparrow
Signed sealed and deliv'ed
in the presence of us
Thomas Drewe   John Epes

Md It is added and condiscended by me Charles Sparrow abovesd that in case of Decesse of the sd Elizabeth Tye dureing her minority the sd 1000 acres of Land above given and graunted w'th all my rights and previledges thereof shall descend and come by hereditary succession to the surviv'r or surviv'rs of the orphanes of Capt Richd Tye aforesd decd witnes my hand this first day of Sept: 1659
Test
Thomas Drewe   Charles Sparrowe

                    rec. 7'br. 8. 59
                    (8th September 1659)

page 203.

                Att a Co'rt at Weynoke Sept: 10: 1659
Present   mr Tho: Drewe
      mr Antho: Wyatt   mr Cha: Sparrowe
      Capt Tho: Stegge   Capt Robt Wynne

page 203. Whereas Arthur the orphane of mr Wm Lawrence dec'd haveing certeine chattells in his mothers hands to be de'lred at his full age and departed this life in his minority not possest of any the premisses; Itt is therefore the opinion of this Co'rt that the sd chattells do and shall belong to Peter Plumer who married the relict and ex'rix of the sd mr Lawrence

page 204.

           Att a Co'rt holden att merchts hope Octobr. 3. 1659
present   mr Thomas Drewe
      mr Anthony Wyatt   Capt Robert Wynne
      Capt John Epes

page 204. Abstract. Thos. Holford to be pd 450 lb tobo from est of Nicholas Poole decd with one year's interest.

page 204. Abstract. Dif betw Wm Hill plt and Jo: Cogan deft to next Court.

page 204. Mr Hill present

page 204. Abstract. Lt. John Howell bound with Mary Ast, 10000 lb tobo to protect the Court from claims of orphans of Jno. Ast dec'd.

page 204. Elizabeth Short widd confesseth Judgmt to mr James Crewes for fifteene good large beav'r skins in season to be pd him or his ass's the first day of Jan'ry next als exec for the same and costs

page 204. Coll: Hill, mr Holmwood
        and mr ffrancis Epes present

page 204. The suite of Edd Hatcher agst Capt Edd Mathewes is referred to the next Co'rt, and order to passe agst the sherr for what shalbe found due in case of nonappeance of the sd defte

page 204. Abstract. The suit of Nicholas Perry agst Capt Edd Mathewes to next court. Entry worded as above.

page 204. Wm Lambson ordered to pay Capt Henry Perry esqr 420 lb tobo due by bill to Capt Bishopp with 5 yrs int.

page 204. Ordered that Wm Lea pay unto Richd Taylor 350 lb of good legall tobbo. and cask Due per a bill of his predecessor Thomas ffelton w'th costs, als exec.

page 205. Ordered that Henry Gerard stand comitted till he enter into bond w'th good caution for his good abearing and appeance at the next Co'rt.

page 205. The difference betweene Jane Wms plt and Henry Gerard Defte is refferred to the next Co'rt

page 205. Abstract. Dif. betw. Richard Carter plt. and Thomas Stevenson deft. to be tried by Jury.

"Jury impanelled vidzt
mr Geo: Potter foreman   John fflowers
mr ffran: Grey   Morgan Jones
mr Jo: Drayton   Moris Rose
mr fferd Aston   John Howell
Wm Justice   Walter Holdsworth
Wm Sanders   Augustin Willyard

The verdict
We find for the plt tenn pounds of tobbo Damages, and the defendt and his wife to ask the plt and his wife forgivenesse in open Co'rt
     The Cort giveth Judgmt according to this verdict, wth costs to be pd by the defendt, als exec. "

page 205. Abstract. Mr. Jno Drayton admr of Wm Robinson dec'd ord to pay Jas Salmon 250 lb tobo for 'accomodacon' of sd Robinson.

"Ordered that Mr John Drayton admr of Wm Robinson dec'd pay to John Burton for endeavo'r of cure of the sd Robinson 250 lb tobbo out of the estate, als exec.

page 205. Ordered that John Thompson adm'r of Xpofr Greenfield be first pd his charges and disbursemts as shall appe' due out of the Decedts estate

page 205. Abstract. Com of admr of est of Richd Bayley decd to Dorothie Bayley widow.

page 205. Abstract. Mr Jno Cogan and Wm Hill conf judgt for 5000 lb tobo and to agree to settlement of dif by Coll Edd Hill esqr and Mr Theoderick Bland.

page 205. Abstract. Mrs Hanna Aston by her attor Mr Walter Aston conf judgt to Mr Thos Drewe for L 1: 7: 6.

page 206. Thomas Stevenson hath in open Co'rt asked forgivenesse for his abuse and slander of Richd Carter and his wife acknowledgeing to be heartily sorry for the same
page 206. Abstract. Johanna Stevenson as above. Duplicate wording.

page 206. Abstract. Com of admr to Wm Edwards of est of William Stadword decd, he having married the relict.

page 206. Abstract. Mr Stephen Hamelin ord to pay Mr Tho Drewe 342 lb tobo and L 5. 7. 6 sterl with costs of suit agst Jno Gilham in case Gilham does not appear.

page 206. Abstract. Comm'rs to meet 25 Oct at Merchants Hope for proportioning levies.

page 206. Abstract. Francis Grey to pay Capt Tho Stegge 200 lb tobo in settlemt of dif.

page 206. Abstract. Mr Tho Drewe to settle dif betw Peter Plum'er and Mr Jno Drayton.

page 206. Abstract. Robt Evans a/c of est of Mr John Gibbs approved. Quietus est, he paying debts and the widow her thirds.

page 206. The deposit' of Mary Samborne aged 31 yeares or thereabouts ex'aed and sworne sayth that about the 15th of Aug. last I heard Tho. Stevensons wife call Richd Carters wife whore many times, and Stevenson and his wife did hold up their hands and told her she was knowne to be a whore from Kicotan to the falls and said the child in her armes was a bastard and she sayd she fluttered and flourished in Birds feathers ev'ry day and called her bitch and bid her go home to her whelpe, and sayd if her son came on their ground she would criple him or pull off his eares, and at their parting she told her she would be revenged of her and would do her a mischiefe by day or night, and the night foll' the sd Carters wife being in the pasture Stevensons wife came to her againe and told her she would give her a whores mark ere it was long, and Stevenson called her husband old rogue many times, and further saith not.

Note: My goodness! - How would you like to join the Colonial Dames or the Colonial Wars on that item ?   B.F.

page 207. Wm Justice hath proved right by Indentures and testimony produced to 1200 acres of land for the importacon of 24 persons Vidzt

Wm Edds	Elizab: Harris	Peter Plumer
Tho: Atwell	Marian Chance	Mary Plumer
Robt Midleton	Richd Clark	Alexander - -
John Crowe	Olliv'r Hunt	Ann Plumer
Alex: Hewett	Edd Hanscome	Mary Cooper
Wm Price	Cornel' Clemence	Ann Lucai
Edd Beck	Jo. Hatley	Sara Stiles
Mary Durdaine	Tho. Llewellin	Rebecca Heatham

Proved vidzt per Indentures	10
by mr Astons oath	2
by Wm Justice oath	1
by Peter Plum'ers oath	11

Jur in Cur 8 br 3. 1659
Test Hoel Pryse Cl

page 207. Abstract. Business to next Court in December at Westover.

page 207. Abstract. Deposition of Wm Dollin aged 40 yeares or thereabouts , same as that of Mary Samborne re. the Stevenson - Carter quarrel. Dollin prob. gives the key to the mischief in adding "That about the 15th day of Aug. last Tho. Stevenson and Sara the wife of Rich: Carter being in the Pasture a talking together the sd Stevensons wife came up the hill to them and presently called the sayd

Carters wife whore " etc.
  Rebecca the wife of Wm Dollin, aged 26 yeares or thereabouts, deposition in duplicate of foregoing. Her's signed Rebecca x Dowlin.

Jur Coram me
7 br 3. 1659
Charles Sparrowe   Rec 8. 29 sequ.   (29 October 1659)

page 208.
           Att a Co'rt holden att merchts hope 8 br 25. 1659
Present   mr Thomas Drewe
       mr: Antho: Wyatt   Capt Robt Wynne
       Capt Tho: Stegge   mr Edd Hill
       Capt John Epes

Ordered that 29 lb tobbo per poll be forthw'th collected by the sherr (by distresse if needfull) on the tytheables of the whole Com and paid as foll Vidzt

	lb tob
Coll Edd Hill esqr for burgesse charge	3300
mr Warham Horsmonden per	3300
mr Hamelin for charges	0430
Howell Pryse for arreares &c	2218
to him for c'op publick proceedings &c	1100
Morgan Jones for 2 wolves	0200
mr Holford for 1	0100
Richd Baker and Tho: Parham for 3	0300
Henry Newcome for 1	0100
Capt Wynne for Wm Reynes for 1	0100
Henry Gilham for 1	0200
Lt Howell for 1 wolfe and boate hire	0200
Sam'll Ealle for 1	0100
Capt John Epes for boate hire	0060
James Parham for Com service	0100
to the sherr' to pay 2 men for 6 dayes apiece	0120
to him for Com list	0500
To Sallery for Collecon	1230

	13558
to mr Hamelin for S'r Wm Berkeley per ord'r	1500

And that 10 lb tobbo per poll be likewise levied and collected on the South side of the Com and pd as foll   vidzt

To Capt Tho: Stegge for arrears	1870
to Lt Banister for 10 cutts timber	0300
to mr Thos Drewe for nailes	0600
cr To Sallery	0277

	3047

(continued)

County Expenses 25 October 1659. (continued)
page 208.

And on the north side the Com 4 lb per poll and pd vidzt
To Coll Edd Hill esqr for cov'r the Co'rt howse   700
to Sallery   70

                                                          770

page 209.
And on Westov'r parish in particular 14 lb per poll and pd vidzt
To Coll Edd Hill esqr per ord'r   1100
To Howell Pryse per order   1650
To Sallery   275

                                                         3025

page 209. Abstract. Attachmt to Mr Charles Sparrow 5511 lb tobo agst est of William Short decd.

page 209. Abstract. Order dated ar Westover 21 Dec. 1652 binding Richard the orphan of Peter Holmes decd to Mr Wm Worsuham to be extended to include his heirs, exors or assgs for the term.

page 209. Abstract. Indenture. 10 Oct 1659. John Cogan of Merchants Hope in Cha. City Co. chirurgeon, sells Anthony Wyatt of Chaplines Choice in same Co. gent., for bond for L 240. Sterling, dated 1st Sept. 1659, the plantation "whereon he now dwelleth", 5 negro servants, crops, etc.
Wit: signed   Jno Cogan
Robert Wynne
Howell Pryse Cl   Rec. 28 Oct. 1659.

page 211. Abstract. Robert Nicholson discharged from guardianship of Robert the orphan of Robert Herdman "he now being at full age".
   Robert Herdman, also shown in the entry as Hardman, releases Robt Nicholson from bond to Capt Tho Stegge and Mr War Horsmonden for delivery of estate. Dated 20 October 1659
Wit:
Warham Horsmonden   signed   Robert Hardman
Samuell Smith
                  Rec. 28 Oct. 1659

page 212. Abstract. Agreement dated 3 April 1656. betw William Short and Amee Symonds widow. Wm Short "will take into my tuicon the two boyes Symon Symonds and Samll Symonds and the bigger girle called Margarett Symonds till they come to age and the younger girle called Elizabeth Symonds to be as my owne finding them w'th meat drinke and apparell dureing the time aforesd, and to keepe her the abovesd Amee Symonds wth Dyett and apparell dureing her life". Amee Symonds makes over plantation, cattle etc to Short, with the provision that the children return to her in case of his death.
Wit:
Georg x Dowglas   Signed   Wm x Short
ffoulk Moulson   Ame x Symonds

                    Recorded 28 October 1659

page 213. These presents oblige me Arthur Graunt to Carry Thomas Poythres in my ship this yeare for England and at his arrivall there in case mr George Laud shall not accomodate him w'th Dyett and lodging, I do hereby oblige my selfe to do it untill the retorne of the next shipping to this Countrey of Virginia, w'ch I am to do gratis w'thout expecting any pay, and the next yeare to bring him into this Countrey againe he paying for his passage inward as others doe. To the performance whereof I bind me my heires ex'rs and adm'rs and In testimony thereof have hereunto put my hand this 30th of November 1659
Wit: Arthur Graunt
John Stith
Thomas Malory   rec 10'br 3. 59

page 213.
                At a Co'rt holden at Westov'r Dec. 3, 1659
present   mr Tho: Drewe
           Capt Tho: Stegge   Capt Edd Hill
           mr Cha: Sparrow   mr Jo Holmwood

page 213. Abstract. Attachmt to John Gilham agt Antho: Tall's est for 1100 lb tobo per bill.

page 213. Whereas a warrt issued that John Burton should deliv'r a woman serv't belonging to Tho: Mudgett, and he fayled therein, the Co'rt doth therefore hereby appoint the sherr to seize the sd servt out of the sd Burtons hands and render to the sd Mudgett or his assgs.

page 213. By reason of the bad weather and inconvenience for accomodacon of the Com'rs and others at this time and place, This present Co'rt (and all dependencies to it) is adjorned and referred to be held and had at Merchts hope the second Day of January next.

page 213. Abstract. Jno Stith ord to appear and explain neglect of duties.

page 213. Abstract. 15 Nov. 1659. John Tomson releases Isaac Ebbs from service for a year.
Wit: signed   John x Tomson
Willm Stenton
                        Rec. 3 Dec. 1659

page 214. Abstract. Bond. 14 March 1658/9. 300 pounds lawful money of England. George Potter, Wm Hatcher and Henry Randolph of Virginia, gents., to Willm Breuton "of Newport in Rode Island", merchant and Mathew Burne of Boston in New England marin'r. Payable 1 May 1659.
Wit:
Rich Webley   signed   George Potter
Ho: Pryse   Will Hatcher
John fflowers   Henry Randolph
                        Rec. 4 Jan 1659/60

page 215.
            Att a Co'rt holden att mer'chts hope Jan'ry 2: 1659
present   mr Thomas Drewe
         mr Antho: Wyatt   Capt Robt Wynne
         Capt John Epes   mr ffrancis Epes

page 215. Abstract. Com of admr of est of Thomas Tanner deceased to Lt John Banister.

page 215. Abstract. Mr John Dibdall conf. judgt to Mr Thomas Drewe for 1410 lb tobo and L 3: 14 Sterl money.

page 215. Abstract. Capt Otho Southcot conf. judgt to Mr John Dibdall minister for 480 lb tobo.

page 215. Whereas Wm Tottersell now servt to mr Antho: Wyatt and Joseph Stepp now servt to Capt Thomas Stegge came into this Country w'thout Covent apper-rit on their part for their service. And whereas by lre of mr John Bird of London a Credible man, and a sealed contract on his parte, it appereth that the agreemt w'th the sd servts parents or other friends was for eight yeares each of them: Itt is therefore ordered that the sd Tottersell and Stepp shall serve and complete the time of eight yeares aforesd from their arriveall, except an agreemt shalbe produced and proved from England for a different time

page 216.

Brother Stegge

My love &c Inter salia. According to yo'r Desire I have sent yu 2 lustie lads out of our towne of Edmonton, one his father is a shoemaker his name is Tatersoale I beleeve yu nev'r met w'th such an arch youth, and the other his father is a Chapman I desire yu may write to me of them, if they come safe because of my pleaseing their fathers

Ultra The boyes I being so sick could not bind them but agreed for eight yeares and have signed and sealed my Indentures and gave my vucle (sic) order to bind them aboard

        Yo'r ev'rlo: Brother to Comand
London 21. 8ber 1658   John Byrd

    rec Jan'ry 11. 59
     (1659/60)

page 216. Abstract. Rice Hoe conf. judgt to Mr John Dibdall for 410 lb. tobo.

page 216. Abstract. Phillip Ellyott, for himself and Wm Ranger, conf. judgt. to Capt John Wall for 800 lb. tobo.

page 216. Abstract. Judgt granted Capt Jno Wall agst est of Capt Wm Odeon for 349 lb tobo and 3 yrs interest.

page 216. mr Sparrowe present

page 216. Abstract. Thomas Warren and John Toppin conf. judgt. to admrs of Joseph Dunne decd for 400 lb tobo.

page 216. Abstract. Mr Cha. Sparrow to settle dif re land betw Thos Morgan and Edw Richards page 216. Abstract. That a Jury decide dif betw Wm Johnson and Thos Richman

page 217. Abstract. Henry Leadbeater ordered to pay Mr Jno Cogan 816 lb tobo.

page 217. Morgan Jones hath undertaken in Co'rt to keepe and mainteine Jane the orphane of Thomas East dec'd for the rest of her time according to the Indentures made w'th her by John Griffith, w'ch the Co'rt confirmeth

page 217.
    The humble peticon of Thomas Stevenson
    To the worp'll Board   Humbly sheweth
That whereas yo'r hath his bond lying out and another man bound w'th him for his good behavior, Now all things being agreed and att a period, he doth humbly beseech the worp'll Board he may have the bond in to release his security
                      And yo'r pet'nr shall pray &c
rec Jan'ry 11. 59

Upon peticon of Thomas Stevenson of Martins Brandon all the recognizances for the yeare and good behavior taken and acknowledged before mr Charles Sparrow or at Co'rt for and agst the sd Stevenson are hereby released and made null

page 217. Ordered that John Griffith be first pd and satisfied out of the estate of Alexander Maior decd for the trouble and charge of buriall of the sd Maior

(Alexander Maior ie Major)

page 217. Abstract. Jno Epes to be pd 300 lb tobo from est of Alex: Maior decd.

page 217. Abstract. John fflowers having become security of Richd. Parker at suit of Capt Tho Stegge for 4743 lb tobo and no appearance made, payment is ordered.

page 217. Abstract. "John Maine a poore exempted person" released from this levy.

page 218. Abstract. Jno fflowers security for Richd Parker at suit of Robt Rowse, 530 lb tobo, and no appearance made by deft, is ordered to pay.

page 218. Ordered that mr John Cogan retorne Joseph Reynolds to the place or parish whence he first recd him, and discharge this Com of him, w'ch done the Contract and ord'r agst him are hereby released and made null

page 218. Abstract. Nonsuit granted Martin Quelch agst Richd Parker

page 218. Abstract. Nonsuit granted Tho: Stevens agst Mr John Holmwood

page 218. Abstract. Unfinished business to next Court 3rd Feb. at Merchants Hope.

page 218.
  To the Hono'ble Gov'nor and Counc'll &c
  Wm Johnson humbly sheweth
That Thomas Richman haveing beene accused and apprehended for the fellonious takeing away of the petn'rs goods and burning of a howse, whereupon he fled and was taken w'th the goods is remitted according to law to receive his tryall, but (may it please yo'r Honors) the vast charge and expence of attendance in this place of inevitable high costs will easily exceed all possible compensacon that can be made by the sd defendt
  Wherefore the Petn'r humbly prayeth yo'r Hon'rs so to prevent future expence in the premisses as to remitt and reffer the tryall and decision of the matter to the next Co'rt for Charles Citty Com
       And so shall ev'r pray &c
rec Jan: 20. 59

page 219.
    James Citty 9 br the 29th 1659
The w'thin menconed peticon is reffered to the Co'rt of Charles Citty Com who are required to examine the cawse therein expressed, and if the sd Co'rt shall find suffict cawse to remitt the same to the Governor and Councell otherwise to determine the same as to their discrecons shall seeme requisite and agreeable to Law
       Test Tho: Brereton Cl Cur
rec. Jan: 20 sequ

page 219.

Walter Brookes aged 36 yeares or thereabouts exai'ed and sworne
  Saith
That Jervis Dicks called to the dept and sayd there was the fellow agst whom there was a huy and cry issued, whereupon the Dept put

forth w'th his boate and Robt ffarm'r and the depts servt and pursued the fellow, who turned into a creeke, whereupon the dept called one Lewis Greene a neere neighbor to come wth his cannow because the boate would not flote there, who came, and w'th him and the aforesd persons the Dept made pursuit, and the fellow left his cannow and tooke the swampe but at last the dept and the rest neere ov'rtakeing the fellow, he came to meet them, and had w'th him a rapier and about 1/2 l of powder the dept saying he thought an honest man should not turne out of his way, and then apprehended the fellow and desired him to go along w'th us, and the fellow prayed to have his cassock and blankett so the dept conveyed the fellow to his howse for that night, and the next day rendred him to the Constable of that precinct, and further saith not

         Walter X Brookes his mark

Jur in Cur Jan'ry 2. 1659
Test Hoel Pryse   Cl
     rec Jan'ry. 20. sequ

      The Jury vidzt
Ca Otho Southcott foreman	mr Tho: Broome
mr Jo. Drayton	mr Richd Taylor
mr Jo. Banister	mr Ja: Blamore
mr Tho: Holford	mr Wm Sanders
mr Rice Hoe	mr Tho: Calloway
mr Jo. Stirdevant	mr John Gilham

      verdict vidzt
    We find it a trespasse

page 220
   Att a Cort holden att merchts hope ffebr: 3. 1659
present   mr Thomas Drewe
   mr Anthony Wyatt Capt Robt Wynne
   Capt John Epes mr ffran: Epes

page 220. Abstract. Wm Rawlinson conf judgt to Geo. Barfoote 1050 lb tobo.

page 220. Abstract. James Rayner conf judgt to Geo. Barfoote 473 lb tobo.

page 220. Abstract. Theophilus Beddingfield conf. judgt. to William Rawlinson 524 lb tobo.

page 220. Abstract. Order that Thomas Mather pay Jone Thomas 470 lb tobo due, "and if any goods belonging to the sd Mather or his wife be in the hands of the sd Jone Thomas that they be rendered unto him"
    Jone Thomas assigns right in above to Mr John Beauchamp, Feby 3rd 1659/60.

page 220. Abstract. Jury to try case betw Wm Johnson and Thomas Richman. Also to inquire re "damages of Thomas Richman for his restraint and imprisonmt".

page 220. Abstract. Tho Warren and John Toppin to peaceably have a cow purchased from Thos Mather. They conf. judgt. to Mather 176 lb tobo.

page 221. Abstract. Deed. 25 Sept 1657. Patrick Jackson and Richard Baker sell James Ward 100 acres, part of 1500 acres patented by Mr Richard Jones, minister. "bounded as followeth: North upon the merchts and running in Length along the heads of Thomas Wheelers land till it extend it selfe from the merchts land to the mark'd trees of Capt Richard Tye, w'ch makes the length to runne due South, and the breadth East upon Wheeler and West upon our owne land". Refers to the plantation that Richard Baker is seated upon.
Wit:
Richard x Colsyth   signed   Patrick Jackson
                                                  Richard x Baker

                     Rec. 15 Feby 1659/60

page 222. Abstract. Anna Church servant to Jane Williams having absented herself 160 days, has that time doubled.

page 222. mr Edd Hill present.

page 222. Abstract. Wm Wilkins ordered to release to Mrs Frances Letherland a parcel of her land now held by him.

page 223.
> Jury Inter Johnson and Richman
> mr John Drayton foreman   mr Tho: Holford
> mr James Crewes   mr Willm Hill
> mr Tho: Malory   mr Ja: Ward
> mr Jo: Beauchamp   mr Tho: Mather
> mr Jo: fflowers   mr Jo Stirdevant
> mr Tho: Crane   mr John Gilham

The 36. act of Assembly how presents charges are to be borne
whereon indorsed
> The Juries verdict vidzt

We of the Jury do deliv'r our verdict to be according to the act of Assembly whereof the inclosed is a copie
> Judgemt is graunted on this verdict.

page 223.
A list of the men impanelled upon a Jury by me James Warradine this 2. day of ffebr 1659   (1659/60)
> mr Richd Taylor   Thomas Ham'ond
> mr James Ward   Tho: Dowglas
> mr Rice Hoe   Henry Bankes
> Wm Sanders   James Wallis
> Sam: Lucie   Tho: Tomlinson
> Thomas Crooke   Edd Amas
> Verdict

We find the corps cleere w'thout any bones broke or any wounds
> Rich: Taylor

page 223. Itt is ordered that Walter Hind servt to mrs Hanna Aston shall according to the act for Irish servts serve continue and complete the full tearme of six yeares from the time of arriveall, and make good the time neglected.

page 223. Abstract. Wm Bush ord to pay Mr Jno Beauchamp 1000 lb tobo.

page Md. That Anthony Gardiner arrived in Virginia by his owne report in Co'rt the first day of 9 br last.

page 224. Abstract. Wm Vaughan conf. judgt. to Mr Jno Beauchamp for 610 lb tobo.

page 224. Abstract. Dispute regarding a cow betw Richard Pace and Jno Drayton to be settled by Mr James Ward and Mr Richd Taylor page 224. Abstract. Elizabeth Short widow conf judgt to Lt. John Banister for 552 lb tobo.

page 224. Abstract. Judgt and exec to Jno Gilham agst est of Antho: Tall for 1100 lb tobo.

page 224. Abstract. Capt Edward Hill permitted to keep an Indian.

page 224. Abstract. Order renewed Jno Flower agst Capt Wm ODeon in October 1658 for 2 hhds tobo.

page 224. Abstract. Mathew Hogson for Wm Lea confesses judgt to Mr Jno Drayton for 645 lb tobo according to bill assigned from Mr Henry Randolph with 2 yrs interest.

page 225. Abstract. Power of Atty. 6 Jan. 1659/60. William Lea to "my loveing frd" Mathew Hogson to conf. judgt as above.
Wit:
Jno. Gittings　　　　　　　　　　signed　William Lea

page 225. Whereas Richd Parker obliged him selfe in 5000 l tobo to give his attendance on mr Thomas Drewe and his family once each fortnight for twelve monthes and at each other time he should be desired and bestow use and administer his best skill and meanes for the sd mr Drewe and his family, but hath failed in the premisses so that the sd mr Drewe was enforced to have recourse to other men.
  Itt is therefore ordered that the contract be henceforth null, and that the sd Parker shall lose his reward for the few times he hath attended or adm'red meanes, and pay to the sd mr Drewe all that shall appe' to be occasionally expended on other practicon'rs by reason of his neglect and what app'eth due on acco't from him to mr Drewe w'th all costs, als exec.

page 225. Coll Edward Hill esqr hath proved right to 1100 acres of land for the charge of importacon of 22 persons underwritten vidzt

Edd Hill Junr	Jo: Jacob	Joseph, Richd, John
Elizab: Hill	Jo: Merywether	3 negroes
Susanna Brett	Tho: Moore	Long John
Sam: Russell	Walter Maloyne	Thomas Merywether
Walter Rowland	Dorothy Henton	2 Scotch men that dyed at
Jo: Hall	Jo. Barber	James Citty

Note: We hope indeed that the Hon. Coll. Hill, esqr, etc. did not intend to cheat his Sacred Majesty.　　　　　　　　　B.F.

page 225. A refference is graunted to Capt Edd Mathewes till the next Co'rt to produce and prove a statute for illegalitie of raceing wch if he faile then to do Judgemt to passe agst him for mr Hatchers claime, and that the sayd Mathewes give good caution for his appereance at the next Co'rt

page 225. Willm Clay sworne Constable for Weynoke parish

page 226. Abstract. Mrs Susan Nicholas widow of Richd Nicholas ordered to pay Mr John Beauchamp 3551 lb tobo and 6 lb good beaver due from her husband.

page 226. Abstract. Capt. Robt Wynne promises to hold debts of Mr Thos Nothway to John Stirdevant until the next shipping.

page 226. Abstract. Appeal to Gen'l Court granted Walter Hind. (see page 63)

page 226. Abstract. Tho Richman ordered to pay Mr Stephen Hamelin 3000 lb tobo "for the charge of his imploym't and accomodacon".

page 226. Abstract. Richd. Parker to pay Capt Tho Stegge 4743 lb tobo due. Also to pay Robt Rowse 530 lb tobo due.

page 226. Abstract. Nonsuit granted Capt Edd Mathewes agst Nicholas Perry.

page 226. Abstract. Suit of Geo. Douglas agst Elizabeth Short to next Court.

page 227. Abstract. Jno fflowers released from security for Richard Parker, he having appeared at Court.

page 227. Abstract. Edmond Shipdham through Howell Price, his atty, confesses judgt to Mr Saml Smith for 1273 lb tobo. Power of Atty dated 18 Jan 1659/60.

page 227. That mr Anthony Wyatt attorney for mr George Potter hath made tender and offer of paymt in Co'rt of fowr poultry (being actually brought hither and presented by the hands of Daniell Holicrosse) for two years quitrent of and for the land at Jordans whereon mr Potter dwelleth, for the use of mr Theoderick Bland the now proprietor of the sd land

page 227. Coll Edd Hill esqr hereby comandeth and requireth the present sherr to deteine the person and armes or weapons of Capt Edward Mathews untill the sd Mathewes shall enter into bond w'th good Caution for his good abearing and appean'ce at the next Co'rt

page 227. Abstract. Suit of Wm Hunt agst George Douglas to next Court.

page 228.

Att a Co'rt holden at Westov'r ffebr: 20. 1659

present
    mr Thomas Drewe
    mr Antho: Wyatt   Capt Robt Wynne
    Capt Tho. Stegge   Capt Edw. Hill
    mr Cha: Sparrow

page 228. Abstract. Mr Anthony Wyatt, Capt John Epes and Mr Charles Sparrow recom. to the Gov. and Council, one to be app. sheriff.

page 228

Mr Drewe
    At y'r last rayseing the levie the clearke absolutely forgott to include S'r Wm Berkeley's ord'r of 1500 lb tobbo Due this yeare to be satisfied out of our levie. If you please to subscribe this, These may authorize the Clearke to add 3 lb tobbo more in Liewe of that towards paymt:

S'r we are yo'r lo: frds   Edw: Hill
                                Thomas Drewe
To the Com'rs of Cha: Citty   Thomas Stegge
Com & so to mr Howell   Edward Hill Junr
Pryse Clearke of the Co'rt   Anthony Wyatt
                                Francis Epes
                                Robert Wynne
                                John Epes

Record: April: 20: 1660

Att a Co'rt holden at Westov'r April 3. 1660
present   mr Thomas Drewe
      mr Anthony Wyatt   Capt Robt Wynne
      Capt John Epes   Capt Edward Hill

page 229. Abstract. Order that Lt Jno Banister repay to Richd Baker and Thos. Parham 408 lb tobo, they to "make publick acknowledgem't at the next arrivall of Capt Robt ffoxe that the sd tobbo rec'd was of their crop and makeing, and not of Lt Banisters"

page 229. Abstract. Order that John Thompson pay Mr Francis Grey 792 lb tobo due per bill. Also that Thomas Tomlinson pay Grey 311 lb tobo at Martins Brandon due by bill.

page 229. Ordered that Edward Heming continue and serve w'th Richd Parker according to his Indentures to him assigned untill Willm Hunt shall make appeare a better right to the sd servt.

page 229. Whereas Willm Hunt hath contemned a writt sent to him by Capt Edward Hill for his convention before him as appe'th by two positive oathes: Itt is therefore ordered that the sd Hunt shall rest in the custody of the sherr till he enter into bond w'th security for his good abeareing, and pay one thousand pounds of tobbo fine, w'th costs thereof.

page 229. Abstract. Mr Charles Sparrow to settle dif betw. John Thompson and Willm Copeland.
      Wm Copeland ordered to pay Jno Thompson 398 lb tobo.

page 230. Abstract. Richd Mosby ordered to pay Alexander Seares 420 lb tobo due.

page 230. Abstract. Mr James Crewes exor of Mary Ast dec'd authorized to recover all debts and other estate of the dec'd.

page 230.
          To the worp'll Co'rt of Cha: Citty Com
          Wm Hunt humbly presenteth
That being justly censured by yo'r worp's for a contempt, he humbly recanteth his error so unadvisedly comitted by (him) and is very sorry for the same
     And therefore humbly implore the favourable lenity of this worp'll Co'rt so as to release and remitt the sd censure, and the

C 11

petn'r promiseing more civill demeano'r for the future
Shall ev'r pray &c
William Hunt

rec Apr: 7. 60

Upon peticon and submission of Wm Hunt and his recantacon of his rash error and contempt The Co'rt is pleased to remitt and release the censure this day past agst him, he paying the costs hereof

Note: Captain Hill may have been a most considerate young gentleman, but to William Hunt he was just another overbearing young squirt. And this petition is just another thing that would not have to be after the Revolution.   B.F.

page 230.
To the worp'll Com'rs of Cha: Citty Com
The humble peticon of Edward Mathewes
Sheweth
That yo'r peticon'r the last Co'rt misbehaveing himselfe was by yo'r worp's bound to good behavior at w'ch time y'r petn'r was ov'rtaken w'th drink and is very sorry for his misdemeanor
Wherefore yo'r petn'r humbly Craveth release from the sd bond and he shall &c
Edd Mathewes

Upon the humble pet'n and submicon of Capt Edd Mathews and his recantacon of his rash error comitted at the last Co'rt for w'ch he was bound to the good behavior, wch error he confesseth to have beene comitted through his excesse of drink, The Co'rt doth release his bond for his good behavior and ord'r that he pay 50 lb fine for his sd confest ebriety according to act, w'th all costs hereof, als exec

page 231. Abstract. Mr John Cogan this day giving "security for the state of Capt Tyes children" is released of former security.
(again the final 'e' omitted from next word)

page 231. Abstract. Receipt. 25 Feb 1659/60. James Drysdall to Augustine Willyard for cattle belonging to Mary Herdman. Witnessed by Walter Houldsworth and Richard x Hamlet. Recorded 7 Apl. 1660.

page 231. Abstract. Augustin Willyard released from bond as guardian of Mary Herdman orphan, who has married James Drysdall, her property delivered to her husband.

page 231. The next Co'rt is agreed and concluded to be held att Westov'r and so to Continue till October Co'rt, and all the winter Co'rts to be kept at mer'chts hope.

page 232. Richd Parker aged 31 yearea or thereabouts exaed & sworne saith
That haveing brought a warr't from Capt Edd Hill for convention (contempt) of Wm Hunt to appe' before him the dept Delred the sd war't to the sd Hunt in presence of Tho: Davies and another man, and the sd Hunt, instead of obedience to the writt, answered that he had somew't else to do then to wait on Com'rs warrts, saying further that he admired Capt Hill being made so sensible of the businesse, would graunt his warrt to that purpose, but, sd he, Capt Hill is a young Com'r and I suppose he will graunt his war't for any thing: Whereipon y'r depo't told the sd Hunt the danger of Contemning the war't to w'ch he replyed that the dept went about a businesse of such difficultie that if he had an order of Co'rt for the serv't then in question he the sd Hunt would not deliv'r him, and further saith not
                                    Rich Parker
Jur in Cur April 3. 1660
Test Hoel Pryse Cl.

page 232. Tho: Davies aged 22 yeares or thereabouts exaed and sworne saith that being w'th mr Parker when he read and del'red a war't to Wm Hunt for his appeance before Capt Edd Hill about a servt w'ch he deteined the dept heard the sd Hunt answer that he had no time to wait on Com'rs war'ts (or to that effect) whereupon mr Parker telling him the danger of contempt, the sd Hunt replyed, he cared not, and added If yu had an ord'r of Co'rt for the servt I would not deliv'r him and further saith not
                            Tho: x Davies   his mark
Jur in Cur April: 3. 1660
Test: Hoel Pryse   cl

page 232.
        At a Quarter Co'rt held at James Citty the 27th of march 1660
                    S'r Wm Berkeley knt Gov'rne'r
            mr Richd: Bennett   Coll ffrancis Morison)
            Coll: Hen: Browne   Lt Coll Jo: Walker   ) esq'rs
                        Lt Coll Edward Carter

mr John Holmwood is no'iated and appointed to be sheriffe of Charles Citty Com for this ensueing yeare and to be sworne at the next Co'rt there held
                            Test Tho: Brereton   Cl Con
rec April 20 sequ

page 233. Abstract. Mr Theod Bland gives verbal security for Holmwood.

page 233. Robert Rowse is sworne under sherr according to eleccon and appointmt of mr John Holmwood the present sherr
Abstract. Capt Robt Wynne gives verbal security for Rowse.

page 233.
    Att a Co'rt holden at Westov'r Jun: 4: 1660
Present   mr Thomas Drewe
    mr Antho: Wyatt   mr Stephen Hamelin
    Capt Thomas Stegge   Capt ffrancis Epes
    Capt Robt. Wynne

page 233. William Harrison hath proved right by testimony produced in Co'rt to 550 acres of land for the charge of importacon of eleven persons underwritten

Gilbert Kerr	Tho Browns	Edd Wright
Alice Bury	Wm Robinson	Robt Manell
Martin Quelch	Tho: Prince	John Mackale
Sam: Boston	Nicho: ffarr	

page 233. Abstract. Com of admr of est of Henry Gilham decd to Mr Thomas Drewe as formerly made over.

page 233. Capt Jo: Epes and mr Cha: Sparrow present

page 233. Abstract. Attachmt to Mr Steph Hamelin agst est of Nicho Perry for 2000 lb tobo.

page 234. Abstract. The sheriff ord to seize the person of Nicholas Perry and a boat he has taken belonging to Mr Jno Richards.

page 234. Abstract. The sherr ord to seize the estate of Phillip Ellyott, pay Capt Jno Wall and release the person of Ellyott.

page 234. Abstract. Dif betw Willm Bird and John Stith to next Court. Also dif betw Richd Parker and Wm Hunt.

page 234. The inquest of the violent death of John Adams late of Westov'r Carpenter dec'd, and the Inventory of his estate are ordered and appointed to be presented to the next Quarter Co'rt att James Citty where the regnizeance of the premiss's properly apperteine.

page 234. Abstract. Nonsuit to George ffarley agst Nicho Perry. Also attach to Tho Hunt agst est of Nicho Perry for 550 lb tobo.

page 235. Abstract. Mr James Crewes trustee for est of Mary Ast decd ord to pay Mary Thomas widd 350 lb tobo due per bill.

page 235. Abstract. Thos Richman ord to pay Howell Pryse 616 lb tobo "fees of his late Criminall businesse".

page 235. Abstract. "The peticon and complt of Persivall Barton and Ann Holsey servants of Nicholas Perry of their violent abuses and dealings w'th and by their sd master and mistresse is referred to be exaied and decided by mr Charles Sparrowe, And in the interim the sd servts to be and remaine w'th mr Cha: Sparrowe aforesd or where he shall appoint them, if he shall see just cause for the same" Also concerns judgt for Howell Pryse agst Nich: Perry for a filly.

page 235. Abstract. By mutual consent Dan: Holicrosse is released from service to Mr Geo Potter he "to pay the sd serv't the accustomed allowance of corne and clothing".

page 235. Abstract. Judgt to Mr Theod Bland agst Nich: Perry for 1800 lb tobo.

page 235. Abstract. Nonsuit to Richd Davies agst Wm Wilkins.

page 235. Abstract. Henry Hawkins conf. judgt. to Jno Cogan 350 lb tobo.

page 236. fferdinando Aston aged about 34 yeares and Ann Redford aged about 28 yeares both exaed and sworne
Say
    That they the depts were present w'th mr Richard Nicholas shortly before his decesse, and heard him deliv'r and declare a Nuncupative will in these or the like tearmes.
    That he made his wife Susanna Nicholas whole ex'rix and gave to his Daughter Susanna Nicholas the elder of his two young mares w'th

all her increase, six cowes to be chosen out of his penn w'th all
their increase, 5000 lb tobbo (to buy her servants) when she should
come to full age or marriage, 2 feather beds w'th sixe pare of sheets
and all furniture belonging to them, And all his land after the
decesse of his wife

Also he gave and bequeathed to mr Antho: Wyatts youngest
daughter (his the deced'ts God daughter) one young heyfer.

ffurther he requested and desired that mr Warham Horsemonden
and mr Francis Redford would be Overseers herof and se the premisses
performed, And further they cannot depose

        ffer: Aston
        Ann A Redford
         her mark

Jur in Cur Jun: 4. 1660
Test Hoel Pryse Cl
      rec Jul: 17 sequ:

page 237.

  Att a Co'rt holden at Westov'r Aug: 3. 1660
present
       mr Thomas Drewe
   mr Antho: Wyatt Capt Edward Hill
   Capt John Epes   mr Steph: Hamelin
   Capt Robt Wynne

page 237. Abstract. Dif betw Thos Richman and Wm Johnson to next
Court.

page 237. Abstract. Jno Stith security for appearance of Thomas
Stevens conf judgt to Mr John Holmwood attor of Mr Tho: Branch for
300 lb tobo.

page 237. John Edwards is hereby exempted and reliesed (by reason
of his impotencie to get his subsistance) from all future publick
and Com Levies and taxes.

page 237. Abstract. Rice Hoe ord to pay Mr Jno Cogan 175 lb tobo
"for damages of a boate lent to the sd Hoe"

page 237. These are to Certifie that Thomas Peters of this Com of
Cha: Citty cowper hath entered into bond w'th responsible security
for the keeping and educacon of the orphanes of Dan: Washborne late
of Isle of Wight Com decd, and for securing and deliv'ry of their
sev'rall por'cons and estates according to the Lawes of this Countrey

page 237. Abstract. Judgt to Mr Steph: Hamelin agst est of Nicholas Perry for 2000 lb tobbo.

page 237. Abstract. Order that present sheriff pay Mr Francis Grey 1180 lb tobo with 3 yrs int and all costs incident for the debt of Edmond Shipham arrested at his suit and not appearing, except the sheriff produce the person or sufficient estate to pay.

page 237. Abstract. Mrs Sara Hoe ord to pay Mr Jno Cogan 300 lb tobo due by bill.

page 238. Knowe unto all men by these presents that I Henry Comly of Bysport in the Com of Somersett husband of Judith Comly formerly knowne by the name of Judith Clarke, being daughter unto Mary Clark of Temple parish of Bristol dec'd do hereby constitute x x my welbeloved friend Mr John Tofte of the Citty of Bristoll chirurgeon to sue arrest and implead all manner of men unto and indebted either by bill bond certificate concordacon or otherwise, especially Robt Bird of Warwick Squeeke (sic) in James riv'r in Virginia, or to recov'r from him the sd Robt Bird or any other all that my right estate and interest in right of my wife aforesd, all such lands goods and chattells sum and sums of money as shall appe unto me due from any by vertue of an inheritance by the decease of my brother in the law Robt Clarke dec'd, And haveing recov'ed the same to passe unto them or any of them a perfect acquittance x x x witnes my hand and seale this 24th Day of August in the yeare 1659
Testes Rich Phelps
     Charles Moone   Henry Comly the seale
                                     the marke of
                              Judith x Clark the seale

                rec Aug: 20. 1660

page 238. Due to Sam: Harwell for a wolfes head Certf'd by Capt Wynne
Due to Coll Hill for 2 Cert by Capt Ed Hill
Due to Capt Southcott for his boate 3 dayes - 45

page 238. Abstract. Court adj to 3rd Oct next.

page 239. The declaracon of Susan'a Langworth taken by me this 3th of July 1660 being brought before me Sayth

That matter of 6 weekes agoe Thomas Calloway her master did lay and had the use of her body in carnall copula'con agst her will, and makeing a noise in crying notw'thstanding did abuse her: and further declares that the sd Calloway will not let her rest in any peace for the same intent, and had the use as formerly of her once since that time, and told me if I was w'thchild it should be layne to Nicholas Marselles, and so far I declare witnes my hand the day and yeare above written

          Susanna x Langworth   mark

Declared before me
S: Hamelin   record: Aug: 20: 1660

page 239.
To the right worp'll Co'rt of Cha: Cittie Com
The humble peticon of Susan Langworth

 Whereas Clays Nicholas Marselles hath sev'rall times inveagled me to lay a slander on my master and to say my master hath got me w'th child and to lay it to him, and by that meanes he should get me free and would marry me, and likewise advised me to go to mr Hamelin to complaine that my master had forced me to ly w'th me agst my will: I utterly deny any such accon ev'r comitted by my sd master and that I was saduced to say so by the instigacon of the sd Clays.

Itt is ordered that Susan Langworth the serv't of Thomas Calloway who accused her sd master w'th an indecent demeano'r and persecu'con to have had the use of her body violently, but since denied her sd calumny shalbe punished w'th 20 lashes on her bare back for her acknowledgedgem't of the offence of fornicacon by her (w'th whomsoev'r) asked or comitted.

page 239. Howell Pryse hath proved right by testimony produced to 1550 acres of land for the charge and importacon of

Dorcas Young	John Allmand	Dannell -- --
Ann Chandler	Henry Tyre	Hugh Moris
Ralph Jennings	Wm Baker	Neale Griffen (?)*
Hugh Jones	Margaret Smith	Bridget Carter
Robt Mercer	Mary Sly	Walter ffloyd
Robt Grey	Rebecca Jackson	Jane Alder
Michael Terrell	Richd Beake	Thomas Mann
James Wragg	John Glover	Bernard Wynne
Jone Harrison	Henry Peterson	Tho: Castle
John Edwards	Isaac Warren	Edd Richardson

   (one name missing from original record)

* Possibly 'Grishmen'.

page 240.

      Att a Co'rt holden att mohts hope Sept: 14: 1660
present   mr Antho: Wyatt
                  Capt John Epes
                  Capt Robt Wynne

page 240. Abstract. Dif. betw. Thos Drewe and Martha Greene to next Court.

page 240. The peticon of Morgan Jones about Jane the orphane of Tho: East dec'd is refferred to the next Com Cort.

page 240. Ordered that Thomas Douglas who married the relict of Wm Sanders dec'd shall produce and present to the next Com Co'rt the testimonies of the nuncupative will, and the Inventory of the estate of the sd Sanders.

page 240. Abstract. Absent Com'rs to be fined

page 240. Abstract. Quietus est to Jno Stirdevant of est of Samuel Woodward decd, he having given bond for overplus for use of the orphans, and releasing him from admr obtained by his wife in her widowhood.

page 240. Due to Capt Jo: Epes for 2 wolves heads testified by Capt ffrancis Epes.

page 241. Wittnes these presents that whereas Wm Sanders lately dec'd by his last will before sufficient witnesss did bequeath unto his sonne Wm Sanders Junr one yoke of steers already broken w'th a cart and the tackling belonging thereunto to be made good to him when he comes to age and one gunne wch he called by the name of Isaac, And for the remainder of the estate he did bequeath unto his loveing wife Joane Sanders to give as she thought fitt to the rest of the children saying as they prove dutifull according to her discre'con
    Wherefore to fullfill the will of my late dec'd husband I the aforesd Joane Sanders now in my widdowhood do make ov'r unto my children these goods and cattell after following
    Imprimis To my sonne William two cowes one called ffortune about five yeares old and the other called Nancie about three yeares of age
        It To my daughter Susan one cow called Coll about six yeares

old and one heyfer called Dazie about two yeares old: more one feather bed and bolster and rug and blanket and 1 pare canvas sheets and fowr pewter dishes

It To my daughter Jane one cow called Browning nine yeares old and one heyfer called hope-well and foure pewter dishes

It ffor my daughter Joane one cowe called Blackneyes and one heyfer called Jugg and four pewter dishes: And in case of mortality of any of the children their por'con to come to the youngest child

Wittnesse these presents that I Thomas Douglas God willing intended to marry to Joane Sanders do hereby bind and oblige my selfe to performe w'tsoev'r hath been given to the children by their fathers will and this present act of their mother, and this I do bind my selfe to record to them in cor't, and in case that I faile to record this then I do consent to forfeit tenn thousand pounds tobbo to the children. Wittnesse my hand this third of September 1660

        Thomas x Douglas his mark
        Joane x Sanders
         mark

Signed and sealed in the presence of
Patrick Jackson
James Blamore   rec 7 br: 21. sequ.

page 242. Whereas it Apeares there is noe Coroner in this County, and John Adames is Come to A violent end In such cases wee the Commition are to take Cognizance of such matters when it pleseth god to suffer them to fall out

These are In the name of his highnes the Lord protector to will and Requier you James Hayms to summon those under written as A Jury of Inquest to Inquier After the death of the sd John Adames hereof faile not as you will Answare the Conterary

  given under my hand this 24th: of 9 ber 1659
        John Holmwood

     The names of the Jury
Mr John: Dibdall Min'r foreman   Joseph Bradly
Mr The: Bland   Geo: ffarlow
Capt: Otho: Southcutt   Andrew Meldrum
Capt: Rich: Dibdall   Willi: Clark
John: Marshall   Samson: Craford
Daniell Scott   Tho: Stronge
Sworne by me this 24th of 9 ber 1659
        John: Holmwood

page 243. That upon the whole matter duly examined by us wee finde that the 24th day of this instant November in the yeare of our Lord 1659, betwone seaven and eaight of the Clocke in the fore noone, the said John Adams being very sick and weake, did Drinke A peuter cup of sack of halfe A pint or there abouts afterwards, did with a knife which wee value to bee worth sixe pownds of Tobacco Give himselfe a mortall wound in the throate upon the left side, the bredth of three Inches, the debth quite threw his winde pipe and of which hee did die, and murther him selfe by his owne hand

         John: Dibdall: 1

page 243.
    Att a Co'rt holden at mer'chts hope Octob'r: 3: 1660
present   mr Thomas Drewe
   mr Antho: Wyatt   Capt Robt Wynne
   Capt John Epes   Capt ffran: Epes

page 243. Abstract. John Jones servt to John Hardway absented himself 8 1/2 months. Has his time doubled.

page 243. Abstract. Dif betw Mr Wm Johnson and Thos Richman to next Court on account of Johnson's "present Debility".

page 244. Mr Thomas Drewe mr Anthony Wyatt Capt Thomas Stegge Capt John Epes Capt Robert Wynne Capt Edd Hill mr Stephen Hamelin and Capt ffrancis Epes were this day sworne Com'rs for the Kings Ma'tie the sd oath being admr'ed unto them by Coll: Edward Hill esqr

page 244. Abstract. Deed of Gift. 28 April 1660. Marke Avery, planter in Martin Brandon, to Thomas Reynolds, chirurgeon in Surrey Co., 50 acres adj. Jeremyah Lamping and Robt Murray.
Wit:
Robert Murray   Signed Marke A Avery
James R Rainer   his marke
 his marke
      "Recognit: in Cur' Octobr: 3. 1660 by
      Marcu Avery supradt:
        Test. Hoel Pryse Cl
        Rec. 8br: 20: sequ:

page 244. Abstract. Order that Jane the orphan of Tho. East, dec'd., dwell and serve with Morgan Jones till 21 or marriage.

page 245. Abstract. Inventory of est of Mr Charles Sparrow decd, to be presented at next Court.

page 245. Abstract. John fflowers gives bond for estate of Walter Daux decd for "carefull keepeing and educating the orphanes of the sd Daux dureing their minority".

page 245. Abstract. Deed of Gift. 3 Oct. 1660. John Wall "unto his sonne in Law Charles Clay" 2 ewes.

page 245. Abstract. Court adj. to 20th Nov. next.

page 245. Abstract. Judgt to Howell Pryse agst est of Nichol Perry for 550 lb tobo and 4 yrs interest assigned from Tho: Hunt.

page 246.
        Att a Cort holden att merchts hope 9 br. 10: 1660
present   Coll Edward Hill esqr
    mr Tho: Drewe   Capt Robt Wynne
    mr Antho: Wyatt   Capt Edd Hill
    Capt Tho: Stegge   mr Steph: Hamelin
    Capt Jo: Epes   Capt ffrans: Epes

page 246. Abstract. Prob of will of Michael ffletcher to Wm Garrett who m the relict. He ord to give security.

page 246. Abstract. Admr of Mr. Charles Sparrow ord to repay Mrs Jane Egbrough amount overpd by her on her late husband's obligation

page 246. Abstract. "The deposition of Tho Dennington aged 56 yeares or thereabout"
Concerns Sparrow-Egbrough a/c. "being at mr Sparrows when mr Randolph and mrs Egbrough came to him", etc. 1st Nov. 1660.
        Signed Tho: Dennington
I Henry Randolph am ready to depose the same as Tho Dennington.
        Signed Henry Randolph
Wit:
Will Drummond
Tho Loving
        rec 13 Nov. 1660.

page 247. Jane Hall the relict of Oswin Hall dec'd confesseth Judgemt before me and Capt Robt Wynne for six cowes and their female increase to be equally divided betwixt three children being the orphanes of the sd Oswin as foll

Impr's To my Daughter Jane the eldest two cowes named Motherlesse and Dazie

It To my daughter Ann two cowes named young Nancie and Cherrie

It To my daughter Hellena two cowes named Motherlike and Sloe

And two steers of fower yeares old per steere wth a piece of broad cloth conteyning two y'ds and a halfe, and a cloth suite, wch we value at eleavn hundred pounds of tobbo and caske, wch tobbo is to be equally divided amongst them toward their schooleing if need require or if I shall endeavo'r to educat them my selfe then they shall enjoy each her sev'rall propor'con when they shall attaine to the age of seaventeene yeares or married, and if any of the sd children shall Dye before they attaine to the age afore men'coned then that parte to be equally divided betwixt the survivors: This as my lawfull act I Desire to be recorded As witnesse my hand 8 br the VIth Anno D'm 1660

Testis
Anthony Wyatt
Robert Wynne
Tho: Cranes
    mark
Morgan M Jones

        mark
Jane H Hall

Rec. 9 br 13. sequ

Page 247. Abstract. Order that admr of Mr Charles Sparrow decd pay Mr Thos. Dennington and John Allam Chirurg' 2320 lb tobo " for meanes and attendance administred to the sd Decedt by them". Also to pay Thomas Roynolds chirurg' 1540 lb tobo due for same

page 247. Abstract. Vestry of Martins Brandon ordered to raise and pay 10 lb tobo per tytheable to Wm Rawlinson admr of Mr Charles Sparrow "for the burgesse charge of the sd mr Sparrow according to his agreement wth them".

(Note: There is no page 248. Page 249 is the other side of page 247)

page 249. Abstract. Deed. 11 Febry 1659/60. Richard Pace of Powells Creek, planter, sells Wm Wilkins " a certeine Neck of Land lying betweene the branch comonly called the Westowne branch of fflower de hundred Creeke and the bottome comonly called by the name of reedy bottome, and running up to Blands path at the head conteyning by estimacon two hundred acres of land ".

Wit:
Thomas Bigge
Thomas Parrham

Signed Richard Pace

Rec. 16 Nov. 1660

page 250. Abstract. Settlement of a/c of Stephen Hamelin as sheriff.

page 250. Abstract. Com of admr of est of Tho Mather decd to Elizabeth Mather his relict.

page 250. Itt is ordered that mr John Drayton shall produce and present to the next Co'rt an Inventory of the state of John Burdon dec'd and then, in case of no opposicon of a widdowes right, to have adm'racon thereof graunted

page 251. Abstract. Order that the relict of the admr of Tho Tanner dec'd pay Mr Wm Bird 5 lb beaver due, and give a/c of Tanner's est at next Court.

page 251. Abstract. Attachment agst the King of Weynoke for 15 lb beaver due to Tho Tanner now dec'd referred to the Governor and Council.

page 251. Abstract. Edmond Shipdham (sic) conf. judgt 1093 lb tobo to Capt ffran: Grey.

page 251. Abstract. At suit of Mr Steph: Hamelin in October last, Martin Quelch agreed to produce the person of Thomas Busby or pay 10 lb beaver and 500 lb pork. Having failed to do so order is issued that he should.

page 251. Abstract. Order that burgesses limit their charges to 100 lb tobo a day hereafter

page 251. Abstract. Capt Tho Stegge and Mr Steph: Hamelin to settle dif betw Edward Mosby plt and Curtis Laud and James Nicholls defts.

page 251. Abstract. Dif betw Mr Tho Drew and Martha Greene to next Court.

page 252.
Itt is ordered that 77 lb of tobbo per poll be forthwth levied by the sherr on each tytheable person in this Com, by distresse if needfull, and paid as foll vidzt

	lb tob
mr Theod: Bland for 40/s expended	0400
mr Theod: Bland for Burgesse charge	8758
Capt Robt Wynne per eod	7213
Coll Edd Hill esqr for 3 wolves	0300
Sam: Harwell for 1	0100
Capt John Epes for 2	0200
Morgan Jones for 5	0500
Richd Baker for 2	0200
Capt Otho Southcott for his boate	0045
John Howell forgot last yeare	0070
John fflowers omitted last yeare	0090
Howell Pryse for Acts of march Assembly	1100
Ditt: for last acts	1100
Lewis Greene for wolfe	0100
Tho: Blankes for wolfe	0100
mr Bland per acco't of the mens charges	2199
mr Taylors man Caesar for 2 wolves	0200
Tho: Tanner behind of his Debt Due	0500
Patrick Jackson behind	0196
Wm Hunt for 19 dayes roweing the burgesss	0190
Capt Southcott 4 dayes	0040
Geo: ffarley 6 dayes to Wm Hill 6 dayes 60	0120
Gibson 6 dayes 60 Andr: Meldrum 4 dayes 40	0100
Samuell Phillips 4 dayes	0040
Wm Bayly 15 dayes	0150
Robt Jones his mate 9 dayes	0090
Roger Reese 9 Dayes	0090
The sherr for takeing the list	2500
Tho: Beedles for rowing burgesses 6 Dayes	0060
James Moore 2 dayes	0020
mr Steph: Hamelin per arreares	1462

	26233

page 253.

Sum brought ov'r	26233
Robt Rowse per assignemt 2 wolves	00200
Wm Justice 2 dayes rowing the burgesses	00020
mr Antho: Wyatt for getting timber	00500
mr Drayton for a drown'd man	00200
Tho: Reynolds for arreares	00093
Howell Pryse for arrears	00265
Ditt for fees about a pre'son'r	01160
mr Bland for boate 15 dayes	00225
Capt Wynne for boate	00150
Robt Rowse for keeping the Co'rt howse	00500

(forward)

C 11   82

(forwarded)

Jos: Woodham for service	00095
Ho: Pryse for furniture for the Co'rt house	00400
mr Holmwood for the like	00750
Ditt: for Com charge	02200
John Hatley for service	00070
John Stith for arreares	00960

	34021
The sherr for Sallery	03402

	37423

page 253. Capt ffrancis Grey is sworne Com'r for this Com according to elec'con

page 253. The Cort Doth request and intrust Coll Edd Hill esqr to endeavo'r the purchaseing and procureing of the tann howse and appertenances at Bermooda hundred, w'ch for the present may be an introduccon and beginning of manufactures for both these upper Counties

page 253. Abstract. Order "that a sequestracon be made of the estate and porcon of Susanna the daughter of Richd Nicholas decd, according to his nuncupative will, out of the hands of mr Rice Hoe who married the relict of the sd Dece'dt". Capt Tho: Stegge and mr Steph: Hamelin to appoint two men to select the cattle and Hoe to give security "untill the full age or marriage of the sd orphane".

page 254. Abstract. Wm Rawlinson who m the relict of Mr Charles Sparrow authorized to transact the business of the estate until further order "or at the arrivall of Selby Sparrow the heire of the Decedt".

page 254. Abstract. Mr. John Holmwood the present sheriff to conf judgmt 60000 lb tobo to the Court " to save them harmlesse " re - collections.

page 254.
           Att a Cort holden at merchts hope Dec. 3, 1660
present   mr Thomas Drewe
          mr Anthony Wyatt   mr Stephen Hamelin
          Capt Robt Wynne   Capt ffran: Grey

page 254. Abstract. The est. of John Hardway decd to pay Jno Nothway merchant 902 lb tobo. Also 138 lb tobo to Capt Robt Wynne.

page 254. Abstract. Rice Hoe ordered to pay Mr Tho: Drewe 5776 lb tobo and L 3. Sterl due.

page 254. Abstract. Robt Scott ordered to pay Wm Rawlinson 520 lb tobo.

page 255. Abstract. Order that est of Jo: Hardway decd pay Wm Pierson chirurg, attorney of Robt Washington, 700 lb tobo due.

page 255. Abstract. Wm Hughes ordered to pay Mr Tho. Drewe 300 lb tobo due.

page 255. Abstract. Dif betw Mr. Antho Wyatt plt and Mr Rice Hoe deft to next Court.
    Also the dif betw Sara Whitmore plt and Robt Scott deft.

page 255. A Comicon of adm'racon of the state of John Burdon dec'd is graunted to mr John Drayton according to Law, he giveing caution as is accustomed
    And his acco't of 1050 lb tobo and caske exhibited agst the sd estate is confirmed and allowed by the Co'rt.

page 255. Abstract. The est of John Hardway decd ordered to pay Mr John Beauchampe 302 lb tobo.

page 255. Abstract. John Hughes ordered to pay Mrs ffran: Bland 350 lb tobo due.

page 255. Abstract. Order that Wm Dollin's specialty of 1390 lb tobo formerly in hands of Mr Cha: Sparrow decd, in relation to the est of John Gallis decd, be delivered to him, he to give bond "for the sd Gallis his orphane".

page 255. Abstract. Nonsuit to Jo. Stith agst Wm Bird.

page 256. Abstract. Estate of Jno Hardway decd to pay Mr Tho. Drewe 765 lb tobo.

page 256. Abstract. Nonsuit to John Pigott agst Mr Jno Dibdall.

page 256. Abstract. Est of John Hardway to pay Mr John Cogan 300 lb tobo due by specialty and 700 lb tobo "for meanes paines and attendance".

page 256. Abstract. Power of Atty. 29 July 1660. "Robert Washington of Wapping in the parish of Stepney and Com of Middlesex marin'r" to "my very loveing friend Wm Pearson chirurgeon" to collect debts. This is an exceedingly long entry.
Wit: Signed   Robert Washington
Lancelot Simpson scr
Richard Simons
Robt Streete   Rec 8 December 1660

page 257. Abstract. Prob of will of Macam Currey decd to Alse Currey relict and extrx. Richd Braine and Tho Peeters to val inventory and div it according to the will. They sworn before Capt Francis Grey 3 Dec 1660.

page 258. Exors Bond. 3 Dec 1660. Wm Rawlinson for est of Mr Charles Sparrow decd. 20000 lb tobo.
Wit: Signed   William Rallinson
John Drayton   Elias Osborne
H Pryse Cl   Maurice x Rose

page 258. Abstract. John Tippett discharges James Ward of 6 head of female cattle "as they are recorded in Co'rt for my wife in her minority". 17 Nov. 1660.
Wit: Signed   John x Tippett
Richard Taylor
John Barker   Rec 29 Jan 1660/1

page 258. Abstract. Court cancels bond of James Ward as guardian of Winifred Rosser an orphan who m John Tippett.

page 258. Abstract. Mr Jno Holmwood ordered to pay from the est of Jo: Hardway decd 300 lb tobo "for use of mr Edd ffoliott Clerk".

page 259. Abstract. Petition of Jno Cogan, who having paid Thos. Boyce, asking for discharge acknowledged in Court by Boyce 3rd Dec. 1660. Boyce also acks "full satisfaccon of all his estate and porcon from Capt Richd Tye dec'd".

page 259.
> Elias Osborne sworne and ex'aed Sayth

That Rob't Scott sayd Sara Whitmore had the pox and he would not be so sure of a clap w'th a french fagot stick for a thowsand pounds or some such sum, and he saw a swelling in her secret parts and further saith not
Jur in Cur 10br 3. 1660   Test
        H Pryse   Cl

page 259.
> Wm Rawlinson sworne and exa'ed saith

That Rob't Scott sayd Sara Whitmore had the pox, and he would not be so sure of a clap w'th the french fagot stick for some certeine sum he named, and he saw the pox in her secret parts, and further sayth not
Jur in Cur 10br: 3. 1660
Test: Hoel Pryse   Cl

page 259.

```
              mr John Burdon &c              tob & cask
for 5 weeks Dyet according to agreem't         0250
for the Doctor 100. for a sheete 150           0250
for his attendance and extraordinaries in
    his sicknesse                              0350
for fun'rall charge                            0200
                                              -----
                                               1050
```

page 259. Abstract. Sheriff ordered to pay Ho. Pryse 491 lb tobo due for fees and arrears of levies from Tho: Calloway

page 260.
> Att a Cort holden at merchts Hope ffebr: 4. 1660
> present   mr Thomas Drewe
>   mr Anthony Wyatt   Capt Edward Hill
>   Capt John Epes   mr Stephen Hamelin
>   Capt Robt Wynne   Capt ffrancis Grey

page 260. Abstract. Prob of will of mr Rich'd Dibdall decd to Mrs Sara Dibdall the relict and extrx.

page 260. Abstract. Willm Chamberlin conf judgt to Morris Rose for 300 lb tobo.

C 11   86

page 260. Abstract. Francis Trehan conf judgt to Mr Tho Drewe for 3018 lb tobo.

page 260. Willm Reynes by reason of sicknes age and long continuance is hereby exempted and released from all future publick service and taxes in his owne person, except parish dues.

page 260. Abstract. John Coale, by his atty Mr John Dibdall minister, conf judgt to Edward Mosby for 400 lb tobo. Coale's order dated 2nd Feby 1660/1. Signed John x Cole, wit by Thomas Marston.

page 260, Tho: Douglas sworne Constable for merchts hope precinct

page 260. Abstract. Order that a/c of Jane Williams agst est of Mr Charles Sparrow be referred to Capt Francis Grey and reported to next Court.

page 261.
Mr Drewe: w'th the rest of the old Com'rs of Cha: Citty Com, yo'r serv't Saluteing yu These are to certifie yu that mr John Holmwood yo'r high sherr not long since being at my howse gave me notice of three accons ag'st me, one of ffrancis Gray one Henery Briggs, the other I have forgotten, yet howev'r as I acknowledge the sumons I desire an appeale to the Quarter Co'rt for tryall before the Govern- o'r, this note ingageing me to answer under my hand, where I shall God willing appe' according to law, but for appereing att yo'r Cort I must not do, neither will I untill I have a reparacon for my form'r Injuries, and then it will and must be knowne where a Perrey hath seene madd or the people of Cha: Com
    not else but rest
        Yo'rs Nicholas Perey
(sic)   or Perry

page 261. Abstract. Order that security be given for the cattle of Symon Symonds "or else that the sd cattell be then appointed to be sold at an Outcry".

page 261. Abstract. Wm Rollinson trustee for the est of Mr Chas. Sparrow decd ordered to pay John Richards mercht 1059 lb tobo.

page 261. Abstract. Dif betw Richd Braine plt and Thos Mudgett deft to be settled by Capt Francis Grey and Wm Bird.

page 261. Abstract. That Edw Mosby pay Wm Chamberlain 500 lb tobo.

page 261. Abstract. Dif betw Edmond Smith and Edmond Shipham to next Court.

page 262. Abstract. Richd Mosby to pay Robt Rowse 630 lb tobo to settle suit.

page 262. Abstract. That Capt Thos Stegge be given security by trustee of Mr Charles Sparrow's est for admr of Major Jno Westhrope's est. "wherein he was co obliged w'th the sd Mr Sparrow".

page 262. Itt is ordered that Katherine Hughes the orphane of Tho. Hughes decd be and remaine w'th Wm Chamberlin chirurg: for and dureing the full time and space of five yeares next to come. In consideracon whereof the sd Chamberlin is hereby obliged to use and exercise his best skill meanes and endeavo'r for the cure of all Defects and maladies of the sd orphane, and discharge the parish from the sd orphane, and give bond to the Co'rt to that purpose, and for all her accomadac'.

page 262. Abstract. Tho: Rowe to give bond for est of Jo Hardway and care of the orphan.

page 262. Abstract. John Hodges exempt from pub services and taxes, except parish dues "by reason of lamenesse and inability to labo'r"

page 262. Abstract. Wm Vicars to pay Tho: Hamond 325 lb tobo.

page 262. Abstract. Mr Jno Holmwood sheriff to pay Moris Rose 368 lb tobo for nonappearance of Martin Quelch

page 263. Abstract. Order that Geo: Gibson pay Humfrey Allen 2400 lb tobo w'ch he was to pay in Surry Co., he to have remedy agst Capt Geo Jordan and Mathew Battell who were originally to pay.

page 263. Phillip Courtney exempted from pub. serv. and taxes, except parish dues "by reason of his lamenesse and age".

page 263. Abstract. Dif betw Theod. Bland plt and Jo: Harris deft to next Court.

page 263. Abstract. Mr Anthony Wyatt, Capt John Epes, Capt Edd Hill and Lt Howell Pryse recommended to the Gov. for appointment as Sheriff.

page 263. Abstract. Est of Thos: Tanner dec'd intrusted to Mr Antho: Wyatt until a/c be called.

page 263. Abstract. Mr Rice Hoe to appear and "answer what shalbe objected agst him on behalfe of the orphans of Richd Nicholas deed".

page 263. Abstract. Dif betw Mr Tho Drewe plt and Mr Jno Dibdall deft to next Court.

page 263. Abstract. Nonsuit to Wm Rallinson agst Thos. Culmer

page 264. Abstract. Mr Rice Hoe ordered to pay Mr Anth: Wyatt 281 lb tobo due for fees.

page 264
          Att a Cort holden at Westov'r April: 22: 1661
present   mr Tho: Drewe
    mr Antho: Wyatt   Capt Robt Wynne
    Capt Tho: Stegge   mr Steph Hamelin
    Capt John Epes

page 264. Abstract. Capt Edd Hill sworn sheriff 3 April 1661 before Mr Tho: Drewe, Capt Stegge and Mr Antho: Wyatt. Recorded Apl 23. Robt Rowse sworn under sheriff.

page 264. Abstract. Lawrence Biggins ordered to pay Wm Rollinson trustee for est of Mr Cha: Sparrow decd 595 lb tobo.

page 264. Abstract. 3 Jan 1660/1. Receipt for cattle belonging to orphans of Slayde delivered by Anthony Tall. Signed Wm x Edwards, witnessed by Thomas Rowe. Recorded 23 April 1661.

page 264. Abstract. Prob of will of Richd Hamelet (sic) dec'd to Elizabeth Hamlett (sic) relict and extrx.

C 11

page 265. Abstract. Deed. 22 April 1661. Walter Aston of Cha: Citty Com, gent, sells Wm Edwards a parcel of land adj land of sd William Edwards, Jo: Hardway, Kemidges Creeke, Walter Shipleye.
Wit:
Tho: Crane   Signed Walter Aston
Chris: Woodward
Wm Alford   Rec. 23 April 1661.

page 266. Abstract. John fflowers conf judgt to Nicholas Church for 2300 lb tobo on condition he "keepe harmlesse the sd Church from a bond wherein he is co-obliged wth the sd fflowers to James Jannoie and Jo: Beauchamp merchts for 1150 lb of tobbo and cask".

page 266. Coll Edd Hill esqr present cum caeter

(Note: This Latin abb. not clear to me. Broadly it may be "present with the rest". B.F.)

page 266. Abstract. Dif betw Mr Tho Drewe and Martha Greene to next Court.

page 266. Itt is ordered that Wm Rollinson trustee for the state of mr Charles Sparrow decd pay on the 10th of November next to Thomas Culmer chirurg 1200 lb of good tobbo and caske for physick and Chirurgery imployed adm'red and exhibited to the wife of the sd mr Sparrow, wth costs als exec

page 266. Abstract. Order that Elizabeth Short widow deliver to George Midleton all cattle and other estate belonging to Symon the orphan of Symon Symonds dec'd.

page 266. Abstract. Edmond Shipdham conf judgt to George Barfoote for 350 lb tobo. Contra a/c to be settled 10th Nov.

page 266. Itt is ord'rd that all the servants of mr Rice Hoe appeare personally at the next Co'rt, by whose exai'acon the comp'lt of Tho: Cooke agst his m'r may be Decided and determined

page 266. Abstract. Dif betw Wm Justice plt and Wm Harrison deft to next Court.

page 267. Abstract. The sheriff ordered to sell all cattle "belonging of late to Mary the orphane of John Minter dec'd" now in the possession of Ralph Poole.

page 267. Abstract. Nonsuit to Thos. Stevenson agst Wm Bird.

page 267. Abstract. Edward Bushell attorney of Thos. Culmer chirurg' assigns to Robt Rowse 1000 lb tobo collected from Wm. Rollinson. Entry signed and dated 22 April 1661.

page 267. Abstract. Phillip Ellyott ordered to appear in Court or render up the cattle of Daniell the orphan of Hugh fforshaw to Cornelius Clemence.

page 267.
Itt is ordered that mr Thomas Drewe receive the list of tytheables
    from Chepekes Creeke to Powells Creek:
Capt Robt Wynne from Powells Creeke to the head of Appomattock riv'r:
Mr John Holmwood from Turky Island Creeke to Herring Creeke, includ-
    ing the sd Creeke, Westov'r, and Buckland, beginning at Swin-
    house planta'con and including the same, to the lower end of the
    Com on that side:
And that the Constables in their sev'rall precincts sumond the house
    keepers before the sd sev'rall gentlemen (when they shall
    appoint) according to Act of Assembly.

page 267. Wm Harrison is sworne Constable ffor fflower de hundred precinct Curtis Laud sworne Constable for Weynoke precinct.

page 268. Abstract. Bond. 100000 lb tobo. Coll Edward Hill esqr and Capt Edward Hill for the latter as sheriff. No date shown.
Test   Signed Edward Hill Junior
Hoel Pryse Cl   Edw: Hill

page 268. Abstract. Mr Rice Hoe to pay Mr John Cogan 500 lb tobo due. Also to "forthw'th pay to Jo fflowers or his ass'gs one case of good London Drams confessed due in Co'rt".

page 268. Abstract. On request of Mr Theod: Bland suit of William Bayly agst him to next Court.

page 268. Abstract. Dif betw Richd Prise and Isaac Tatham, on deft's request, to next Court.

page 268. Abstract. 100 lb tobo to Tho: Tomlinson from sale of cattle "late of Mary the orphan of John Minter decd". To Howell Pryse 137 lb tobo for fees.

page 268. Abstract. Mr Stephen Hamelin to settle dif betw Howell Pryse and Thomas Calloway.

page 268. Abstract. Nonsuit to Wm Chamberlain agst Edd Mosby. Also John Stith agst Wm Bird.

page 269. Abstract. Mr Thos Drewe and any one or more Com'rs to settle dif betw Wm Rawlinson trustee of est of Mr Cha: Sparrow and Robt Scott.

page 269. Whereas mr John Dibdall hath conveyed away Daniell the orphane of Daniell Scott decd, who hath sev'rall relacons, and some small estate due, in this Com.
It is therefore ordered that the sherr or his deptie by virtue hereof sumon require and comand the sd mr John Dibdall to make his personall appearance at the next Com Cort at Westov'r before the Com'rs then and there to answer to what shalbe objected agst him on behalfe of the sd orphane, And that he bring w'th him likewise the person of the sd orphane

page 269. Abstract. Order that 1 bu corn per poll for Westover Par. due to Mr Edwd ffoliott minister be brought by the Inhabitants of the South-side to the mill at Powell's Creek, and of the North side to Mr Cook's mill. The church wardens to give notice to house keepers "who in case of neglect are hereby censured to pay for each barrell and the colleccon 110 lb tobbo".

page 269. Abstract. Inhabitants given respite of 14 days for paymt "of the Gov'rn'rs corne".

page 270.

Children baptized in the parish of Martin Brandon A'o 1660

Maurize the son of Richd Hamlet	Apr	4th
Mary the Daughter of Walter Houldsworth	May	16
Wm the son of Roger Lucas	May	16
Mary the daughter of Thomas Huxe	June	13
Elias the son of Benjamin Waid	Aug	12
Sara the daughter of Thomas Stevenson	Septbr	19
ffrancis the son of ffrancis Hogwood	9 br	12
Elizab: the daughter of Thomas Mudget	Jan'ry	9
Mary the daughter of Theophilus Beddingfield	febr	6

Marriages in Anno 1660

John Cunliffe and Johan Mountain	Aug	7
Dennis Kigan and Phebie Banks	Aug:	8
Wm Rawlison and Jane Sparrow	September	16
Walter Houldsworth and Naomie Davis	Octobr	11

Burialls in Anno 1660

Lawrence the son of Lawrence Seares	May	7
Mary the wife of Walter Houldsworth	May	11
Charles Sparrow	Septembr	11
Margaret Bottle	Aug:	26
Ellino'r the daughter of Ralph Poole	October	19
Naomie the wife of Ben: Waid	Octobr	22
Hugh Gubbins	Octobr	11
Wm Doelitle	March	1
John Cunliffe	march	14
Ellino'r the wife of Thomas Mudgett	march	15
Mary Minter	march	15

record: May 3. 1661.

Note: Mrs. Sparrow-Rawlinson, etc., did not have so very much on the collector of these abstracts (and other miseries) when it came to making quick decisions. A lady no doubt of my own kind and understanding.
　　　　And to any who doubt that the Colonial Virginians were a most remarkable people I would respectfully submit the Houldsworth miracle.
　　　　　　　　　　　　　　　　　　　Beverley Fleet.

page 270. Abstract. Defts to all actions depending to submit answers in writing.

page 271.
        Att a Co'rt holden at Westov'r April ulto 1661
present   Coll Edward Hill esqr
       mr Thomas Drewe   mr John Holmwood
       Capt Robt Wynne   mr Steph Hamelin

page 271. Abstract. Wm the orphan of Evan Roberts dec'd by his own consent bound to ffrancis Trehan.

page 271. Abstract. One cow of the estate formerly of David Ramsey dec'd, being the third belonging to his widow, and delivered to her second husband Wm Greene, to be delivered to Mr Tho: Drewe for one year in part paymt of Greene's debt to him.

page 271. Abstract. Thos Chappell acks to have received of James Wallis, who married the widow of Lt. John Banister decd, a legacy given by Banister in his will to sd Chappell's child. The legacy being 3 cows and 1 heifer. Thos. Chappell ordered to give security for cattle left his child "and by him recd for her use".

page 271. Itt is ordered that the parish of Westov'r pay mr John Dibdall 120 lb tobo for the charge of a window necessarily ordered by him in the Church of the sd parish

page 271. Abstract. Parishoners of Westover ordered to pay Mr John Dibdall arrears

page 272. Abstract. Order that Mr John Dibdall deliver, at Westover, to Howell Pryse, Daniell the orphan of Daniell Scott dec'd, by Jan 1st next with suitable clothing, etc. Also that he deliver a cow and calf "for the use of Elizabeth and Daniell the orphanes of Daniell Scott".

page 272. Abstract. Wm Rollinson, not appearing to settle dif betw Robert Scott and himself, is ordered to pay 1780 lb tobo from est of Charles Sparrow, dec'd. And that he also pay "to the sd Scott for a winters worke in fenceing, for nine months Dyett of a serv't, three bushells of Indian corne and one cowes milke by indifferent valuacon".

page 272. Abstract. Memo: that Coll Edward Hill esqr, at this Court did give to John Poyt'res the son of Capt ffran Poythres Dec'd, 50 acres at Jordans, adj the land now occupied by Capt Robt Wynne.

page 273.

    Att a Co'rt holden att Westov'r Jun: 3. 1661
present   mr Thomas Drewe
    mr Anthony Wyatt   mr John Holmwood
    Capt Robt Wynne   mr Stephen Hamelin

page 273. Abstract. Isaac Tatem ordered to pay Richd Price 480 lb tobo due by "bill assigned from John ffeepes" with one year's int. Tatem appeals and is ordered to give bond.

page 273. Abstract. Dif betw Capt Jno Wall plt and Phillip Ellyot deft to next Court.

page 273. Abstract. Thos Stephenson ordered to pay Wm Bird 310 lb tobo.

page 273. Abstract. Samuell Johnson sumoned and not appearing ordered to pay Capt John Wall.

page 273. Abstract. Mr Jno Beauchamp security for Richard Parker to pay Mr Thos Drewe 1100 lb tobo.

page 273. Capt John Epes present

page 273. Abstract. No cause for action in dif betw Wm Bird and John Stith.

page 273. Abstract. Prob of will of Thos Rands decd to "Margaret Moore widd form'ly the relict and extrix of the sd Rands"

page 274. Abstract. Deed. 15 Aug. 1654. John Gundry of Elizab: City Co., gent and Ann his wife sell Willm Edwards cooper, 333 acres in Henrico Co., adj land of Richard Cox and Samuell Woodward
Wit:
Edw: Hallywell   Signed   John Gundry
Tho: Sellery   Ann gundry

Ack in Court by Daniel Llewellin for John and Ann Gundry 1 May 1655.

Wm Edwards having already sold 100 acres part of above, "next adjoyning to mr Cocks land", to John Ewen, and 50 acres to Ewen, leased for life. The remaining acreage now transferred to Mr John Beauchamp and Mr James Crewes. Dated 3 June 1661. Signed Willm x Edwards. Test Hoel Pryse Cl. Cur. Recorded 11 June 1661.

page 275. Abstract. Deed. 10 Aug 1654. Samuell and Sara Woodward sell to Wm Edwards cooper, all their int in a third part of 1000 acres "purchased of mr Richard Cooke and given unto the sd Sara by will of her dec'd father mr Robt Hallam, vidzt, that part lying next to the land downwards wch was purchased by the sd Edds of our brother John Gundrey"

Wit: Signed   Samuell x Woodward
Daniell Llewellin   Sarah Woodward
Margaret Llewellin

Ack by Dan'l Llewellin for Saml and Sarah Woodward 1 May 1655.
                          Test: Hoel Pryse Cl Cur pre'dt
Wm Edwards conveys above to Mr John Beauchamp and Mr James Crewes 3 June 1661. Signed Wm x Edwards. Recorded 11 June 1661.

page 276. Abstract. Com of admr of est of Thomas Callyons decd to Maryan Callyons relict. She to produce inventory.

page 276. Itt is ordered that Wm Chamberlin performe the cure ingaged for on the person of Katherine Hughes by the 25th Day of December next, to hold firme or continue till the twelth of May following, and then to render her to Wm Clay for the rest of her five yeares service. And that thereupon mr Stephen Hamelin for the parish of Weynoke pay to the sd Chamberlin seaven hundred pounds of tobbo and cask for the sd cure

page 276. (Entry faded) John Stokes by reason of his great age is exempted from all future personall service and taxes except parish dues.

page 276. James Hardway by reason of excessive sicknesse and lamenesse is hereby exempted from all future personall service and taxes except parish dues.

page 276. Abstract. John ffloweres having collected paymt for 2 hhd of tobo shipped by Walter Daux, from the est of Capt Wm ODeon, during his absence "and whereas now it apper'eth that the sd tobbo was legally deliv'red or disposed in London" is ordered to refund.

page 276. Abstract. Prob of will of John Pratt senr to John Pratt Jr.

page 276. Tho: Douglas sworne constable for merchts hope precinct.

page 277. Whereas Samuell Grey slanderously reported that Edmond Shipdham and others intended privately to runn away and convey certeine goods beside their owne Itt is therefore ordered that the sd Grey be forthwth punished w'th twenty lashes inflicted on his bare back by the sherriffs officer

page 277. Abstract. That Phillip Ellyott give security for 2 cows and a calf belonging to Daniell fforshaw an orphan in chg of Cornel: Clemence and deliver them to him at his full age.

page 277.
        To the worpll Cort of Cha: Citty Com
Edward Mosby humbly presenteth   That he hath necessarily pd out of the state of Judith Parsons for her parte of sev'all debts recov'ed and allowed as per record appeareth the sum of 5123 lb tobbo and caske as per ac'ot &c
    Wherefore he humbly craveth a discompt and deduccon of so much out of her estate for w'ch he is obliged at the Same rate in money as the sd estate is valued to him by Capt Perry and Capt Stegge
                     And he shall pray &c

```
The estate of Judith Parsons Dr                        wth cask
For tobbo pd Capt Stegge for her part of )
12000 lb tob recov'ed for mr Adenbrook   )              2666
for tobbo allowed John Stith for         )
her part of Debts recorded there and     )              1544
in the Countrey as by record             )
tobbo pd Howell Pryse for her parte of fees             0913
                                                        ----
                                                        5123

Reduced into money as the estate
was valued by Capt Perry and                            l   s    d
Capt Stegge at 12/s per C: is                           30: 12: 09

Per Contr Cred'r
Besides her share of cattell                            lb tob
For goods and servts and debts                          9422
at 12 s per Cwt as per record
                      is                                56: 10: 08
Debt per Contr Deduced                                  30: 12: 09
                                                        ----------
Rests due to her                                        25: 17: 11
                                                        ----------
                                                        56: 10: 08
```

                Jun: 3: 1661

                Rec. July 15, 61

                (see next page)

page 278. Abstract. "Whereas Edward Mosby Guardian of Judith Parsons one of the orphanes of Joseph Parsons dec'd" having pd from her estate several debts due from her father's estate, amounting to 5123 lb tobo, order that this be allowed.

page 278. Abstract. Respite allowed in dif betw Jno fflowers and Capt Wm ODeon, until Capt ODeon "shall come into these parts of the Country".

page 278. Abstract. Entry faded. Dated 11 May 1660. Robert Wynne, being intrusted by Mr Steph: Hamelin, agent for the relict of Mr John Gibbs, to settle an a/c with Robt Evans of - thousand six hundred lb tobo, comes to an agreement that paymt be made in 1661 and 1662.

```
Consented to By                 Signed    Robert Wynne
  S hamelin
Consented to By
  Robert Evanes
Test  Hoel Pryse  Cl
```

page 279.

```
        Att a Cort held at James Citty 12th June 1661
              ffrancis Moryson Esqr Gov'nor
    Thomas Ludwell secret
    Coll Henry Browne       Col Read
    Coll Wm Bernard         mr Nath: Bacon
    Coll Tho: Pettus        Coll Wood
    Coll Edd Hill           Coll Hamond
    Coll Tho: Swann         Capt Warner
```

Whereas the unsetlednesse of the militia the uncerteinties of Allarmes and the want of fixed armes to Defend the people in time of em'gent dangers are principall causes of those feares and terrors that so frequently disturbe the peace and quiett of the Inhabitants of this Countrey upon the least rumor of the Indians comeing against us, how uncerteine soev'r the same may be. Itt is therefore Ordered by Right Hono'ble the Gov'nor and Counc'll that for prevencon of the like occasions of feares hereafter and for our defence when a war cannot be avoyded, ffirst that whosoev'r shall falsely raise any rumor or reports that may tend to the disturbance of the Countrey shalbe fined 5000 lb of tobbo and suffer one whole yeares impr'omnt

2. Because confidence grows chiefely out of the knowledge of our thoughts, Itt is ordered that ev'y house-keeper in the Countrey be

provided of so many fixed guns and a competent proporcon of powder and shott as he hath men able to beare armes in his family.

3. ffor the fixeing unserviceable armes Itt is ordered that no smith in the countrey shall refuse to fix such guns as shalbe brought to him for that purpose but that he apply himselfe wholly to that worke untill the occasion ceaseth. And in case any smith shall Deny to fix the guns brought to him, he the sd smith if (a freeman) or his master (if a servant) shall by warrt from any Com'r to whom the complt shalbe made, be comitted to prison, the sd Com'r being hereby authorized to issue out a warrt accordingly

4 That a muster be made upon three sev'all dayes in each Com beginning by the last of July next at three such places as by the officers of the militia shalbe appointed and who are hereby required to take a list how many fixed armes how many free men and how many servants are able to bear them, and to make retourne thereof to the Gov'nor by the last of August next ensueinge   And because the whole Reg'mt cannot conveniently at one time upon any suddaine occasion be brought together Itt is therefore ordered that there be an eighth parte of the number of tytheable persons chosen out of the whole Regim't to be as a trayned band always ready in armes, w'ch trayned bands are to be proporconed into three companies consisting of freemen or servants of undoubted ffidelity, liveing as neare as maybe to the places appointed for their Rondervous upon an Alarme made.

5   ffor the better distinguishing when Allarmes are made and that it may be knowne there is a necessity for the trayn'd bands reporting when ev'r they are made, Itt is ordered that the distinct f-eing off of three guns shalbe an allarme, and that the same shal not be made upon any other occasion then some forceable assault made by the Indians, or house fired by them, or one or more persons being wounded or killed

6   Itt is further ordered that the Com'rs of the Militia of each Com appoint three such places in each of their precincts as are most fitt to oppose an invasion of the enemy and to communicate assistance and supply to such persons or places as shall first want it, and that they appoint Comand'rs to receive the soldiers comeing thither upon Alarme, and march wth them to the assistance of such whose necessities shall require it

7   That upon Allarmes made the trayned bands report im'iediately to those places they are respectively appointed to belong to and there accordingly to their Ordrs given by such officers as shalbe appointed to receive them to march under his com'and to the rescue of such distressed places or persons as he their Comand'r shall Direct

page 281.

8 That a propor'con of horse vidzt to ev'ry footeman one horseman be added to augment the number of the trayned bands who are to be Comanded as the foot

Whereas there are comands out of England and from the Assembly how to administer the oathes of alleageance and sep'rmacie to all tytheables in the Countrey, in regard of the conveniencie that wilbe of putting the same in execucon att the sev'all musters Itt is therefore ordered that two Justices at least of the Comicon of each Com give their attendance at the places appointed for the musters and administer the same accordingly

Orders that no minister shall officiate nor any other person be admitted of the vestry that shall refuse to take the oathes of allegeance and supremacie and subscribe the following
As I do acknowledge my selfe a true sonne of the Church of England, so I do beleive the articles of faith there professed, And oblige my selfe to be conformable to the Doctrines and discipline there taught and established
                              Rec July: 15: 1661

Note: Here follows a long, and to me, very tiresome letter from Francis Moryson, 'Gov'nor and Capt Gen'all of Virga' recapitulating the foregoing papers, attempting to quiet the fears of the people and yet making provision for their defense. This letter is recorded in full, pages 281 - 282 - 283, 15th July 1661.   B.F.

then follows:

page 283.
            By the Gov'nor and Capt Gen'all of Virga
To all whom these presents shall concerne, Know yee that I ffrancis Moryson Esqr Gov'nor and Capt Gen'll of Virginia
    have authorized and impowered Coll Abraham Wood Lt Coll Thomas Drewe Major Wm Harris Capt John Epes Capt Wm ffarrar Capt Peter Jones Capt Edd Hill Junr and Capt ffrancis Grey to be the Com'anders of the Regim't of the trayned bands in the Counties of Henrico and Charles Citty, And Capt Thomas Stegge to be Comander of all the horse listed in the troope to be raised in the sd Counties, ffor the exercise of w'ch power according to the order made att a meeting of the Counc'll at James Citty the 22th of June last this shalbe their sufficient power and warrent untill a formall and full Comicon be graunted to them particularly: Given this fourth of July 1661.
                              Francis Moryson

            Rec: July 15. 1661.

page 284.
     Att a meeting of the Militia att
      Westov'r July 12: 1661
present   Coll Abraham Wood Esqr
   Lt Coll Thomas Drewe Capt Thomas Stegge
   Major Willm Harris   Com'ander of horse
   Capt John Epes
   Capt Edward Hill
   Capt ffrancis Grey

page 284. Itt is ordered that the sev'all companies of this Regiment for the present be Divided proporooned and distinguished as foll vidzt

1. The Collonells companie to be from the Citty Creeke to Bykers Creeke on the Southside of James River

2. The Lt Collonells Companie to be from Powells Creek to Wards Creeke on the Southside of the river, and on the North side from Capt Stegges Creeke to the Lowest extent of the Countie on that side the riv'r

3. The Majors companie to be from Powells Creeke in Henrico Com to the falls of James riv'r on the South side thereof and Curles plantacon to four mile Creeke

4. Capt John Epes his companie to be from Swin house to Capt Stegges Creeke (includeing the same) and all Sherley hundred Island, and from Bykers Creeke to Powells Creeke on the South side of the river

5. Capt William ffarrars company to be from Turkey Island Creeke to the falls on the North side except Curles aforesd

6. Capt Peter Jones his companie to be from Citty Creeke to the falls of Appomattock riv'r on the south side, And from Powells Creeke to the sd falls on the North side

7. Capt Edward Hills companie to be from Swinhouse Creeke to Turky Island Creek, except Sherley hundred Island.

8. Capt ffrancis Greys company to be from Wards Creeke to the lowest extent of the Com on that side the river

page 285. Ordered that Capt John Woodleife, as Capt Lt of this Regmt have the leading and com'and of the Collonells company according to ordrs and direccons

      (see next page)

page 285. The sev'all places appointed for report of the trayned bands upon allarmes made are Capt Stegges plantacon at the falls of James riv'r, ffort Henry, and Moris Rose his plantacon att the head of Wards Creeke

page 285. Howell Pryse by reason of his occasioned attendance and imploymt as Clearke to the Regiment is hereby exempted and excused from all personall military services and comands

page 285. Itt is ordered that all the freemen inhabiting in Henrico Com, except Bristol parish, shall meet and appe att a muster to be made at Roxdall on the 22th of this Instant July about nine of the clock in the forenoone w'th their armes, and there give in their names, and lists of all their armes fixed and unfixed, servants and serviceable horses and mares, w'th acco't of theire sev'all ammunicon, from wch none to be exempted but Com'rs and sherr, who notw'thstanding are to send in their lists and accots as aforesd: And all unfixed armes are to be forthwith carried to the smiths next inhabiting, by the sev'all owners thereof, to be repaired, w'ch if refused forthwth to be done, the party grieved to prosecute the smith, or his master, according to order of the Right Hono'ble Gov'nor and Counc'll Dated the 12th of June last

page 286. Itt is also further ordered that Capt Wm ffarrar be assistant to Major Wm Harris in the sd muster, that they cause to be there published the Gov'nors Remonstrance and take an exact list and acct of the persons, armes, horses and municon as abovesd, And by their warrant com'and the Constables to sumon the sev'all Inhabitants to the sd muster.

Itt is further ordered that mr Richd Cook and mr Christofer Branch give their attendance at the sd muster, and then and there tender and administer oaths of allegeance and supremacie to all the sd Inhabitants, and to comitt to the sherriffs custody untill farthur order, all or any person or persons that shall refuse the same. And that Major Harris give timely notice and warning to the sd Com'rs for their attendance for the purpose aforesd

And itt is further ordered that after performance of all the premisses Major Wm Harris and Capt Wm ffarrar aforesd appoint and nominate by their sev'all particular names an eighth part of the freeman so listed to be a setled trained band, and those to be such whose habitacons are neerest to the allarme place at Capt Steggs plantacon at the falls, as also to ev'y four footemen to add one horseman, and they to be in continuall readinesse and preparacon to march away w'th all possible speed upon allarmes made (w'th armes defensive and offensive and each man furnished w'th one pownd of powder, and four pounds of shott) unto the Allarme place aforesd, there to observe and performe the com'ands and direccons of Capt Thomas Harris appointed for that place one of the Capts of the guard of the Counties

page 286 (continued)

And the said Major Wm Harris and Capt Wm ffarrar are to give and present an accot of their proceedings in all the premisses under their hands (together w'th the gen'all lists) w'th all possible speed to Coll Abraham Wood esqr att ffort Henry. And to be very wary and circumspect that no amunicon be spent - wast at the sd muster but onely false fires to be given to prove the readinesse of their guns.

page 287. Itt is further ordered that so often as any allarme shalbe made by the dischargeing of three guns distinctly, the Inhabitants of the next plantacon answer the same by the shooting of three distinct guns and so to passe from plantacon to plantacon throughout the whole regim't: And the next adjoyning Comicon officer to the place where any default shalbe made forthw'th to take out a warrt from the next Com'r Directed to the sherr for present apprehension of the party deficient, and detencon of his person in safe custody untill he shall have answered his contempt therein

And that this Order be published at each sev'all muster

Itt is ordered that the like muster be made by the sayd Major Harris w'th the assistance of Capt John Epes of all the freemen Inhabitants of Bristoll parish, and of the South side of James River downe to Powells Creeke and of the North side downe to Queenes Creeke on the 24th of this instant July att Charles Citty, and list and accots be taken and returned as abovesd. And that mr Anthony Wyatt and Capt Robt Wynne haveing timely notice from the sd Major Harris give their attendance att the sd muster, and before tender and administer the oathes of allegeance and supremacie to all the sd Inhabitants and comitt the party or parties refuseing to take the same into the sherr custody

That an 8th part of the sd Inhabitants be selected and listed for a trayned band, w'th addicon of horse, and provided as aforesd, to report to ffort Henry upon occasion of allarme and there to be comanded by Capt ffrancis Epes one of the Capts of the Guards of the Counties

And that the sd Major Harris and Capt Epes observe and performe all other comands and direccons as in the fore menconed muster is exprest

page 288. Itt is further ordered that the like muster be made by the sayd Major Harris w'th the assistance of Capt ffrancis Grey of all the freemen Inhabitants from Powells Creeke on the South side, And from Oldmans Creeke on the North side to the lower extent of the Com upon the 5th of August next att fflowriday hundred, and that lists and accots be taken and returned as abovesd; That mr John Holmwood and mr Stephen Hamelin haveing timely notice from the sd Major Harris

(continued)

page 288 (continued)

give their attendance att the sd muster and tender and administer the oaths of allegance and Supremacie to the sd Inhabitants and imprison by their power in the sherr' custody all persons refuseing the same

That an 8th part of the sd Inhabitants be selected and listed for a trayned band, wth addicon of horse as aforesd, and provided as before directed to report upon occasion of allarmes to Moris Rose his plantacon on the head of Wards Creeke, there to be comanded by Capt John Wall one of the Capts of the guard of the Counties

And that the sd Major Harris and Capt Grey observe signifie and follow all other comands and direccons as in the first branch hereof is expressed for the first muster

page 288. On request of Major Willm Harris Itt is ordered that Thomas Calloway be taken out of the Company of Lt Coll Drewe, and added to the sd Majors company, by reason of his military experience and the greate use the sd Major shall have of such a person.

. . . .

Note: The next Court was held at Westover on the 3rd of August 1661. Abstracts of the proceedings will be continued in Vol. 12 of this series.   B. F.

INDEX

Abernethy, Robt. 6. 22
Adams, Jno. 12. 15. 71. 76. 77
Adenbrook, Mr. 96
Alder, Jane 74
Alford, Wm. 89
Allcock, Basil 21
Allen, Antho. 9. 42
Allmand, Jno. 74
Alsop, Ben 27
Allam, Jno. 79
Allen, Humfrey 87
Amas, Edd 63
Andrewes, Jno 28
Annis, Joice 33
Ardington, Edd 11. 32
Armore, Phill: 28
Armstrong, Andrew 28
          Geo. 22
Arwood, Wm. 28
Ashwin, Tho. 33
Ast, John 45. 50
    Mary 45. 50. 67. 71
Aston, Mr 53
    Ferdinando 17. 18. 35
        45. 51. 71. 72
    Mrs. Hannah 19. 29. 30
        52. 63
    Col. Walter 15. 19. 52
        89
Atkins, Benefield 28
      Geo. 1. 2. 3.
Atwell, Tho. 53
Avery, Mark 12. 77

Bacon, Mr. Nath: 97
Badger, Isaac 27
Baker, Richd. 54. 62. 67. 81
    Wm. 74
Banister, Jone 17. 24
    Lt. John 6. 20. 24.
        31. 45. 54. 57. 61
        64. 67. 93
Bankes, Henry 63
Banks, Phebie 92
Barber, John 64
Barefoote, Geo. 8. 61. 89

Barker, Eliz. 24. 30
    Henry 24
    James 1. 7. 9. 10. 12.
        24. 32. 33. 84
    Margaret 24. 27
    Michael 30
Barriss, James 28
Barton, Persivall 71
    Tho: 27
Basterd, Henry 12
Baston, Theoph: 28
Batt, Christopher 4
Battell, Mathew 87
Batts, Henry 39
    Thos 38. 39
    Wm 39
Baugh, Wm 8. 41
Bayly, Mr Arthur 8. 12. 13. 14
Bayley, Dorothie 52
    Fortune 17
    Jas. 33
    Jane 16
    Richd 14. 16. 52
    Thos. 11. 49
    Thos. Sr. 48
    Wm. 81. 90
Beake, Richd 74
Beaseley, Wm 17
Beauchamp, Jno. 44. 62. 63. 65
        83. 89. 94. 95
Beck, Edd 53
Beddingfield, Mary 92
      Theoph: 61. 92
Beedles, Tho. 81
Benfield, Edd 28
Bennett, Gov. Richd 69
Berkeley, Sir Wm. 5. 6. 7. 54
    66. 69
Bernard, Col. Wm 97
Berry, Hugh 27
Bigge, Tho. 79
Biggins, Lawrence 30. 88
Bill form 1657. 32
Bird, John of London 30. 58
    Margaret of Bristol and
      of Virginia 27
    Robt of Warwick Creek 73

Bird, 9. 13. 30. 70. 80 83
  86. 90. 91. 94.
Bird's feathers 53. (personal and
  private family memo. Historians
  and nosey genealogists kindly
  mind their own business. B.F.)
Bishop, Edmond 47
  Capt John 27. 51
Blackbird (barque) 35
Blamore, Ja: 61. 76
Blanks, Tho. 47. 81
Bland, Mrs Frances 83
  Theoderick 8. 9. 10. 11.
    32. 45. 52. 66. 70. 71
    76. 81. 87. 90.
Bland's Path 79
Blessing, Ralph 21
Blyth, Ellinor 33
Burgesse, Robt. 33
Booker, Roger 47
Bonaccord 31
Bond, Capt. Richd of Bristol and
    Virginia 27. 48
Boston, Sam 70
Bottle, Margaret 92
Bourcher, Susan 22
Boyce, Thos. 84
Bradly, Jos. 76
Braine, Richd. 31. 84. 86
Branch, Christopher 41. 42. 101
  Tho. 41. 72
Brereton, Tho. 5. 7. 60. 69
Brett, Susanna 64
Breuton, Wm of R.I. 35. 57
Brewer, Eliz. 40
  Geo. 6. 23. 31. 37. 41. 42
Briggs, Henry 14. 86
Brooke, Walter 6
Brookes, Walter 60. 61
Broome, Tho. 61
Browne, Hen: 69. 97
  Rich. 33
  Tho. 70
Bryans, Wm. 22
Buck, Agnes 22
Bunne, Mathew 35. 36
Burdon, Jno. 80. 83. 85
Burgis, Robt. 46.
Burne, Mathew 57
Burton see Burdon
Burton, Jo: 24. 31. 51. 56

Burgesses to limit expenses 80
Bury, Alice 70
Busby, Tho: 80
Bush, Wm 63
Bushell, Edw. 90
Butler, Jo. 11
  Mary 11

Calloway, Tho. 15. 28. 61. 74.
    85. 91. 103
Callyons, Maryan 95
  Thos. 95
Cammock see Cormack
Carter, Bridgett 74
  Richd. 51. 52. 53. 80
  Sara 53. 54
Cartwright, Benj. 2. 3. 20
Case, Roger 28
Castle, Tho. 74
Chamberlin, Dr. Wm. 40. 42. 85
    87. 91. 95
Chance, Marian 53
Chandler, Ann 74
Chappell, Tho. 17. 18. 93
Chappell orphanes
Church, Anna 62
  Nicho: 89
Clarke, Richd 42. 53
  Tho. 3
  John 15
  Judith 73
  Mary 73
  Robt. 73
  Wm 76
Clay, Charles 78
  Wm. 65. 95
Clemence, Cornel: 53. 90. 96
Coale, Jno. 86
Coalman, Robt 19
Cook, Mr. 12. 94
  Richd. 8. 14. 39. 41. 94
    101.
Cook's Mill 91
Cogan, Dr. John formerly of
    Bristol. 27. 37. 44. 45
    48. 50. 52. 55. 59. 60
    68. 71. 72. 73. 84. 90
Coleman see Coalman
Collett, Sam. 28
Colsyth, Richd 62

Comly, Henry 73
    Judith 73
Communion Silver for Martin's
    Brandon Parish 80
Cooke, Fran: 22
    Tho: 89
Coolish, Thos. 25, 26
Cooper, Mary 53
Copeland, Wm. 67
Cordell, Jone 44
Cormack, Danl. 27
Court House and Prison. 39, 46
    54, 55, 81, 82
Courtney, Phil: 87
Covell, Robt. 33
Cox, Richd. 94
Coxe, Jo: 41
Cradock, Robt. 47
Craford, Samson 76
Crane, Tho: 1, 26, 31, 63, 79
    Walter 89
Crewes, Jas. 8, 10, 22, 29, 45
    50, 63, 67, 71, 94
    95.
Crooke, Thos: 63
Crowe, Jno. 53
Cuerton, Tho. 29
Culmer, Thos: 88, 89, 90
Cunliffe, Johan 92
    John 92
Currey, Alse 84
    Macam 84

Davies, Richd. 71
    Thos. 69
Daux, Ann 10
    Mary 10
    Richd of London 22
    Susan 10
    Walter 9, 10, 16, 22, 30
    39, 47, 78, 95.
Daux orphanes 39
Daniell, Jno. 3
Darnham, Walter 17
Davies, Amy 33
    Richd. 71
    Tho: 6, 69
Davis, Naomie 92
Dawdin, Sara 21
Deffell, Robt. 49

Dekem, Seger 12
Denne, Jno. 27
Dennington, Tho. 78, 79
Dessell, Robt of Bristol 27
Devall, Jno. 23, 37, 39, 41, 42
Dibdall, Rev. John 2, 8, 11, 12
    17, 22, 32, 33, 57, 58, 76
    77, 83, 86, 88, 91, 93.
    Mrs. Jone 34
    Richd. 33, 34, 76, 85
    Mrs. Sara 22, 34, 85
Dicks, Jervis 60
Dimity drawers 24
Dobson, Seth 27
Dodford, Jno. 27
Doelitle, Wm. 92
Dollin, Rebecca 54
    Wm. 53, 54, 83
Dolbens, R. 24
Donnalls, Rich 21
Donne, Jno. see Denne
Douglas, Geo. 56, 65, 66
    Thomas 63, 75, 76, 86, 95
Dowlin see Dollin
Drayton, Jno. 4, 19, 29, 37, 38,
    43, 47, 51, 52, 61,
    63, 64, 80, 81, 83,
    84,
Drewe, Thomas 2, 4, 6, 7, 11, 12,
    20, 28, 29, 31, 33,
    37, 40, 43, 49, 52,
    54, 57, 64, 66, 70,
    75, 77, 80, 83, 85,
    86, 88, 89, 90, 93,
    99, 100, 103.
Drewe, Thomas as a Commissioner
    1, 7, 10, 14, 15, 19
    20, 23, 28, 31, 33,
    40, 42, 43, 46, 47,
    50, 54, 56, 57, 61,
    66, 67, 70, 72, 77,
    78, 82, 86, 88, 91,
    93, 94.
Drowned while bathing. 14
Drummond, Wm 39, 78
Drysdall, James 14, 68
Duckett, Jas. 27
Dunne, Ann 49
    Joseph 2, 3, 29, 58,
Duraine, Mary 53
Dyer, Tho. 33

Ealle, Sam 6. 54.
East, Jane 59. 75. 77
    Thos. 59. 75. 77
Edds, Wm 53
Edenborough, Mr 10
Edmonton in England 58
Edwards, John 72. 74
    Margaret 44
    Wm. 12. 37. 39. 44
      52. 53. 88. 89
      94. 95
Egbrough, Mrs Jane 78
    Wm. 37
Elcock, Jane 28
Elliott, Phill: 37. 48. 58.
    70. 90. 94. 96.
Ellis, Edd 9. 46
Epes, Francis 1. 10. 11. 19
    20. 21. 30. 35. 46. 50
    57. 61. 66. 70. 75. 77
    78. 102
Epes, Captain John 9. 11. 31
    49. 54. 59. 66. 75. 81
    88. 99. 100. 102
    Capt. Jno. as Commissioner
    1. 10. 15. 21. 28. 31
    37. 46. 47. 50. 54. 57
    61. 66. 67. 70. 72. 75
    77. 78 85. 88. 94.
Epes, Thomas 11
Evans, Hugh 1
    John, Sr. 48. 49
    Robt. 35. 45. 52. 97
Ewen, Jno. 94

Farley, Geo. 29. 71. 81
    Jone 33
Farlow, Geo. 76
Farmer, Arth: 48
    Henry 28
    Robt 61
Farr, Nicho 70
Farrar, Wm. 41. 42. 99. 100
    101. 102
Feepes, Jno. 94
Felton, Thos. 51
Fenn, Hen: 33
Ferdinan, Robt. 48

Fisher, Wm. 18. 22
Fitzgarrett - 2
Fitzgerald, Edw. 8. 11. 15. 16.
    17. 18. 22. 24.
    28
    Mary 28
Fletcher, Michaell 21. 78
Flower, John 9. 10. 11. 13. 16.
    22. 30. 36. 37. 38. 44
    47. 51. 57. 59. 63. 64
    65. 77. 81. 89. 90. 95
    97.
    Mary 10
Floyd, Walter 74
Foliott, Rev. Edw. 84. 91
Forshaw, Danl. 90. 96
    Hugh 90
Fort Henry 37. 101
Fox, Capt. Robt. 67
French pox 85

Gallis, Jno. 22. 83
Gardiner, Anth: 63
Garrett, Wm 78
Gay, Ro: 33
Gerard, Henry 51
Gerey, Roger 27
Gibbs, Jno. 35. 36. 52. 87. 97
Gibson, - 81
    Peter 28
Gilham, John 52. 54. 56. 61. 63
    64. 70.
Gillard, Wm 31. 32. 43
Gittings, John 64
Glasbery, Tho: 28
Glover, Jno. 74
Graunt, Arthur 56
Greene, Jas. 28
    Lewis 61. 81
    Martha 75. 80. 89
    Wm. 1. 43. 93
Greenfield, Christopher 35. 52
Greenhough, Jno. 3
Greenwood, Edd 9. 38. 46
Gregory, Charles 23
Grey, Francis 4. 11. 46. 51. 52.
    67. 73. 80. 82. 84.
    85. 86. 99. 100.
    102. 103.

Grey, Robt. 74
    Saml. 96
Griffen, Neale 74
Griffis, John 14
Griffith, John 59
Gubbens, Hugh 14. 92
Gundry, Ann 94
    John 94

Hacker, Jno. 2
Hackett, James 33
Haines, Jas. 22
    Robt 33
Hall, Ann 79
    Bernard 28
    Hellena 79
    Jane, Jr., 79
    Jane, Sr., 79
    John 64
    Oswin 79
    Steph: 21
Hallam, Robt 94
    Sara 94
Hallywell, Edw. 94
Halsey, Steph: 28
Hamelin, Stephen 1. 4. 10. 39
    47. 48. 52. 54. 65.
    70. 73. 80. 81. 95.
    97. 102.
Hamelin, Steph: as Commissioner
    9. 10. 14. 15. 19. 21
    22. 23. 28. 31. 33.
    70. 72. 74. 77. 78.
    80. 82. 85. 88. 91.
    93. 94.
    Stephen, Jr., 47
Hamlet, Eliz: 88
    Maurize 92
    Richd. 14. 68. 88
    Robt. 92
Hammond, Tho. 1. 15. 63. 87. 97
Hampton, Wm. 33
Hanscome, Edd 53
Harard, Jos. 14
Hardman see Herdman
Hardaway see Hardway
Hardway, James 12
    John 77. 80. 82. 83
    84. 87. 89. 95
Harmore see Armore
Harper, Major John of Bristol 27

Harris, Elizab: 53
    George 26
    Jo: 10. 87
    Capt. Thos. 101
    Maj. Wm. 41. 99. 100.
        101. 102. 103
Harrison, Jone 74
    Rebecca 28
    Wm. 2. 70. 89. 90
Hart, Gabriell 28
Harwell, Sam 73. 81
    Wm 27
Harwood see Arwood
Harwood, Jno. 28
Hatcher, Mr 65
    Edd 51
    Wm 36. 57
Hatley, Jo 53. 82
Hawkins, Hen: 71
Hayes, George 28
Heath, Julian 33
Heatham, Rebecca 53
Heming, Edw. 67
Henton, Dorothy 64
Herdman, Robt. Sr. & Jr. 55
    Walter 68
Heriman, Danl. 21
Herman, Susan 28
Hermison, Isaac 4. 6.
Hewett, Alex: 53
Heynes, Tho: 28
Heynet, Robt. 21
Heywood, Roger 27
Hide, Robt. Jr. & Sr. 28
Highways 8
Hill, Col. Edward. 19. 37. 43.
    45. 46. 50. 52. 54. 55
    64. 66. 73. 77. 78. 80
    81. 82. 89. 90. 93. 97
    99
    Edward, Jr. 44. 64. 73. 88
    90. 100
    Edward, Jr. as Commission-
      er. 38. 43. 47. 50.
      54. 56. 62. 66. 67.
      69. 72. 78. 85
    Elizabeth 64
    William 17. 20. 50. 52
      63. 81
Hind, Walter 63. 65
Hinton, Timothy 33
Hodges, Jno. 6. 32. 87

Hoe, Rice 15. 29. 30. 38. 45.
    58. 61. 63. 72. 73.
    82. 83. 88. 89. 90.
  Mrs. Sarah 29
Hogson, Math: 64
Hogwood, Francis Jr. & Sr. 92
Holdsworth, Walter 4. 9. 51.
    68. 92
Holford, Tho: 6. 11. 39. 50.
    54. 61. 63.
Holicrosse, Dan 66. 71
Holmes, Peter 55
  Richd 55
Holmwood, John 8. 12. 15. 21.
    23. 28. 43. 44. 46.
    47. 50. 56. 60. 69.
    70. 72. 76. 82. 84.
    86. 87. 90. 93. 94.
    102.
Holsey, Ann 71
Honny, Martha 33
Hookes, Robt. 33
Hopper, Wm 25
Horsley, Wm 21
Horsmonden, Warham 10. 19.
    45. 54. 72
Horsmonden, War. as Com'r.
    9. 19. 31. 32. 45.
    55
Houldsworth, Mary 92
    Naomie 92
Houldsworth see Holdsworth
Howell, Lt. John 29. 30. 38
    43. 50. 51. 54. 81
Hoxsteed, Sam 21
Hughes, Jno. 83
    Kath: 87. 95
    Tho: 87
    Wm. 83
Hunt, Oliver 7. 53
    Tho. 71. 78
    Wm. 15. 66. 67. 68. 69
    70. 81
Hunter, John 33
Huntley, Jno. 9
    Millisent 9. 12
Huxe, Barbara 16
    Mary 92
    Tho. 10. 16. 22. 92

Indian Invasion threatened 97
Isham, Henry 41. 42

Jackson, Patrick 19. 62. 76. 81
    Rebecca 74
    Tho: 33
Jacob, John 17. 64
Jannice, Jas. 89
Jennings, Ralph 74
Johnson, Luce 27
    Saml. 94
    Wm. 59. 60. 62. 63. 72. 77
Jones, David 35
    Edd: 27
    Hugh 74
    Jno. 77
    Lewis 33
    Rev. Richd. 62
    Robt 47
    Morgan 6. 51. 54. 59. 75
        77. 79. 81
    Capt. Peter 99. 100
    Robert 47. 81
Jordan, George 87
Justice, Wm. 24. 25. 31. 51. 53. 81
    89.

Kemidges Creek 89
Kent, Humfrey 31
Kerr, Gilbert 70
Key, Isaac 33
    Tho. 33
Kicotan 53
Kigan, Dennis 37. 92
    Phebie 92

Lacie, Ralfe 27
Lane - possibly shown as Laud
Lanier, Jno. 33
    Lucrece 33
Lambson, Wm. 46. 51
Lamping, Jere 77
Land - see Laud
Langworth, Susana 74
Lash, John 25 . 8
Laud, Curtis 8. 80. 90

Laud, Geo. of London 1
    George 56
Lawrence, Arthur 15. 50
    Wm. 8. 50
    Orphans 15
Lea, Wm 38. 45. 51. 64
Leadbeater, Henry 59
Lee, Edd 14
    Jas. 28
Leonard, Wm 28
Letherland, Mrs. Frances 30. 62
Lewis, John 21
Ligon, Tho. 4. 7. 41
Llewellin, Dan 8. 9. 22. 94
    Margaret 94
    Thos. 53
Lloyd, Martha 28
Long-John 64
Love, Joseph 33
Loveing, Tho. 8. 22. 78
Lucal, Ann 53
Lucas, Roger 92
    Wm 92
Lucie, Sam 21. 30. 63
Ludson, Tho. 16
Ludwell, Thos. Secry. 97
Lurs, Rowland 22

MacBryon, Dennis 27
MacKenny, Morgan 32
Mackule, Jno. 70
Macocke, Mrs Sara 33
Madard (goodman, wife & dau) 40
Madder, Tho. 42
Maine, Henry 35
    Jno. 59
Major, Alex. 59
Mallard, Humfrey 27
Malory, Tho. 56. 63
M aloyne, Walter 64
Manell, Robt. 70
Mann, Tho. 74
Marrone, Moore 33
Marsellis, Nichol 16. 74
Marsh, Nichol 28
Marshall, Geo. 14
    Jo 9. 76
Marston, Thos. 86
Martin Brandon Par. Reg. 92

Mascall, Richd 4
Matchett, Hen: 28
Mather, Eliz 80
    Tho: 38. 62. 63. 80
Mathewes, Edd 51. 65. 66. 68
Mathews, Gov. Saml 7
May, Jo: 33
Mayes, Jno. 19
Mayor, Rich: 33
Meldrum, Alex. 76. 81
Mercer, Robt. 74
Merywether, John 64
    Thos. 64
Midleton, Geo. 3. 89
    Robt. 53
Minter, John 89. 90
    Mary 89. 90. 92
Moes, Rolan 36
Molesworth, Guy 6. 20
Moody, Tho. 15
Moone, Chas. 73
    Jas. 81
    Margaret 94
    Math: 33
    Tho. 64
Morgan, Tho. 49. 58
    Tho. of Bristol 27.
Morgane, Richd. 27
Moris, Hugh 74
    Wm. 21
Moryson, Gov. Francis 5. 69. 97. 99
Mosby, Mr 19
    Edward 4. 24. 29. 80. 86.
    87. 91. 96. 97.
    Richd. 29. 67. 87
Moulson, Foulk 56
Mountain, Johan 92
Muces, Jos (?) 28
Murrayne, Danl 23
Mudgett, Ellinor 92
    Elizab: 92
    Tho: 56. 86. 92
Mumford, Will 47
Murraine, Dan 45
Murray, Robt. 13. 16. 77

Newcome, Hen: 54
Nicholas, Richd: 17. 47. 65. 71.
    82. 88.

Nicholas, Mrs. Susanna 65. 71. 72
  82
Nicholls, Jas. 80
Nicholson, Robt. 9. 19. 29. 55
Nothway, Tho. 1. 9. 65. 82.

ODeon, William 8. 11. 12. 13
  16. 22. 25. 26. 35. 58
  64. 95. 97.
Old Town 49
Olliver, Wm 32
Osborne, Ellias 14. 84. 85
  Fran: 27
  John 27. 49
Osman, John 21
Owen, Bartlet 4

Pace, Geo. 33
  Richd 3. 33. 63. 79
  Sara 33
Parham, James 6. 40. 54
Parish Reg. Martin's Brandon 92
Parker, Dr. Richd. 2. 3. 8. 18.
  21. 22. 23. 30. 38. 43
  44. 59. 60. 64. 65. 67
  69. 70. 94
Parsons, Jos. 10. 97
  Judith 96. 97
Pate, Thurgood 4
Peibils, Capt. David 47
  Mrs. Eliz: 3. 6
Perkins, Eliz: 18
  Jerem 28
  Lydia 18
  Nichol 18
Perkinson, Ralfe 27
Perram, Tho. 36. 54. 67. 79
Perram - see Parham.
Perry, Nicholas 8. 9. 10. 11
  13. 17. 38. 51. 65. 70
  71. 73. 78. 86.
Pery, Capt. Hen: 7. 10. 12. 13
  21. 27. 46. 47. 51. 96
Peters, Thos. 72. 84
  Wm. 33
Peterson, Hen: 74
Pettus, Coll Hen: 97

Pettus, Col. Thos: 7
Phelps, Rich: 73
Phillips, Saml. 81
Pierces hundred als fflowrday
  hundred. 33
Pierson, Dr. Wm. 83. 84
Pigott, Jno. 83
Plaine, Jno. 10
  Mary 10
  Richd. 21
  Robt. 10
Plumer, Ann 53
  Mary 53
Plummer, Peter (If you had ever
  known a man with this name
  you would never forget him.
                              B.F.)
  9. 11. 50. 52. 53
Pollard, Tho. 28
Polson, Jno. 21
  Richd. 28
Poole, Ellinor 92
  Nicho: 7. 50
  Ralph 89. 92
Poultry 66
Poythres, Thos. 56
Porter, Elias 33
Posled, Jno. 4
Potter, Geo. 12. 16. 21. 32. 35
  36. 51. 57. 66. 71
  Robt. 35. 36
Powell, James 32
Poythress, Fran: 93
  Jno. 93
Pratt, John 14
  John Sr & Jr. 95
Price, Richd. 27. 49. 90. 94
  Tho: 27
  Wm 53
Prince, Jane 20
  Tho: 20. 70
Pryor, Jno. 28
Pryse, Howell 3. 4. 5. 6. 9. 10
  14. 20. 22. 27. 32. 36. 37.
  39. 44. 48. 57. 65. 71. 74.
  78. 81. 88. 91. 93.

(For Howell Pryse as Clerk of
the Court see next page)

Pryse, Howell - as clerk. 6. 13.
17. 18. 19. 23. 24. 25. 31.
33. 34. 36. 43. 44. 48. 53.
54. 55. 61. 66. 69. 71. 72.
77. 81. 82. 84. 85. 90. 94.
95. 96. 97. 101.

Quelch, Martin   29. 40. 60. 70.
80. 87.

Races. Legality questioned 65
Radford see Redford
Rainer, Jas. 14. 77
Ramsey, Wm. 93
Rands, Margaret 94
    Thomas 7. 31. 94
Ramage, Jas. 48
Randolph, Henry 5. 36. 38. 57.
64. 78
Ranger, Wm 58
Rawlins, Roger 10
Rawlinson, Jane 92
    Wm. 61. 79. 82. 83.
84. 85. 86. 88.
89. 90. 91. 92.
93.
Rayner, Jas. 2. 61
    Jno. 2
Read, Coll Geo. 7. 97
Redford, Ann 16. 71. 72
    Francis 8. 11. 15. 16
22. 31. 32. 35. 43
72.
Reese, Roger 81
Reeves, Wm 33
Reyner, Jas 14. 77
Reynes, Wm. 11. 54. 86
Reynolds, Jane 12
    Jos. 44. 60
    Tho. 3. 6. 8. 11. 14
77. 79. 81
Rhodes, Rebecca 33
Rice, Robt. 33
Richards, Edw. 58
    John 10. 70. 86
Richardson, Edd 74
Richman, Thos. 59. 60. 62. 63.
65. 71. 72. 77.

Roaffe, Jno. 21
Roberts, Evan 93
    Wm 93
Robins, Col. Obed: 7
Robinson, Wm. 47. 51. 70
Rogers, Johanna 28
Rose, Moris 6. 13. 14. 51. 84
85. 87. 101. 103
    Phebe 14
Rosse, Tymothy 27
Rosser, Winifred 84
Rothwell, Robt. 16
    Wm. 12. 16
Rowe, Thos. 80. 87. 88
Rowland, Walter 64
Rowse, Robt 1. 2. 3. 4. 10. 18
19. 24. 29. 38. 43. 59.
65. 70. 81. 87. 88. 90.
Rushworth, Jas. 28
Russell, Robt 6
    Sam: 64

Sadler, Wm. 27
Salmon, Jas. 4. 51
    Peter 2. 3. 9
Salter, Walter 1. 2
Samborne, Mary 53
Sanders, Jane 76
    Joane 15. 75
    Joane Sr & Jr 76
    Robt 21
    Sam: 28
    Susan 75
    Wm. 51. 15. 61. 63. 75
    Wm Sr & Jr 75
Sanford, Peleg 36
Scott, Danl. 6. 76. 91. 93
    Elizab: 93
    Robt. 83. 85. 91. 93
Seares, Alex: 67
    Law: Sr & Jr 92
Seaward, Robt. 28
Sedgrave, Walter 28
Sellery, Tho. 94
Sharpe, Tho. 4. 9
Sheffield, Robt. 27
Shepard, Jas. 28
    Richd. 21
Shipdham, Edmond. 65. 73. 80. 87.
89. 96.

Shipleye, Walter 89
Sholl, Clement 14
Short, Eliz: 50. 64. 65. 89
  Wm. 3. 38. 48. 55. 56
Simons, Richd. 84
Simpson, Lancelot 84
Sinking of Sloop 25. 26
Slaid, Jno. Sr & Jr. 37
Slayd, Jno. 39
  Jno. Jr. 39
  Orphans 88
Sloeman, Jno. 11. 21
Smith, Edmond 87
  Elizabeth 33
  Margaret 74
  Saml. 1. 2. 39. 55. 65
  Wm. 47
Southcott, Otho 18. 57. 61. 73.
  76. 81
Sparrow, Charles 6. 21. 22. 49
  55. 66. 77. 78. 79.
  80. 82. 83. 84. 86.
  87. 88. 89. 91. 92.
  93.
Sparrow, Charles - as Commissioner. 2. 7. 14. 15.
  19. 20. 22. 28. 33.
  46. 47. 50. 54. 56.
  58. 59. 66. 67. 70.
  71.
  Jane 92

Sparrow, Selby 82
Stadword, Joice 44
  Margaret 44
  Wm 52
  Wm. Jr. 44
  Wm. Sr. 44
Stagg see Stegge
Stegge, Tho. 5. 6. 7. 10. 11.
  22. 23. 31. 33. 37.
  38. 39. 44. 45. 46.
  52. 54. 58. 59. 65.
  87. 96. 99. 100.
Stegge, Tho: as Commissioner.
  1. 19. 21. 22. 23.
  31. 33. 43. 47. 50.
  54. 55. 56. 66. 70.
  77. 78. 80. 82. 88.
Stenton, Wm. 57

Stepp, Jos. 58
Sterage, Jno. 23
Stevens, Tho. 60. 72
Stevenson, Johanna 52
  Sara 92
  Thomas 40. 51. 52. 53.
   59. 90. 92. 94.
Stiles, Sara 53
Stinson, Tho. 1. 16
Stirdevant, John 61. 63. 65. 75
Stith, John 1. 10. 22. 29. 30.
  43. 46. 56. 57. 70.
  72. 82. 83. 91. 94.
  96.
Stokes, Jno. 95
  Mary 27
  Sylvanus 27
Stopp see Stepp
Stroete, Robt 84
Stronge, Tho. 76
Swann, Col. Thos. 97
Suicide of John Adams 76. 77
Symonds, Amee 56
  Eliz: 56
  Margaret 56
  Saml: 56
  Symon 56. 86
  Symon Sr & Jr 48. 89
  Wm 4
Syphilis 85

Tall, Antho: 17. 39. 40. 56. 64.
  88.
Tame, Mary 28
Tams see Tame
Tanner, Thomas 3. 6. 8. 9. 19.
  41. 42. 45. 57. 80. 81.
  88.
Tattersole, Wm. 58
Tatham, Isaac 90. 94
Taylor, Mr. 81
  Christopher 48
  Jo: 14
  Math: 28
  Richd: 45. 51. 61. 63. 84.
Terrell, Michael 74
Thomas, Jone 17. 62
  Mary 71
Thompson, Jno. 35. 52. 57. 67

Thompson see Tomson
Thorne, Wm 33
Thweyt, ffranc: 28
Till, Thos. 16. 17. 20.
Tippett, Jno. 84
Tobacco Warehouses for Co. 20
Tofte, Jas: 27
     Jno: 73
Toke, Richd 28
Tomlinson, Thos. 3. 63. 67. 90
Tompkins, Elizab: 27
Tomson, Jno. 57
Toppin, Jno. 58. 62
Tottersell see Tattersole
Townsend, Ann 16
Trained bands 98
Trehan, Franc: 86. 93
Trenser, Simeon 46
Tucky, Ellinor 28
Turner, John 9. 11
     Tho: 29
Turvile, Thos: 27
Twyford, Rich: 33
Tye, Eliz: 49
    Mrs Joyce 23
    Richd: 4. 6. 7. 15. 19. 23
          37. 39. 49. 62. 68.
          84.
    Orphans 68
Tyns, Bernard 21
Tyre, Hen: 74

Varnham, Ellin 35
      Geo: 35
Vaughan, Wm. 4. 12. 63
Vicars, Wm. 87

Waid, Ben 92
    Elias 92
    Naomie 92
Ward, Jas: 62. 63. 84
    Richd: 41. 42
Walker, Lt. Coll. John 69
Wall, John 3. 9. 13. 35. 58. 70
      78. 94. 103.
Waller, Peter 33
Wallis, Jas: 63. 93
Walls, Tho: 2. 11

Walter, Roger 48
Ward, Robt. 27
Warner, Coll 97
Warradine, Mr. 13
     Mrs. 13
     Jas: 11. 37
Warren, Isaac 74
    Nick 48
    Thos: 58. 62
Washborne, Dan 72
Washington, Robt. 83
Webb, Ellias 22
    Gregory 28
    Nichol: 41
Webley, Rich: 36. 57
Webster, Henry 28
Wells, Robt. 28
Welsteed, Roger 48
West, John 6. 11
    Mary 11
Westhorpe, Jno. 30. 87
Westover - window in Church, 93
Weynoke, King of 8. 45. 80
Wharton, Jane 33
Wheeler, Tho: 62
    Wm. 2. 13. 14
White, Chas: 4. 24
    Jno: 4. 13. 27. 47
    Ralph 10
    Tim: 22
Whitmore, Sara 83. 85
Wickerson, Jo: 33
Wigge, Tho: 33
Wilkins, Josias 28
    Wm. 62. 71. 79
Wilkinson, Geo: 28
    Tho: 21
Williams, Mr 10
    Jane 3. 8. 11. 51. 62.
      86.
    Jo: 21
Willyard, Augustin 51. 68
    Austin 14
    Bridgett 16
Wilson, Jane 33
    Mary 21
Wishert, Jas: 38. 44
Wolverton, Edw: 37
Wood, Col. Abra: 4. 6. 7. 37. 97.
      99. 100. 102.

Woodham, Joseph 82
Woodhowse, Ham'on 31
Woodleife, Capt. John 6. 21. 30
                 32. 100
Woodward, Christopher 46. 89
       Saml. 28. 46. 75. 94.
          95.
       Sara 28. 95
Worsuham, Wm. 11. 41. 42. 55
Wortham see Worsuham.
Wragg, Jas. 74
Wray, Marg: 33
Wright, Edd 70
Wyatt, Antho: 1. 2. 3. 4. 6. 9.
      12. 19. 20. 22. 29. 30.
      31. 33. 40. 45. 46. 47.
      55. 58. 66. 72. 79. 80
      81. 83. 88. 102
Wyatt, Antho: as Commissioner.
      1. 7. 10. 14. 15. 19. 20
      23. 25. 26. 27. 28. 31.
      33. 37. 43. 47. 50. 54.
      57. 61. 66. 67. 70. 72.
      75. 77. 78. 82. 85. 88.
      94.
Wyatt, Anthony's daughter 72
Wynne, Bernard 74
    David 27
    Robert 1. 3. 6. 7. 9. 12
       19. 21. 29. 30. 31. 39.
       54. 55. 65. 70. 73. 79.
       81. 82. 93. 97. 102
    Capt. Robt. as burgess 19

Yeamans, Fran: Jr., 27
Young, Dorcas 74
Younge, John 27

www.ingramcontent.com/pod-product-compliance
Lightning Source LLC
Chambersburg PA
CBHW020647300426
44112CB00007B/272